T0330010

China's Economic Development

China's Economic Development

Institutions, Growth and Imbalances

Ming Lu, Zhao Chen, Yongqin Wang, Yan Zhang, Yuan Zhang and Changyuan Luo

Fudan University, China

Edward Elgar

Cheltenham, UK • Northampton, MA, USA

Originally published in Chinese as *China's Development Path as a Large Country* by China Encyclopedia Press, Beijing, 2008

Published by
Edward Elgar Publishing Limited
The Lypiatts
15 Lansdown Road
Cheltenham
Glos GL50 2JA
UK

Edward Elgar Publishing, Inc.
William Pratt House
9 Dewey Court
Northampton
Massachusetts 01060
USA

A catalogue record for this book
is available from the British Library

Library of Congress Control Number: 2012948157

This book is available electronically in the ElgarOnline.com
Economics Subject Collection, E-ISBN 978 0 85793 509 0

MIX
Paper from
responsible sources
FSC
www.fsc.org   FSC® C018575

ISBN 978 0 85793 508 3

Typeset by Servis Filmsetting Ltd, Stockport, Cheshire
Printed by MPG PRINTGROUP, UK

Contents

Acknowledgements

This book is the outcome of research conducted by the Fudan Lab for China Development Studies. The authors gratefully acknowledge funding from the National Social Science Funds (11AZD084 and 12AZD045) and the National Natural Science Funds (71133004). This research is also supported by the Shanghai Association of Philosophy and Social Science and the Shanghai Leading Academic Discipline Project (B101). Changyuan Luo thanks the financial support from National Social Science Funds (11CJL039) and Fudan 985 Project (2011RWSKQN004 and 2011SHKXZD002).

The book is rewritten from its Chinese version *China's Development Path as a Large Country* (translator: Wu Jiaming), published by China Encyclopedia Press (Beijing, 2008). The translation and publication of this book was financially supported by the Chinese Fund for the Humanities and Social Sciences (12WJL001).

1. Introduction: the reform and opening-up of a large, developing country

Rapid growth accompanied by unbalanced development is the best way to describe the path taken by a large, developing country over the past 30 years – China. Even today, China is constantly adjusting its system to accommodate ever-changing challenges.

In 1978, China had just completed the Great Proletarian Cultural Revolution and the country was in the very earliest stages of its reconstruction. The green shoots of change began to appear quietly in the spring, although at the time most people did not notice. In December, the Communist Party of China (CPC) held the Third Plenary Session of the 11th Central Committee, which announced the prolog of the reform and opening-up policy.

Eleven years later, after the serious political disturbances of 1989, the whole country regarded the concept of market-oriented reform with great suspicion and mistrust. In 1992, Deng Xiaoping, speaking in southern China, remarked, 'For a big, developing country like China, rapid economic development cannot always be accompanied by smoothness and stability ... Development is the foremost and essential principle' (Deng Xiaoping, Vol. III, 1993, p. 377).

Beijing's hosting of the 29th Olympic Games in the summer of 2008 was a coming of age, showing that China had grown from a developing country characterized by poverty and backwardness to an economic giant. This was not only the year after the 17th Party Congress but also the 30th anniversary of the launching of the reform and opening-up policy. Thirty years earlier, 'Olympic' was a term that was unfamiliar to the Chinese people. By 2008, however, the map of the world's economy had changed and China had undergone a great deal of development.

Not only has the world's economic map changed since China began its reform and opening-up, but also, as described by US political scientists Townsend and Womack (1986) in their comments on Chinese-style socialism, there is a strong belief that China has taken a different route toward development from other countries. For this reason, China should be considered a unique case. After more than 30 years of reform and opening-up, China's achievements and response to challenges not only inspire awe, but also raise many questions, including what are the differences between China's path toward development and those taken by other countries, whether China can realize sustainable economic development, and what other developing countries can learn from China's model.

Like China, the former Soviet Union and countries in Eastern Europe have had planned economies. These countries also began radical transitions into market economies in the late 1980s, though these may have differed from China's 'exploring through practice' reform strategy. At one time, economists thought that China had achieved success through a gradual and smooth progression of incremental reforms and that this strategy had prevented the economic recessions that can be caused by hasty actions. Today, from a viewpoint of standard economic theory, China's transition could be considered a basic establishment of a market economy system characterized by the free determination of prices and free mobility of factors. The private sector accounts for an overwhelming amount of China's whole economy. However, China's development path is more complicated than a simple transition from a planned to a market economy. We must reevaluate the meaning of 'development' and then analyze China's 30-year experience of reform and opening-up from a much wider perspective, taking into account its status as a large, developing country.

In this book, we analyze China's economic process on the basis of the system structures of a large country. We here interpret 'development' as changes in the interactions between the economy, politics and society. It is our view that two key factors that have affected China's economic path are that it is large and that it is a developing rather than a developed country. Because it is large in terms of population, territory and economic scale, it has a broad domestic market that leans toward scale effects and a significant supply of public goods (including the development of national defense, technology and strategic industries). In order to realize the advantages of its size, China has favored political centralization because it promotes national unity, political stability and policy implementation. In order to overcome the disadvantages of heavy centralization of power, the central government supports economic decentralization, which offers local governments more autonomy to make local economic policies and to share the increased tax revenues produced by the development of the local economy. Thus, China's mode of governance is in accordance with its status as a large country. Within this kind of system structure, market-oriented reform and opening-up can foster stunning economic growth. However, it can also cause two types of imbalances: internally, there is uneven development not only between the urban and rural areas but also across regions, and imbalances in the distribution of public services within the country; externally, trade surpluses and external imbalances may be created.

As a developing country, China has another structural feature: strong social relationships in almost all transactional processes. Some scholars call China a 'relationship-based society'. In the early stages of economic development, social connections can lower transaction costs. However, once the social network becomes embedded in the new market system, it can aggravate social inequality and provide a structural background for internal and external imbalances during periods of rapid growth. These inequities may be rendered more intense by the combination of political power and social relationships. Under decentralized economic systems, the localization of social relations can strengthen the localization of the economy, which does not favor market competition or scale economy.

For sustainable economic development, the challenge of dual imbalances can serve as an impetus to promote further adjustment of system structures and to improve the market economy system. China's development involves interactions among the economy, politics, and society as well as the construction of a socialist market economy with Chinese characteristics. China has selected the market economy system as its fundamental method of resource allocation. However, this system must be tailored to China's long and rich history and to all the particular issues of large, developing countries.

1.1 CHINA'S 30-YEAR PATH TO REFORM AND OPENING-UP

The report of the 17th CPC National Congress summarized China's achievements over the past 30 years. It described how large-scale reform and opening-up were why China had 'successfully realized a great historical transition from a highly centralized planned economy system to a dynamic socialist market economy; from an isolated, to a semi-isolated system to a fully opened-up one'. The policy of reform and opening-up has transformed the market economy system into a basic form of resource allocation, allowing the economy to develop vigorously. However, the existing political and social structures have also had an undeniable effect on this newborn market economy system. This has caused many distortions in the market economy system and some imbalances in development.

According to traditional views, it is indisputable that the transition from a planned to a market economy system was a rough one. China still has regulated exchange and interest rates, a relatively inflexible cross-regional flow of the labor force, and a segmented interregional commodity market, but it is likely that these issues will all be solved in the foreseeable future. In view of various drawbacks found in the current market economy system and the challenges posed by economic development, we may conclude that there is no direct or necessary connection between a traditional planned economy and the various drawbacks and challenges currently faced by China. In other words, in order to understand the current problems, it is necessary for us to consider economic transition as a much wider type of development, one that includes but also goes beyond the traditional view of a mere transition from a planned to a market economy. In this section we first outline China's 30 years of transition from a planned to a market economy.

According to traditional economic theories, China has completed two major tasks during the past 30 years of development, the implementation of reforms at home and the opening-up to the outside world.

Reforms at Home

History has proved that planned economies can be inefficient. There are two reasons for this inefficiency. First, in a planned economy system, the central government decides on prices and allocates resources, and information asymmetry can have huge effects (Hayek, 1945). Second, planned economy systems are often troubled by incentive problems. Because of the information asymmetry that is common in certain types of organizations, inefficiencies such as shirking and free riding become universal unless proper price mechanisms and incentive mechanisms are put in place (Stiglitz, 1994). Leaders like Deng Xiaoping drew similar conclusions after years of practical experience. After several years of experiments and arguments, the Central Committee's Decision on Economic System Reform was unanimously adopted in the Third Plenary Session of the 12th CPC Central Committee. Among other points, the committee agreed that 'a reasonable price mechanism should be established, thus the price could sensitively reflect changes in labor productivity and the relationship between supply and demand' and that 'only if we fully develop the commodity economy, can the economy be dynamic and enterprises be more efficient, more flexible, and more sensitive and adaptable to complicated social needs'. China's market-oriented reform and opening-up was designed to fundamentally correct the disadvantages in the planned economy system.

Marketization has changed the allocation of economic resources. China adopted a dual-track system that incorporated both market-determined and planned prices as a transitional way of realizing price liberalization in the commodity market. It did not truly establish a factor market until the second half of the 1990s. Specifically, 1994 was the watershed year. In order to prepare for the market mechanism, reform prior to 1994 first fostered a non-state sector. This system operated according to market mechanisms outside the state sectors instead of following fundamental reform measures toward traditional state sectors. For this reason, some economists referred to China's reform as incremental reform, outside system reform, or a dual-track system (for example, Fan, 1994; Lin et al., 1994; Naughton, 1994). With regard to the reform sequence, many economists considered China to have adopted a strategy of avoiding the important and dwelling on the trivial, or easy first and difficult later.

For the commodity market, from the 1980s to the early 1990s, China adopted a dual-track pricing system. This allowed private enterprises to sell surplus commodities at prices exceeding the planned price so long as they first completed their planned production. In the unplanned market, supply and demand were still marginally allocated by price mechanisms (Byrd, 1989; Yuan, 1994; Zhang, 1997). Dual-track reform not only rendered the planned economy more efficient but also offered widespread benefits to the people without incurring any losses to anyone (Lau et al., 1997, 2000). Although it accelerated the growth of the commodity market, the dual-track system also fostered corruption as the track transitioned from planned to unplanned. After the 1990s, production plans were gradually cancelled, and the dual-track commodity market system was incrementally transformed into a single-track system. This transition continued until China finally realized free pricing in the commodity market. Land, capital and labor are the three main production factors in this type of market. In the 1990s, marketization reforms were also undertaken in the production factor market. A land-leasing market was developed, a stock market was set up and a labor contract system was also enacted. Although these three markets became significantly more sophisticated, it is generally thought that they lag far behind the commodity market and that free flow and market pricing have not yet been fully realized in these areas.

Second, marketization has changed the incentive structure of economic agents. In a sense, the achievements of China's economic reform were a result of correct incentives rather than correct prices (Yongqin Wang et al., 2006, 2007). China's reform involved an effective incentive structure on three levels. At the state administration level, the combination of economic decentralization and political centralization inspired local governments to increase their tax base and local fiscal revenue by developing the local economy. At the same time, governments at all levels assess the governments one level below them on the basis of GDP growth rate and achievements in investment promotion. Both these issues affect the government officials' chances for promotion. This kind of system encourages local government officials to pursue economic growth.

With respect to the way business enterprises are organized, post-reform China has gradually developed an effective enterprise administration structure and an effective incentive system. Since 1985, China has implemented several reforms for state-owned enterprises (SOEs). These include a contract managerial responsibility system, a lease system, and a responsibility system for asset management. By the end of 1987, 78 percent of the enterprises in the country had implemented contract responsibility systems. Of these, 80 percent were large or medium-sized enterprises. Empirical research has shown that the bonus and contract-labor systems were the main reasons for 67 percent of the increase in per capita output in SOEs and 4.68 percent of the increase in total factor productivity (TFP) seen per year from 1980 to 1989. Meanwhile, the management culture changed, rendering managers with poor performance more likely to be replaced (Groves et al., 1994, 1995).

A great number of enterprises suffered losses due to a bureaucratic phenomenon: in the case of losses in practical operation and contract responsibility systems, SOEs deduct a percentage from earnings but they are not required to pay compensation. People recognized that SOEs needed a more thorough reform for enterprise property rights and corporate governance. In the late twentieth century, China underwent a nationwide wave of privatization, mostly of small and medium-sized SOEs. This resulted in the very first reduction in the number of SOEs, from 104,700 in 1993 to 102,200 in 1994. The number of state-owned industrial enterprises was 113,800 in 1996, 98,600 in 1997, and 50,700 in 1999. Nearly all the township enterprises became privatized in a very short period.

In the mid-1990s, economists recommended that entrepreneurs attain the residual claim of enterprise management (Zhang, 1995a, 1995b). Enterprises also needed a competitive product market, a capital market, and a manager market to provide enough information for corporate governance (Lin et al., 1997). Later, reform to invigorate large enterprises and relax control over small ones was implemented, and denationalization of most small and medium-sized SOEs and the merging and restructuring of large and medium-sized SOEs caused the number and range of SOEs to drop significantly. The number of state-owned and state-held industrial enterprises decreased from 64,737 in 1998 to 41,125 in 2002. The number of enterprises run by the central government decreased to 2,790. The rapid privatization of SOEs was related to the incentives obtained by local governments under the decentralization system. The privatization of poorly run SOEs can ease the government's financial burden and increase the tax base by improving enterprise performance. The transformation of enterprises has improved enterprise performance (Bai et al., 2006; Hu et al., 2006).

At the micro level, post-reform China has established a distribution system based on performance. The theoretical basis of the traditional, planned economy distribution system was that labor creates value. However, labor input was mainly measured by time spent, which did not reward labor quality or human capital. Workers had little incentive to invest in their education or return to school. When the system was changed so that rewards would be distributed according to individual performance, workers had an incentive to work harder. The implementation of the Household Responsibility System (*Jiating Lianchan Chengbao Zeren Zhi*) enabled peasants to sell their output over the planned quota at market prices. Studies have found that, from 1978 to 1984, agricultural output increased more than 61 percent, more than three-quarters of which came from the improved incentive mechanism and one-quarter from the improved price system (McMillan et al., 1989). In cities, numerous self-employed households became ten-thousand-yuan households during the 1980s. These were the first batch of people to become rich with the help of market mechanisms. In enterprises, salary reform, the introduction of a bonus system and hourly and piecework wages based on performance produced more incentives for employees and managers to increase work quality. Production efficiency improved dramatically (Groves et al., 1994, 1995). The number of employees returning to school for more education increased significantly after marketization reform was enacted (Li and Ding, 2003; Zhang et al., 2005).

Opening Up to the Outside World

Before 1978, China's main economic goal was to catch up to and surpass other countries. This was achieved by means of speeding up capital accumulation and developing heavy and chemical industries, which could not make full use of China's economic potential. Meanwhile, due to the distorted production system and an exchange rate that overvalued the Chinese currency the renminbi (RMB), products made in China were uncompetitive, forcing the country to maintain its planned economy and remain isolated from the outside world.

China's opening-up policy involved participation in economic globalization, which allowed it to reestablish its comparative advantage. The strategy of opening up to the outside world can be considered indicative of a change in attitude from catching up to establishing a comparative advantage; from import substitution to export orientation. Historically speaking, both 1994 and 2001 were key turning points in the opening-up process.

The period from 1978 to 1994 was the first stage of China's reinvolvement in the international division of labor. During this period, the overvalued RMB exchange rate had not yet been changed substantially; but the Chinese labor market had a serious advantage with respect to costs and quality, quickly outstripping other countries in the international labor market. This caused China's international trade and foreign capital investment to grow rapidly. Before 1979, international trade was under the control of a centrally planned economic system; the central government controlled over 90 percent of trade volume by monopolizing the import and export of more than 3,000 types of goods. By 1991, nearly all imports were decontrolled, and only 15 percent were still controlled by specific trade companies. All exports were decontrolled. By 1994, almost all planned systems for imports and exports had been abolished. Only a very limited number of important goods were still controlled by specific companies.

China has become one of the biggest destination countries for foreign direct investment (FDI) in the world. It is also one of the biggest production bases in the global manufacturing system. In 1979, in order to attract FDI, special economic zones were founded in Shenzhen, Zhuhai, Shantou, and Xiamen. However, little large-scale FDI appeared before 1984, when, in order to attract more foreign capital, another 24 economic open zones, including 14 coastal cities, were made available to foreign investors. From then on, an increasing number of economic open zones were established for the purpose of encouraging foreign investment and technology transfer (Chapter 4). After Deng Xiaoping made his famous remarks during his inspection tour of southern China in 1992, a second wave of FDI appeared in China.

In this way, 1994 was a watershed year for China's reform and opening-up with respect to exchange rate reform. With the execution of reform, including trade system reform, the nominal rate of exchange, which had long overvalued Chinese currency, faced the pressure of extreme devaluation. During this period, in order to encourage exports and increase reserves, China began to adopt the dual-rate system, which involved an internal settlement exchange rate of 2.8 yuan per US dollar for exchange, settlement, and sales while keeping the official RMB exchange rate at 1.5487 yuan per US dollar. The reform of the financial and exchange rate systems required that price controls be eliminated and that the real value of the RMB be determined by the actual exchange rate, which would involve devaluation. Official exchange rates dropped gradually during this period. In 1994, the dual-rate system was formally withdrawn. Unification of exchange rates and the drastic devaluation of the RMB was the new starting point for China's export-oriented strategy.

The year of 2001 was another key point in time for China's opening-up to the outside world. In 2001, China joined the World Trade Organization (WTO), which announced China's integration into the global trade system as a market economy. China was no longer a simple participant in international business. Instead, it began to influence the international cooperation and trade systems as major trading power.

Achievements of China's Reform and Opening-up

The report of the 17th CPC National Congress presented a highly generalized account of the achievements in China's 30 years of reform and opening-up. According to the report,

> [T]he economy of our country boomed from the edge of collapse to the fourth place in the world, with the volume of imports and exports ranking third in the world; the standard of living had improved from starving to well-off, and the number of poor people in the countryside had decreased from over 250 million to around 20 million.

China's achievements could generally be represented by changes in numbers.

First, the economy grew rapidly, with GDP (calculated at comparable prices) growing by a factor of almost 16.5 from 1978 to 2008; the actual growth rate was 9.8 percent annually on average. The reform and opening-up could be divided into two stages according to comments made by Deng Xiaoping during his inspection tour of southern China in 1992. The average growth rate was 9.4 percent from 1978 to 1992 and it exceeded 10 percent from 1992 to 2008. Along with rapid development, China's international economic status also rose quickly. As the economy developed, China's human development index increased sharply from only 0.527 in 1975 to 0.768 in 2004. Even so, it still ranked 81st in the world.[1]

Second, China integrated itself into the wave of economic globalization. The total volume of imports and exports was only US$20.64 billion in 1978 but it increased eightfold to US$165.53 billion in 1992. The increase was even more substantial after 1992, reaching US$2,207.53 billion, which is over 100 times the 1978 value. Since the implementation of reform and opening-up, China's ratio of dependence on foreign trade (the proportion accounted for by total value of imports and exports in the GDP) increased steadily from 10.8 percent in 1979 to 35.36 percent in 1992 and even to 65.17 percent in 2006. It then declined to 44.24 percent in 2009 due to the recent economic crisis. China has already become a genuinely open economy, and the trade-to-GDP ratio in other economies such as the United States, Japan, and India was about 20 percent.[2] At the same time, FDI in China became more and more intense. It amounted to only US$1.769 billion in the period from 1979 to 1982 but, in 2005, it reached US$60.325 billion, and the ratio of FDI to GDP reached 2.7 percent. In 2009, FDI amounted to US$90.033 billion and the ratio of FDI to GDP reached 1.8 percent in 2009 (exchange rate calculated by average annual price).[3] China's status in the international division of labor has consistently grown stronger; the ratio of finished products to total exports was 49.7, 80, 94.5, and 94.75 percent in 1980, 1992, 2006, and 2009, respectively.[4] Although there is a great gap between China and developed countries in terms of manufacturing technology, it is indisputable that commodities made in China are sold almost worldwide.

Third, China has undergone an accelerated process of urbanization and industrialization since reform and opening-up began. Since 1978, the process of urbanization had been greatly promoted and the proportion of urban population increased from 17.92 percent in 1978 to 27.63 percent in 1992. Since 1992, urbanization has proceeded even faster: the proportion of urban population increased to 43.9 percent in 2006 and 46.59 percent in 2009. However, China's urbanization level remains relatively low compared to other countries; rural residents account for about 50 percent of the total population. In contrast, the relative amount of primary industry in GDP has dropped consistently from 28.2 percent in 1978 to 11.8 percent in 2006 and 10.3 percent in 2009. The relative amount of secondary industry in GDP continued to increase from its relatively high level of 47.9 percent in 1978 to 48.7 percent in 2006 and 46.3 percent in 2009. With the increased importance of tertiary industry, the proportion of tertiary industry in GDP increased from 23.9 percent in 1978 to 34.8 percent in 1992, then to 39.5 percent in 2006 and 43.4 percent in 2009.[5]

Termination of Transition?

Thirty years of reform and opening-up has led one-fifth of the world's population down the path of modernization, which almost certainly has worldwide significance.

Over the past 30 years, China has established what can be called a Chinese-style socialist market economy. The period from 1992 to 1994 was an important turning point, in which the reform in marketization grew beyond the preliminary stage. China experienced a serious political incident in 1989, which caused a conservative backlash with respect to marketization reform. During his visit to southern China in the winter of 1992, Deng Xiaoping issued a series of important statements regarding the promotion of continuous marketization reform. These inspired people to support marketization reform wholeheartedly.

During the period from November 11–14, 1993, the 14th CPC Central Committee approved the Decision of the CPC Central Committee on Several Issues Concerning the Establishment of a Socialist Market Economic System, which set a goal of establishing a preliminary socialist market economic system by the end of the twentieth century. In 1994, marketization reform was greatly advanced in four ways:

1. *reform of the financial and taxation systems*: to change the original system of central and local governments taking full responsibility for their finances into the system of tax sharing between central and local governments (including provincial and county governments);
2. *reform of the financial banking system*: to establish a financial organization system in which the SOEs are the mainstay, along with coexistence of various financial institutions and separation between non-commercial (policy) and commercial finance;
3. *reform of the foreign exchange management system*: to unify exchange rates and manage convertibility of the RMB under the current account; and
4. *reform of state-owned enterprises*: to promote further transformation of the enterprises' management mechanisms in order to establish a modern enterprise system able to adapt to the requirements of the market economy characterized by clearly established ownership, well-defined power and responsibility, separation of enterprise from administration, and scientific management.

China's marketization reform made great strides forward in 1994. If the problems addressed by the reforms of the 1980s were mainly related to the development of industrialization and urbanization, then the problem addressed by the reforms of 1994 was system transformation. Substantial development was achieved in terms of establishing the factor market and opening up to the outside. After 30 years of reform and opening-up, China may have reached its goal of transitioning from a planned to a market economy, but several questions remain.

1.2   NEW HISTORICAL STARTING POINTS OF REFORM AND OPENING-UP

At the 17th CPC National Congress, it was asserted that China is encountering a 'new historical starting point' of reform and opening-up, moving toward the goal of a generally prosperous society. The history of transition from planned to market economy is not sufficient to illustrate the opportunities and challenges that China will face with respect to economic, social, and political development in the coming years. China needs to adjust its development goal away from the pursuit of growth and one-sided efficiency toward the pursuit of fairness and general well-being. The government is now moving towards democratic politics that promote a harmonious society. China is attempting to solve the problems left over from the last 30 years of market-oriented reform and opening-up. From our point of view, the contradictions and problems that the country faces today are related to the centralized political structure, decentralized economic structure and relationship-based social structure. These two structural characteristics have not changed substantially, despite the reforms of the past decades. China must solve these problems by adjusting its economic, political and social structures.

Seven Current Challenges

For China to continue developing as a world economy while still pursuing the goals of fairness and prosperity at all levels of society, it must overcome seven challenges.

The relationship between short-term growth and sustainable development

The rapid growth of China's economy, which has lasted more than 30 years, may or may not be sustainable. Under the system of economic decentralization, the assessment and promotion of local government officials was fundamentally dependent on economic growth and the achievements of investment. However, the term of office of local officials usually lasts only a few years, so local governments often ignore many goals that foster continuous economic growth and sustainable social development, including education, health services, and environmental protection, and instead prefer high levels of short-term growth. Under the system of fiscal decentralization, these services require financial support from local government. However, increasing financial support can involve directing funds away from government investments that benefit short-term economic growth, such as investments in infrastructure. As a result, industries that would promote long-term sustainable development but require large amounts of financial support tend to be ignored (Yongqin Wang et al., 2006, 2007; Fu and Zhang, 2007).

The relationship between national and local interests

In an economically decentralized system, it is difficult to avoid conflict between the goals of central and local governments. Central governments tend to represent a nation's interests, while local governments tend to represent local interests. The differences between the goals of central and local governments can manifest in several ways. For example, central governments tend to prefer sustainable development, and local governments tend to focus on short-term goals. The central government pays more attention to peasants' interests, but local governments lack incentives to pay attention to rural development because so much of their incentive is based on growth. The central government tends to prefer to improve the unification of the domestic market, whereas local governments pursue short-term local interests through regional protectionism and market segmentation. In China's case, provincial governments have shown increasing economic power and negotiating skills. This can undermine central policies. One of the advantages of a system of fixed tenure and a rotation of management across regions is that it can reduce the difference between local and central interests. However, this system also has one major problem: local officials then lack incentives to pursue the long-term goals of sustainable development.

The relationship between government intervention and social development
Under the system of economic decentralization, in order to pursue national interests, we need a powerful central government to ensure that central policies are carried out effectively. China has therefore adopted a system of political centralization in order to cooperate with the system of economic decentralization. However, in systems involving heavy political centralization, the strong bureaucratic organizations that give governments much of their practical power tend to manifest at all higher levels of government, but are unlikely to be seen at lower levels. Overly powerful governments and insufficient restraint of personal power can render economic and social development too dependent on specific qualities and abilities of individual government officials. Under the strong government model, the entire society can fail to reach advanced and effective social organization or develop self-organized systems for the allocation of resources and mediation of conflicts. However, many governments are unwilling to permit social organizations to take over responsibility from them, for the sake of their own interests.

The relationship between urban and rural residents: social integration
China's urbanization level is still low. The rapid promotion of urbanization will continue to be an important phenomenon in the development of the economy for several decades to come. However, under the current administration structure, in which the city governs the countryside, urban governments make urban-biased economic policies that protect urban

residents' interests over those of rural residents. This is especially true with respect to public services such as employment, social security, education, and medical care (Lu and Chen, 2004, 2006a). Long-term implementation of policies in support of the urban–rural divide has caused large gaps in income and public services. Increases in both the amount of urban space and the number of migrants lacking local household registration (*hukou*) in cities to which they have moved have translated the urban–rural divide into social segmentation between people with and without local *hukou* identity in urban areas. In cities, the gaps in income and returns on education between residents and migrants have widened (Meng and Bai, 2007; Zhang and Meng, 2007). This may further intensify social conflicts within cities and therefore affect the sustainable development of cities. Improving urban–rural integration and social integration within cities is a major issue.

The relationship between developed and backward areas: market integration

Economic development can differ widely by region. Natural conditions and geographical positions are two important reasons for this. Ports in coastal areas are closer to the international market, which makes it easier for them to attract foreign investment and offers them more opportunities to participate in international trade and realize economic development (Wan et al., 2007). The priorities of economic policy can also account for the wide gap among regions following reform. Until the late twentieth century, the fiscal transfer of central governmental funds was directed more to economically developed areas than to less-developed ones, which intensified the gap among different regions. This situation did not change until the twenty-first century. The widening gap among regions and the ability of local governments to make local policies allowed the proliferation of various market segmentation policies that protected local enterprises and increased employment and taxation (Lu and Chen, 2006b). Market segmentation and regional protectionism are not only harmful to the unity of the market but also make it harder for China to capitalize on the scale of its large population and vast land resources to realize economic growth. Devising a reasonable system that can promote market integration and coordinate the development of a regional economy, therefore presents a major challenge.

The relationship between economic growth and social harmony: interest sharing

The income gap and unequal distribution of public services between urban and rural areas and across regions are all increasing. The combination of public power and social relationships in bureaucratized administrative systems also promotes inequality of political and social resources, which affects income and public services. Income inequality is harmful not only to the sustainable growth of the economy but also to many other aspects, such as the health status of the population, environmental protection, rural and urban poverty, public trust, and social stability (Lu et al., 2005; Wan et al., 2006). Meanwhile, the unequal distribution of public services, such as education and healthcare can lead to inequality with respect to long-term income, which may spread the inequality of human capital and income from generation to generation, decrease social mobility among various groups of people, and produce a series of related negative effects on the harmonious development of society and sustainable economic growth. Therefore, preventing the widening of the income gap and the maintenance of social mobility among all levels of society in order to render the achievements of economic growth more beneficial to more people may be favorable to China's future.

The relationship between internal development and external imbalance
China's speedy economic growth has significant relevance to all human-kind. However, its increased strength has also provoked some anxiety in other countries. China's urban-biased policies, intensive competition in the urban labor market, the low cost of labor, the undervalued RMB, and the government's unilateral pursuit of economic growth, which many consider to be at the expense of laborers' rights and interests, have been problematic for some time. The cost of export products has fallen steadily since the mid-1990s, and labor productivity has increased, strengthening its exports, which began to increase even faster after the country's entry into the WTO. This led to trade imbalances between China and other countries, especially the United States. Although these are largely due to the low savings rate and brisk demand for imports from the United States, the low cost of China's export products is also a significant element. China's investments around the world and its need for global resources have increased. The idea of a harmonious world embodies China's responsibility to the world and its goodwill.

China faces numerous difficulties in its development, each with their own causes.[6] However, all of these problems have a common background in the decentralized political-economic structure and relationship-based social structure. Unequal distribution of political, social, and economic resources can appear among different regions and across different groups of people. This can cause inequality in income and public services, creating internal imbalances. This situation is unfavorable to sustainable development, but it is often ignored by local governments in their unilateral pursuit of economic growth. Because laborers are socially disadvantaged (especially laborers who migrate to cities from the countryside) and because competition in the labor market is intense, the cost of labor has remained low relative to labor productivity, and the volume of both imports and exports has grown quickly. From a macroeconomic perspective, the growth of China's domestic economic consumption has been slower than the growth of its GDP. Thus, China's rapid economic growth depends heavily on investments and exports, which can cause external imbalances.

The problem of internal and external dual imbalances has been part of China's economic development throughout the past 30 years of reform and opening-up. Changes need to be made in order to realize sustainable development, and China must adjust its political and social structures, which have remained unchanged for a long time.

The word 'development' not only encompasses economic development or the processes of industrialization and urbanization but also the all-round development of an economy, political system, and society. More and more economists have recognized that the process of industrialization and urbanization is only one aspect of development. Development is an interactive process incorporating, economy, politics, and society; it cannot be considered independent of political and social change.

On the New Historical Starting Point of Reform and Opening-up

The report of the 17th CPC National Congress announced that the reform and opening-up would create a new historical starting point, allowing China to proceed on a sustainable path through adjustments in the relationships among the government, market, and society.

Changing relationships among government, market, and society

The basic features of the market economy system are, superficially, the marketization of the pricing mechanism and the liberalization of the flow of commodities and factors. However, the current market economy system has certain evident political and social characteristics. Under the system of economic decentralization, the developing model of a strong government has not yet deviated from its roots. Various direct and indirect governmental interventions still exist through the resource-allocation process. Non-market mechanisms are still heavily mixed with market mechanisms. Research shows that the registration of residence, political status, family background, and social network still has important implications with respect to personal income, education, and political participation.

Under the current system, inequalities exist among different people in terms of political and social resources, which in turn intensify the inequalities in income and public services and challenge sustainable economic growth. Therefore, for the purpose of economic growth, China should adjust its political and social structures in two ways.

On one side, the political structure should transition from an administration-oriented government to a service-oriented one. At the early stages of economic development, the support of a strong government is vital to a thriving economy, particularly to the private sector, which was relatively weak in China and could never have created the infrastructure or large-scale industry built by the government. Other economies in East Asia have also been dependent on strong governments early on during economic booms. However, the current phase of economic development is totally different from that of the late 1970s. First, China's private sector has become increasingly stronger, and the importance of government in the promotion of the economy is not as great as it was. Second, the complexity of market information has increased, which increases the government's information disadvantage. Third, the development of infrastructure has reached a sufficiently high level, especially in coastal regions, and the demand for the construction of more infrastructure via government investment can be expected to decrease. With increases in the standard of living, development-oriented demands for education, medical care, social security, and public services may increase. All of these changes require the government to reduce direct interference in economic development and provide more public support for sustainable development. Local governments must also cease intervening directly in order to allow market integration across regions.

On the other side is the transition from a relationship-based society to a society based on rules. During the early stages of economic development, social networks play an important role in coordinating trade relationships, especially for a morality- and family-based society like China. Unlike rule-based societies, relationship-based societies do not need large-scale investments to establish rules and are relatively well-suited for the early stages of economic development. However, the disadvantage of this type of society lies in the limitation of the expansion on market transaction scope. It is therefore not well-suited to the demands of modern economic development (Yongqin Wang, 2006a). Rule-based societies, however, require large-scale investments to set up rules and methods of execution and enforcement (including courts and lawyers). However, once these systems have been established, they can be used to coordinate market transactions on a much wider scale, which is beneficial to modern economic development. China has become more and more adept at setting up rule-based systems, and the demand for a rule-based society has become stronger and stronger. China must gradually establish a market order based on rules and laws. Public power should be strictly confined to the public domain, and private relationships should be strictly limited to the private area.

The current political and social structures and their interactions with economic development will be illustrated in detail in Chapter 2, and the direction of any adjustments to these systems will be discussed.

Sustainable development in China

If adjustments to political and social structures can be made in a timely manner, China may achieve sustainable development. This would involve three transitions.

First, the urban and rural populations must be integrated. For the purpose of realizing economic modernization, China should continue to promote rapid urbanization. Currently, the huge rural population has not shared equally in the benefits of the country's industrialization and economic development. Urbanization is not only an issue of increasing the proportion of urban population, but also a challenge of urban and rural integration, which includes at least three components. The preliminary stage of urban–rural integration involves simply transferring rural residents into cities. Social integration is more complicated. If peasants who move into cities are not treated as equals of the original urban residents in terms of public services, job opportunities, and social security, the traditional urban–rural segmentation will transition into a dualistic society within the cities, which will threaten the construction of a harmonious society and the sustainable development of those cities. One alternative to simply moving people into cities is to provide peasants with equal rights to participate in policy making by means of *political* integration and thus allow them to abolish the economic policies that currently favor cities themselves. The 17th CPC National Congress suggested that the number of National People's Congress (NPC) deputies be selected from urban and rural areas based on population. This would be a critical move toward urban–rural integration.

Second, regional imbalances must be corrected. If the development of the economy continues to widen the gap between regions, interregional income inequality could become rampant. Under a public service system, which is mainly dependent on local budgets, differences in development can lead to differences in social security across regions, which creates barriers to the establishment of a nationwide social security system. This may harm the flow of laborers across regions, so unification of the domestic market should be promoted. This would include integration of the commodity and factor markets. During this process, economic activities would become concentrated in terms of space, which, in the short term, may increase gaps across regions. In the long term, however, it would foster regional balance. According to the developmental experiences of other countries, if factors are allowed to flow freely across regions, the income gap between regions will decrease (Shankar and Shah, 2006). In the meantime, in order to ease the conflicts caused by excessively large interregional disparities, it is important to permit fiscal transfers from the central government, especially for a moderate equalization of infrastructure and public services such as education.

Third, China's economic goals must move away from the pursuit of efficiency and toward emphasizing fairness. Under the current fiscally decentralized system, the objects of economic development are mainly focused on the short term, while objects that will benefit long-term economic development are ignored. Under the current market mechanism, growth and efficiency are the first priority, but inequalities in income and public services between urban and rural areas, between regions, and between different groups of people are intensified. Widespread inequality can harm sustainable development in many ways. When the economy has reached a certain stage, it becomes more important to promote sustainable development that will foster moderate equalization of income and public services. Therefore, China must adjust its system of fiscal decentralization; public finance must take up a larger proportion of the government finance spending in order to provide public services relevant to people's lives. Meanwhile, the government should increase investment in moderate equalization of income and public services, especially for moderate equality of public services between urban and rural areas and between regions. For the moment, the flow of population across these areas and regions is partly motivated by differences in the availability and quality of public services. This is not favorable to coordinated development. If all levels of government adopt some means of fostering moderate equalization in public services, less-developed regions will be able to retain more human capital, which will in turn favor sustainable economic development and decrease the cross-regional flow of laborers (for public services only).

Chapters 3–5 will discuss the issues of urban and rural development, regional development, and public services in detail.

1.3 DRIVING FORCES BEHIND REFORM AND OPENING-UP

After 30 years of market-oriented reform and opening-up, China is facing a new historical starting point. The questions of what the driving force behind deeper reform and further opening-up will be, what kind of universal rule might be used to describe China's journey toward a sustainable system and what lessons other developing countries could derive from China's experience have yet to be answered. In this section, we shall use the concept of a development triangle to illustrate the driving forces behind reform in China.

Development Triangle: Appropriate Institutions, Economic Growth, and Developmental Imbalances

China's development path comprises a development triangle of three variables: appropriate systems, economic growth, and developmental imbalances (Figure 1.1).

At the beginning of reform and opening-up, the goal driving this developmental triangle was the urgent need for growth and the eradication of poverty. As Deng Xiaoping once said, 'poverty is not socialism'. This statement led to a consensus that countrywide development was necessary, and this consensus was visible across all levels of government. After the political disturbances of 1989, marketization reform encountered resistance. Deng Xiaoping then suggested that we should judge everything by the fundamental criteria of whether it favors the promotion of productivity, increases the overall strength of the socialist state, and raises people's standard of living. Market-oriented reform and opening-up resumed and developed further.

The rapid growth observed over the past 30 years owes a great deal to these original goals and to China's political and social structure. However, if growth is to continue, then systems appropriate to the current situation must be built. This will promote economic growth, which will in turn correct developmental imbalances.

The decentralized governments and their focus on short-term economic growth have fostered another cause of internal imbalances – income inequality – which has restrained increases in domestic demand. This is why the rapid economic growth has been mainly dependent on investment and exports. Due to the slow increases in domestic demand, local governments have usually increased their own investments in economic growth. This, however, has increased supplies beyond demand.

From the outside, China's macro economy faces a dilemma. Since 2005, China's trade surpluses and foreign reserves have increased significantly. This has not only brought huge pressure to bear on the revaluation of the RMB but has also exacerbated the problem of surplus liquidity. The joint effect of surplus liquidity and social expectations has pushed up asset prices, especially housing prices.

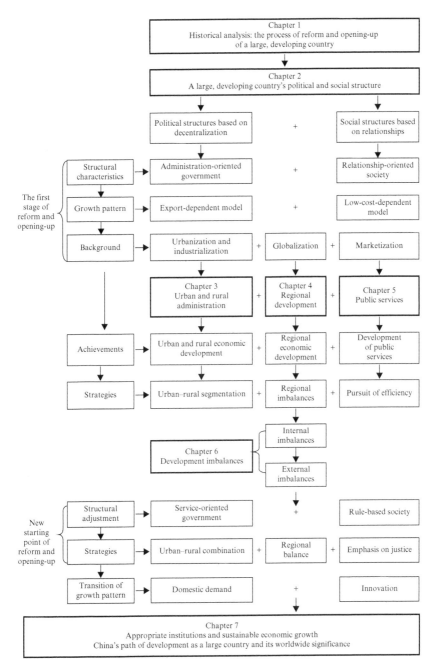

Figure 1.1   China's path toward development

In fact, foreign reserves have caused a series of macro imbalances. These are related not only to undervaluation of the RMB but also to the low costs of labor, environmental degradation, and low prices of basic materials. Between 1994 and 2004, the wages of migrant workers grew very slowly. After 1996, labor market reform took place in many urban sectors, which dragged down costs even further. During the early stages of opening-up, the low cost of labor was a competitive advantage, and China quickly became the world's manufacturing center. Competition in the labor market increased income inequality, which has had a markedly negative influence on the harmonious development of society and sustainable growth in the economy.

China should address the emerging internal and external imbalances by adjusting its pattern of economic growth and political and social structures. The correction of developmental imbalances will lead to economic growth, and growth will lead to new and more appropriate systems. The second stage of reform and opening-up will take place through interactions between the economy, politics, and society. Thus, China will continually improve upon its socialist market economy with essentially Chinese characteristics.

This chapter has looked back on China's path to reform and opening-up and the specific influence of its status as a large, developing country. In Chapter 2, we investigate the political and social structures underlying its economic development and recommend a transition from an administration- to a service-oriented government and from a relationship- to a rule-based society. In Chapters 3–5, we analyze three important aspects of China's development. Chapter 3 analyzes urban and rural economic development in the context of industrialization and urbanization, and examines types of urban–rural governance that would allow China to promote urban–rural integration. Chapter 4 addresses China's regional economic development in the context of globalization, and maintains that China should realize the transition from regional imbalance to regional balance in terms of regional development. Chapter 5 analyzes the reform of public services in the context of marketization, and recommends a transition from the pursuit of efficiency to the pursuit of a fair distribution of public services. Chapter 6 examines the challenges encountered during the 30 years of unbalanced growth from the perspective of economic development, and notes that in order to foster a harmonious society and sustainable economic growth, China must resolve developmental imbalances by adjusting political and social structures and make the transition from its heavily export-based, cost-dependent economy to one driven by domestic demand and innovation. Finally, Chapter 7 examines China's development and its worldwide significance.

China's Path toward Development and the Significance of that Path

China's political and social systems have many quintessentially Chinese characteristics. These have been adapted to its needs as a large, developing country. The progression from the active adjustment of policies under established political and social structures to the self-adjustment of those structures is key to the continuous improvement this or any socialist market economy with Chinese characteristics.

When viewed over time, China's path toward modernization can be said to have involved interactions between politics, economy, and social factors. To continue down this path, China must build and support appropriate institutions, as recently proposed by economists (Djankov et al., 2002; Acemoglu et al., 2006). Chinese scholars, however, have long recognized the importance of the adaptation of existing institutions to national conditions. In his investigation of the history of Chinese political systems, Qian Mu said, 'political systems should develop on their own. Some political systems can be introduced from other countries, but these may not be effective until they are merged into the nation's traditions. Politics cannot exist without life and institutions cannot survive without support' (Qian, 1952 [2001], preface).

China's development has involved unique political and social structures. Under specific historical and cultural conditions, different countries may adopt different developmental paths and still realize very similar goals, in this case, modernization. In terms of traditional viewpoints, some forms of modernization are required. These include democracy, liberty, and private property. However, modern economics has shown that adjustments in political and social structures do not begin until the economy has developed to a certain point. During the early stages of economic development, China adopted market-oriented policies of reform and opening-up, creating an economic boom under established political and social structures. However, China must adjust those of its political and social structures that are relevant to the market economy system if sustainable economic development is to continue. This might explain why modernization can take so many paths.

Academically, studies of China's development focusing on its status as a large country are in accordance with the trends of modern economics. Modern economics no longer considers development as the processes of industrialization and urbanization; economists have recognized that economic development is followed by a series of adjustments in political and social structures. Some scholars are trying to develop a macro-historical theory that can explain the interactive processes of underlying political, social, and economic development in Western countries. They believe that in Western Europe, the early stages of development were 'limited access orders', in which elites exercised privileges in politics, social organizations, and education, and these privileges created a self-sustaining system in which elites actively excluded others. During these early stages, economic development served the interests of the elites. However, as development continued, limited access orders restricted competition and the scope of the market and decreased incentives for economic development. Before further economic development could take place, Western Europe had to enter a stage of open-access social orders, where all political, educational, and social organizations were opened up to the people, and the privileges of elite individuals and organizations were restrained (North et al., 2006).

Strictly speaking, China has never implemented the Western European model of limited-access orders. For the most part, politics and education in China have been open to most people (Qian, 1952 [2001]). Because of these differences, we need to apply different logical models in order to explain China's development.

China's development indicates that established political and social structures might change if the current system cannot maintain the required high degree of social mobility and low degree of income inequality. In other words, the rigidity of the political and social structures may motivate reform. The limited- and open-access orders put forward by North et al. (2006) consider development to be a one-off process of adjustment. The motivation for development is not lost once a society institutes open-access orders. In the development triangle comprising appropriate institutions, economic growth, and developmental imbalances, the interactions among the economy, politics, and society take place continuously. In the sense of the comparative system, if Chinese characteristics do affect the country's modernization, then the differences between the socialist market economy system with Chinese characteristics and other market economy systems will create a new topic of interest for economists.

We have tried to set up a development theory from the perspective of the political and social structures of economic development based on China's history. If the growth strategy concentrates on changes in GDP (size of economy), then we may understand the development process as an interactive process incorporating the economy, politics, and society. The core of modern economics involves drawing boundaries between markets and government. However, adjusting these relationships to promote economic development remains challenging. In traditional economics, knowledge of institutional changes and structural adjustments is limited. In a given situation, there are many static theories that can be used to explain the relationship between the market and government. However, there is no existing economic theory that can explain how the relationship between market and government changes over time and across space. Viewing the development process as an interaction between the economy, politics, and society can enrich comprehension of institutional changes in economics, and then modern economics can be used to analyze the dynamic process of development.

NOTES

1. See UNDP, *Human Development Report 2006*, available at: http://www.undp.org.
2. See *China Statistical Summary 2006*, China Statistics Press; *China Statistical Summary 2007*, China Statistics Press; http://Zhs.Mofcom.Gov.Cn/; *Almanac of China's Finance and Banking 1993*, Almanac of China's Finance and Banking Magazine Co. Ltd; *China Monthly Statistics*, December 2006, China Statistics Advice Center. Data in 2009 are from *China Statistical Yearbook 2010*, China Statistics Press.
3. See *Report of Foreign Investment in China 2006*, Ministry of Commerce of the People's Republic of China; *Almanac of Economy and Trade 2006*, People's Press.
4. See Statistical Communiqué on the 1979 National Economic and Social Development of the People's Republic of China; Results Communiqué on the 1981 National Economic Plans of the People's Republic of China; Statistical Communiqué on the 1992 National Economic and Social Development of the People's Republic of China; available at: http://www.stats.gov.cn/.
5. See *China Statistical Summary 2007*, China Statistics Press. Secondary industry includes industry and construction, tertiary industry includes transportation, storage, postal services and wholesale and retail trade.
6. In his 'On the ten major relationships' in 1956, Mao Zedong described the relationship among heavy industry, light industry, and agriculture, the relationship between industry in the coastal regions and industry in the interior, and the relationship between the central and local authorities. Looking at the challenges and problems China faces today, it is clear that some problems have persisted for a long time and they may continue beyond the transition from a planned to a market economy.

2. Political and social foundations of economic development

During the 30 years that have passed since China first introduced its reform and opening-up policies, its economy has developed rapidly. China's economic miracle has received increasing levels of recognition from the international community, and economists continue to explore its possible causes and implications. To understand the development of China as a large country, we must first understand the behavior of the local governments. In a large country, the central government faces enormous governance costs. China's central–local relationship involves economic decentralization. Politically, China espouses unified leadership in order to execute policies effectively and ensure the political unification of the country. As early as 10 years ago, it became clear to many economists that China's economic performance had outstripped Russia's. Economic decentralization and political centralization are both considered important causes of China's economic success (Blanchard and Shleifer, 2001).

The uniqueness of the Chinese economic system can be traced back to the period of planned economy, when China basically copied the Soviet Union's economic system. However, China paid more attention to the initiative of the local authorities rather than emphasizing the accuracy of central plans, as in the Soviet Union. It could be said that decentralization began shortly after the foundation of the People's Republic of China, even though it changed over time. Chinese leaders recognized that an overcentralized economy regulated by a central authority could be harmful to local initiatives. In his 1956 address, 'On the ten major relationships', Mao Zedong pointed out,

> [T]he relationship between central and local governments is a contradiction. To resolve this contradiction, attention should now be paid on how to empower the local authorities to some extent, providing them with greater autonomy and letting them undertake more responsibilities, on the premise that the unified leadership of the central authority will be advantageous to our task of building a powerful socialist country. Our territory is so vast, our population is so large and the conditions are so complex that it is far better to have the initiatives come from both the central and the local authorities than from one source alone. We must not follow the example of the Soviet Union which concentrated everything in the hands of the central authorities, shackling the local authorities

and denying them the right to independent action . . . For a large country like ours and a big Party like ours, the proper handling of the relationship between the central and local authorities is of vital importance. (Mao Zedong, 1977).

This model of economic decentralization has at its core a system of fiscal decentralization. Local governments were able to benefit from the local economic development that was promoted by the fiscal decentralization in the financial contract system in the 1980s and the tax-sharing system effected in 1994. These systems strongly encouraged local governments to pursue economic development. In order to effectively change the system of fiscal decentralization, motivate economic development, and prevent the decentralized economic systems from succumbing to localism, China regularly appoints and removes local officials, and assessments and promotions are based on relative economic development.[1] After 30 years of high-speed development, China now faces some structural problems. These are to some extent related to the administrative structure, which is in turn related to China's considerable size. In this chapter, we shall analyze the ways in which the administrative structure has managed to promote market-oriented reforms and economic development and how that structure has caused some of the problems that China faces today, such as unbalanced development.

Despite the market-oriented reforms of the past 30 years, the economy is still considerably dependent on social networks. The relationship-based society divides people into insiders and outsiders. Each group has its own bureaucratized structure, many of which are interwoven with the politically bureaucratized structure. During the early stages of China's transition, this reduced transaction costs and promoted economic efficiency. However, the relationship-based society has hindered sustainable economic development in two ways. First, it is embedded in the market mechanism, where it affects resource allocation. Interpersonal relationships vary among different people, and this can aggravate inequality and promote corruption, especially when interpersonal relationships are combined with public power. Second, with further economic development, the scale of the economy and endogenous growth become more and more important. However, the relationship-based society has also limited the extent of economic transactions, and this has had an increasingly negative impact on economic development. Moreover, hidden rules of personal relations are vital in a relationship-based society, which is at odds with the spirit of democracy and rule of law.

In this chapter, we shall analyze the political and social structures underlying China's economic transition. In order to understand the past and future of China's economic development, it is important to note that its political and social structures are related to its status as a large, developing country.

2.1   DECENTRALIZED POLITICAL STRUCTURE AND INCENTIVES FOR DEVELOPMENT

China's political structure, which is based on decentralization, is a basic feature of its market-oriented reform and opening-up. The economic decentralization includes the decentralization of the fiscal system and the separation of government and business, and decentralization from higher- to lower-level governments. Appropriately decentralized management is an important characteristic of economic decentralization, which is also coordinated through a politically centralized system. The main characteristic of this system is vertical management in which the leadership appoints and removes lower management, assesses performance, and organizes the cross-regional rotation of government officials. The combination of economic decentralization and political centralization provides an effective incentive mechanism for the implementation of policies for the early stages of economic development.

Characteristics of China's Decentralized Economic System

The basic definition of 'decentralization' is the devolution of power. For example, before the mid-1970s, the central government almost always controlled the SOEs; the central ministries controlled both production and operation. One change in policy granted power to local enterprises and allowed them to keep a larger share of their profits, and another increased the amount of self-management permitted to local governments. These policies could be considered to be decentralization in the narrow sense that power was devolved. In a broader sense, they could be seen as a re-division of rights and obligations between governments and enterprises.

Economic decentralization includes decentralization of the fiscal system, the separation of government and enterprise, and decentralization in favor of lower-level governments. The government has gradually relinquished control of individuals and enterprises (especially SOEs) and provided local governments with more autonomy. Decentralization of the fiscal system is at the core of this process. From the policy of decentralization and interest concessions in the 1970s to the contract system in the 1980s and tax-sharing reform of the 1990s, the issues of how to reasonably align the interests of central and local authorities and how to stimulate the local government initiatives have been key to reforming the fiscal system.

They have also fostered a breakthrough in the reform of the economic and political systems. If the household contract responsibility system solved the incentive problem of villages and peasants in the 1980s, then the incentives of the urban sector are closely correlated to the local government's devolution of power.

In the early 1950s, the government adopted the Soviet Union's system of fiscal centralization in response to the soaring prices and shortages of materials caused by decades of war. Local governments at all levels handed over all revenues to the central government, which then allocated funds according to strategic demand and development plans. In this system the higher authorities needed to assess local governments' expenditures. The relative sizes of central and national revenues and expenditures indicates that the local governments' authority over fiscal revenues and expenditures was unbalanced before 1978: from 1966 to 1975, local fiscal revenues accounted for 77 percent of China's total revenue but local expenditures were only 43 percent of all expenditures. Although the trend toward local autonomy of partial revenues appeared in some local areas in 1958 and 1970, fiscal centralization was the dominant feature of the fiscal system from 1949 to 1978. The system of fiscal centralization played a major role in mobilizing the country's resources and resolving economic difficulties. However, its disadvantages regarding unified revenue and expenditure began to surface later. This system gave local governments no right to earn or spend, leaving them highly dependent on the central government. The traditional theory of decentralization states that the central government is at a distinct disadvantage in terms of information, which increases the possibility of resource misallocation. Centralized management also tends to overlook differences in local residents' preferences. In China's case, the overwhelmingly large-scale public finance operation incurred high costs. Another problem with a centralized financial system is that the revenue turned in by local governments and the income assigned by the central government did not match, which discouraged local government initiative. Also, the central government invested a great deal of capital in such projects as the Third Front Construction,[2] which left too little disposable fiscal revenue for provinces and municipalities in eastern China. Struggling local fiscal incentives and severe fiscal imbalance made it clear that reform was necessary (Zhang, 2005).

During the planned economy period, the first change to the centralized system (1978–84) involved business, whose decision-making powers were expanded as part of the decentralization and interest concessions policy espoused by the Third Plenary Session of the 11th CPC Central Committee. By the Third Plenary Session of the 12th CPC Central Committee in 1984, reform of the urban economic system was well under way. These decision-making powers were further expanded under the guidance of separating ownership rights from management rights from 1984 to 1986. From 1987 to 1991 the contract managerial responsibility system was introduced to SOEs. The distribution of power between the state and enterprises was adjusted by granting more autonomy to business and allowing them to keep a bigger share of the profits. Surrender of profits was also replaced in part by tax payments. This helped to promote the separation of ownership and management with the use of contracts.

Reform of the fiscal and economic systems took place simultaneously. After pilot projects were found to be successful, the central government began to adjust the distribution of power between central and local authorities. The reform of the fiscal system opened the way for reform of the entire economic system. The fiscal system went through three stages after 1978: the profit-sharing system (before the 1980s); the fiscal responsibility system (1980–93); and the tax-sharing system (after 1994). From 1980 to 1993, the fiscal management system involved 'serving meals to different diners from different pots'. This expression refers to dividing revenue and expenditure between the central and local governments and holding each responsible for balancing its own budget. This made fiscal responsibility the main characteristic of the fiscal management system. This kind of devolution of power played a positive role during the early stages of redevelopment by guaranteeing the financial resources of local governments. However, rather than resolving the fundamental incentive problem of local governments, fiscal responsibility caused conflicts between central and local authorities. It allowed enterprises and individuals to accumulate more wealth and rapidly increased the extra-budgetary funds available to local governments. The ratios of national revenue to GDP and of central to national revenue dropped continuously. National revenue to GDP reached 12.3 percent in 1993, which seriously affected the ability of the central government to function (Figure 2.1).

Since 1994, the central government has popularized a system of nationwide tax sharing. This system divided the tax revenue into central, local, and shared taxes, defined the authority and expenditure scope of central and local governments, and appointed national and local taxation authorities. The central government carried out the measures for a transitional transfer payment starting in 1995. As of 1996, these measures have included partial extra-budgetary funds. In 1997, governmental funds were included. The central authority gradually adjusted the rates of certain types of taxes, collected taxes on interest, cancelled the fixed asset investment control tax and carried out a series of taxation reforms. Thus, central fiscal revenues were rendered stable. The central government

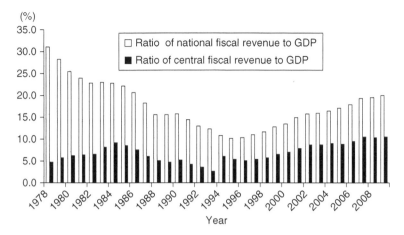

Note: Price subsidies were listed as negative revenue items prior to 1986, but they have been listed as expenditures since 1986. This figure lists the price subsidies before 1986 in fiscal expenditures.

Source: China Statistical Yearbook 2010 (China Statistics Press).

Figure 2.1 Ratio of fiscal revenue to GDP (1978–2009)

also reformed the sharing of income tax revenue in 2002, when it further extended its central share (Figure 2.2).

After the 1994 revolution of the tax-sharing system, income tax-sharing reform was centrally oriented in terms of revenue. However, the government's responsibility for public services has not changed. Statistical analysis of fiscal expenditures also shows that the share of services performed by local governments did not decline. Transfer payments accounted for much of the difference between government income and expenditures, of which tax refunds were a fairly large proportion. Tax refunds tend to be used as base values. All of the consumption tax and 75 percent of the value-added tax collected from the local governments were distributed to local governments. The amounts of these taxes were taken as base numbers for future calculations, and refunds were fixed at a progressive rate of 1:0.3 of the average growth rate of the value-added and consumption taxes in each province. The ratio of tax refunds to transfer payments was 62.1 percent on average from 1998 to 2001, of which the total amount of special fiscal allocations and subsidies accounted for 20.1 percent. These two refunds (value-added tax and consumption tax) and other unconditional transfer payments accounted for the largest proportion of the total transfer payments (Ma and Yu, 2003). Regions in which these two taxes generated

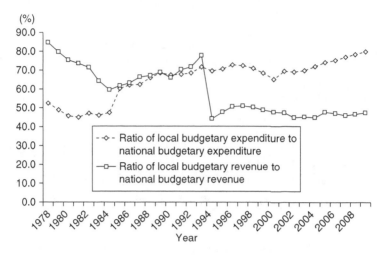

Source: *China Statistical Yearbook 2010* (China Statistics Press). Other values calculated by authors.

Figure 2.2 *Ratio of local budgetary revenue and expenditure to national budgetary revenue and expenditure (1978–2009)*

higher revenues received a higher tax refund. Thus, actual fiscal power can be measured by local fiscal expenditures containing this portion of transfer payments.[3] From a globally comparative viewpoint, the statistics regarding expenditure indicate that local governments retained substantial fiscal power after 1994.[4]

The Vertical Political Administrative System

In addition to economic decentralization, the incentive mechanism under political centralization is also an important driving force behind China's economic growth. The structure of the government is unique. As Qian and Xu (1993) pointed out, China's economy prior to its reform differed from that of the former Soviet Union, whose economic administrative system was vertical and top down. However, the multilayered administrative system, which involves several departments and regions, has persisted in China. During different developmental periods since 1949, vertical and horizontal powers have alternated in being dominant, but the criss-cross M-form structure has always been an important characteristic of China's administrative system. The vertical and horizontal organizational structures and the balance of those two forces have been adjusted in all of the previous institutional reforms. These organizations are constantly resolving conflicts and improving organizational efficiency.

Another important feature of the government's administration is that the political system is organized vertically. In most cases, the appointment and removal of officials is decided on the basis of a popular opinion poll. This has recently attracted attention from researchers. Blanchard and Shleifer (2001) drew a comparison between China and Russia in terms of differences in economic performance. They argued that the combination of economic decentralization and a vertical political administrative system had helped bring about China's success. The central government's power to control local governments is quite weak in Russia; it is difficult to give orders to local governments, so those local governments have little incentive to actively promote the development of the local economy. China's central government, however, can appoint and remove local officials, so its ability to control local governments is much stronger than Russia's.

M-form organizational structures and vertical management comprise China's unique political incentive system. Officials at all levels of government are given incentives to foster local economic development. Specifically, their own promotions are based on the economic success of their districts. The management system involves leaders. Achievements are assessed based on GDP growth, and the mechanism of the cross-region rotation of government officials is important. Political centralization strengthens officials' incentives to develop the local economy, and economic decentralization promotes increased income for businesses and individuals and also creates institutional environments that foster the development of local governments. The combination of economic decentralization and political centralization provides effective incentive mechanisms and methods for the execution of the early stages of economic development. They have become an important driving force behind the country's economic growth. In order to promote better understanding of this incentive mechanism, we must address two issues: what is the source of local government and central government authority?

M-form organizational structure and the reform of government organizations

China has experienced six major government organization reforms since the policy of reform and opening-up was first adopted in 1978. Although each reform had a different focus, from an economic point of view all of them were intended to adjust the relationship between government and market. Generally speaking, the characteristics of all six reforms are as follows:

1. The ability of the government to adjust its relationship with the market was deliberately decreased. This included such things as giving up the right to allocate resources, control prices, and manage enterprises during the early stages of reform and a gradual withdrawal from competitive fields and a transition to service-oriented government more recently. The government has gradually clarified its responsibilities, but it still plays a greater role in economic development than Western governments. This is true of most East Asian economies during the early developmental stages.
2. Vertical top-down management was weakened and regional management was strengthened in order to adjust governmental functions and the boundary between the government and the market. These two reforms enhanced administrative efficiency, invigorated the market (reducing government regulation), and fostered local governments initiative.
3. Top-down management remained powerful; the central government and central ministries have considerable control over local governments and the economy. Although the total number of government agencies has been decreasing for some time, governmental institutions and staff members are still in a strange pattern of streamlining and expansion as they reduce some of the redundancy in governmental structure.
4. In the financial field, the reforms of 1994 attempted to cut the complicated links between banks and local governments. Vertical management was instituted in the financial field, which prevented some of the problems of soft budget constraint on SOEs that were rampant in the 1980s.[5]

Central and local authorities: reform of the cadre and personnel systems

Generally speaking, the authority of the central government comes from two correlated sources: the leadership of the CPC, and the mechanism of performance assessment and promotion for government officials. The reform in the standards for the selection and promotion of government leaders, which was implemented in the early 1980s, connected the promotion of local government officials to local economic development (Li and Zhou, 2005). Thus, local government officials act not only as economic participants who promote local economic development but also as political participants who are under the pressure of promotion.

Since the 1980s, two methods of reform have been decisive to the cadre and personnel systems: the Decision of the CPC Central Committee on the Establishment of a Retirement System for Veteran Cadres; and the development of the system of cross-regional rotation (Zhang and Zhou,

2008). In 1980, Deng Xiaoping pointed out, 'As far as the leadership and cadre systems of our Party and state are concerned, the major problems are bureaucracy, overconcentration of power, patriarchal methods, life tenure in leading posts, and privileges of various kinds' (Deng Xiaoping, Vol. II, 1993). The Party Central Committee, led by Deng Xiaoping, began to explore reform of the cadre and personnel systems during the post-reform era.

The Decision of the CPC Central Committee on the Establishment of a Retirement System for Veteran Cadres was issued by the central government in early 1982. Formal improvements to the tenure system and the method of selecting cadres were suggested by Deng Xiaoping (Zhang and Zhou, 2008). This reform greatly improved the quality of human capital in the government. It became routine for cadres at the provincial and ministerial levels to retire at the age of 65. This means that these officials could be replaced by younger and more knowledgeable successors. The mandatory retirement system provides the central government with the right to make all decisions regarding the tenure of senior government officials. This has had a profound influence on local officials (ibid.). Deng Xiaoping also advocated a system of cross-regional rotation of senior officials, but it was not put into effect until July 7, 1990. On August 6, 2006, the two legal documents – the Provisional Regulations on the System of Fixed Tenures of the Leading Cadres of the Party and Government, and the Provisional Regulations on the System of Withdrawal of the Leading Cadres of the Party and Government – were published formally.

The retirement, fixed tenure, and cross-regional rotation systems are three important components of the personnel system reform, and they have far-reaching institutional implications. First, these systems all favor the regulation of the behavior of government officials and the prevention of corruption. Second, in the context of economic decentralization, the system of cadre personnel management increases control over local governments and ensures that local power is too limited to succumb to localism. Third, these three systems and the system of performance assessment for government officials make promotion the key incentive in the operation of bureaucracy (ibid.). One investigation into the management of government officials since 1978 found that the central government's control over local government officials generally includes two aspects, one dominant and the other recessive (Huang, 2002). Dominant management could be realized by measurable indexes of economic development (such as the growth rate of the domestic GDP and levels of FDI), while recessive management relies more upon the prevention of corruption and disloyalty among government officials, which is difficult to monitor. The central government relies more on recessive management when dealing with senior officials in charge of multiple industries, departments, or regions, such as the secretary of the provincial (municipal) Party committee or the governor of a province (mayor). According to this analysis, recessive management includes the holding of concurrent posts within the Central Political Bureau Committee, direct nomination by central government, tenure control, and the holding of a post in at least one other place. Those systems certainly have some negative effects, such as promoting instant gratification and shortsightedness. However, over the past 30 years, most scholars have accepted the effectiveness of using recessive management to promote economic growth.

In sum, under the M-form governmental structure, central government control of local officials and lower levels of government is sufficiently warranted by the systems of retirement, fixed tenures and cross-regional rotation. The combination of the political incentive and decentralized economic systems forms a unique governance structure.

Positive Effects of the Decentralized Political Structure

Economic theorists have studied the advantages and disadvantages of fiscal decentralization extensively. In short, fiscal decentralization has five key advantages: access to local information, administrative efficiency, reduction in the size of government, retention of marketization, and promotion of fiscal innovation. China is a large country in terms of territory, population, and economic scale, which means that it is very costly for the central government to supervise local governments. Economic decentralization relieves some of this burden. So far, the success of the economic transition can, to a great extent, be attributed to economic decentralization. The more universal experience to be summarized from this decentralization reform is that for economic transition, the most important thing may not be finding the ideal prices because it is impossible to institute correct prices when the market is incomplete. It may be more important to find ideal incentives. The incentive mechanism is a much deeper theme in the economic development, and the price mechanism is nothing but a particular form of incentive mechanism.

Some early researchers maintained that local governments had an advantage over central governments with respect to access to information. Residents choose to live in certain places by judging the quality of public goods provided by local governments. This 'vote-by-foot' mechanism has been shown to optimize the allocation of resources (Tiebout, 1956). The power shift of fiscal revenue and expenditure from central to local authorities can promote economic efficiency, enhance local economic development, and promote economic growth (for example, Buchanan,

1965; Oates, 1972). Under the Chinese-style system of decentralization, local governments have no incentive to bail out SOEs facing bankruptcy or suffering from poor performance, because aiding production with stronger mobility is unfavorable for local governments hoping to improve their own competitiveness (Qian and Roland, 1998). The system of decentralization provides marketized incentives to local governments in order to maintain and promote the process of marketization. This then promotes economic growth and increases tax revenues (for example, Weingast, 1995; McKinnon, 1997; Qian and Weingast, 1997).

Most scholars argue that there is a positive correlation between fiscal decentralization and economic growth.[6] Zhang and Gong (2005) analyzed the data from 1986 to 2002 and found that the tax-sharing system significantly increased the effects of fiscal decentralization on economic growth. However, before China's tax-sharing system was reformed, there was a negative correlation between fiscal decentralization and economic growth. These two factors became positively correlated after 1994. Fiscal decentralization plays a more positive role in areas in the later stages of economic development than in the areas that are less economically developed. The advantages of fiscal decentralization are felt more keenly in the eastern provinces than in the midwest.

Economic decentralization is not the only means of promoting economic development. China's particular political incentives also foster favorable growth. From an economic perspective, we shall focus more on the two characteristics of the political system: the GDP-based method of assessing political achievements and the opinion-poll-based system of appointment and removal (Li and Zhou, 2005). China's economic decentralization is accompanied by political centralization, and promotion-based incentives create a strong driving force that induces local officials to foster fast economic development (Tsui and Wang, 2004). Fixed tenures and cross-regional rotation give government officials strong incentives to boost short-term economic growth (Zhang and Gao, 2007).

The influence of economic decentralization and political centralization on local governments is exerted through yardstick competition among governments. Usually, yardstick competition corresponds to the political system responsible for lower levels of government. The general public and central government almost always know less about the local government's actions than it does itself. However, the voters assess the achievements of the local government in their areas by comparing them to those of other areas. The local government knows this, so it copies and implements successful policies from other areas (Besley and Case, 1995; Baicker, 2005). This kind of yardstick competition is bottom up. Mutual monitoring and sharing of information between governments at the same level could improve the operational efficiency of governmental departments, reduce administrative costs, and prevent abuse of power (Martinez-Vazquez and McNab, 2003). However, in China's political system, the local governments are responsible for the higher levels. In the context of political centralization and the mechanism of achievement assessment, local governments are not only required to ensure GDP growth but are also ranked in accordance with certain indexes, such as GDP. The GDP growth rate incentive system fosters top-down yardstick competition based on the assessment by higher authorities (Zhang et al., 2010). Thus, the government promotes growth by promoting competition for growth.

Negative Effects of the Decentralized Political Structure

A consensus has been reached within the economic community regarding the benefits of decentralization reform (Qian et al., 1988, 1999; Dewatripont and Maskin, 1995; Qian and Weingast, 1997; Qian and Roland, 1998). Existing theories explain how decentralization promotes competition between local governments and boosts economic growth. However, a complete decentralization theory should analyze not only the benefits, such as the positive incentives given to local governments, but also the costs of decentralization. In fact, the outstanding achievements that occurred during the early stages of reform and the many problems that currently exist in China are both related to decentralization reform. Considering the current conditions in China, the negative impacts of decentralization are more prominent. They have three main aspects: first, the widening income gap between urban and rural areas; second, duplicate construction and market segmentation between regions; and third, unfair distribution of public services. These effects will be discussed in detail in Chapters 3–6. The cost of decentralization will be explained from a theoretical perspective in this subsection.

A major difference between China's economic transition and Russia's is that China's central government uses an incentive mechanism similar to that seen in business – decentralization within political organizations. Given the fact that local governments at all levels control a vast number of economic, political, and social resources, providing suitable incentives to local governments and allowing them to share directly in the benefits of local economic development should encourage them to pursue economic growth. This raises the question of whether emulating incentive mechanisms from the business are an effective means of creating incentives for political and administrative systems. To answer this question, a fundamental distinction must be drawn between the incentive mechanisms of political organizations and those of business organizations. This distinction can be used to determine what challenges government departments would encounter when implementing a business incentive mechanism in fiscally decentralized systems.

The incentive mechanisms of political organizations are quite different from those of economic organizations. The principals (the public) have preferences that are different from those of political organizations, but company shareholders generally share the same goals: the maximization of profits. However, in political organizations, each interest group has its own preferences and interests. This makes it difficult to define indicators of government efficiency. Unlike businesses, which focus on maximizing profits, political organizations generally multi-task. In addition to efficiency and economic growth, political organizations also pursue social fairness, income equity, environmental protection, and quality of public services. Theoretically, the pursuit of multiple goals with strong incentives based on a single dimension (task) can be difficult. Assessment based on growth may induce the neglect of social goals, especially when they conflict with short-term economic growth. Third, the heterogeneity of principals and differences in external conditions make it difficult for officials to establish standards for comparison and reference. However, businesses can easily find similar counterparts for reference in terms of achievement and efficiency. It is not reasonable to compare the Chinese US governments because the two countries differ in so many respects. It is possible to make limited comparisons between local governments within China, but these must be made with caution because of the huge differences in conditions.

This illustrates the complexity of the search for indicators that can be used in objective evaluations of government officials, and leads to the fourth difference between political and economic organizations: incentive mechanisms have no single, absolute indicator of achievement. In reality, those at higher levels of government promote local officials by evaluating their achievement with respect to economic development, especially in terms of GDP. Relative GDP growth is probably a suboptimal indicator of the achievements of local government officials. However, the disadvantages of combining fiscal decentralization with relative achievement assessment are even more evident.

One disadvantage is that assessments of relative achievement can lead to fierce competition between local governments. Various methods of market segmentation have been adopted by local governments trying to outperform their neighbors with respect to GDP. The most typical method is regional protectionism, which can take several forms. Protectionism affects resource allocation by limiting the scope of the product and service markets, which in turn restricts the division of labor and specialization.

This is detrimental to China's long-term economic development and international competitiveness.

Overdependence on GDP as an indicator of relative achievement is another reason for China's urban-biased economic policies. Because the secondary and tertiary industries in cities are the country's main sources of economic growth, local governments tend to neglect the economic development of rural areas. A direct indication of this is that the proportion of fiscal expenditure that had been used to support agricultural production decreased sharply from the mid-1990s to 2001 (Lu and Chen, 2006a). When conflicts of interest occur between capital owners and ordinary workers, local governments prioritize the interests of capital owners. As a result, China's labor market is relatively weak. This has a significant influence on patterns of income distribution.

One critical assumption involved in the assessment of local officials using relative achievements is that the objects being assessed have common shocks or risks and that their achievements can therefore be indicated precisely through the relative ranking of their achievements. However, in a large country like China, regions differ from each other in terms of natural resources, geography, history, and culture. Because of this, the assessment of relative achievements involves a great deal of statistical noise, reducing the effectiveness of incentive schemes based on this technique. This could be considered the second disadvantage of a relative achievement incentive.

The third disadvantage is a specific form of the second one. Given its importance, it is analyzed separately. Due to the inherent differences both among regions and in the post-reform policies, differences in economic growth can show an increasing returns effect. In other words, even if there is no other external force, the underdeveloped regions may fall even further behind their neighbors, while developed regions grow more prosperous. This increases the noise in the assessment process, making it difficult for the central government to determine whether the local economic growth is caused by the mechanism of increasing returns or by the endeavors of local government.

Relative assessments of achievement cannot produce incentives for everyone. When competition is based on relative achievement, the number of winners is necessarily limited. Richer areas enjoy more benefits and natural advantages and the mechanism of increasing returns. This means that local officials in less economically developed areas cannot obtain incentives. Even great efforts may go undetected by the relative assessment system.[7] Relative achievement assessment has almost no effect on local officials in less-developed areas. Many government officials respond to this through corruption or inaction. From an economic point of view, the polarization of developed and undeveloped areas will get worse.

There are some difficulties inherent in motivating local officials that have no bearing on the relative achievement assessment. Unlike the managers of enterprises, the achievements of local officials depend more on a group effort than on individual efforts. For this reason, free riders may exist among local officials. These individuals may be reluctant to take responsibility for specific tasks (for example, increasing employment). Corporate managers are often motivated to seek long-term profits because their compensation includes company shares or stock options, but this would not be practical for local officials. As a result, the long-term goals of local economic and social development are ignored. This can take the form of neglecting environmental issues, the income gap, education, or health services.

The economic decentralization and political centralization of China have been the driving force behind economic development for local governments, advances in the marketization and privatization of the economy, and the construction of local infrastructure. The relative achievement assessment system has three significant outcomes: continuous enlargement of the income gap between urban and rural areas, market segmentation between different regions, and insufficient public services. We shall analyze these three problems in detail in Chapters 3–5. In Chapter 6, we point out that the strategy of unbalanced growth adopted by China has caused certain problems, most of them related to the internal and external imbalances affecting the economy. China must adjust its internal structure fundamentally in order to overcome this dual imbalance. In this sense, the challenges faced by the economy are also opportunities for structural adjustment.

Transition from an Administration- to a Service-oriented Government and Inherent Challenges

The challenges China faces in the current political and social environment are related to its status as a large, developing country. Its size makes it hard for the central government to supervise local governments, so the country adopted a system of economic decentralization, which posed its own set of challenges. The way in which China deals with the dilemma of the decentralized system will define its success or failure as a model of a successful large country.

In order to create a suitable stable external environment to foster sustainable economic growth, the solutions to China's problems must be tailored to its politics, economy, and society. In the present situation, the issue of people's livelihoods is becoming more and more serious. These problems pose serious challenges to the government's ability to function.

Several conflicts must be resolved if the transition from an administration- to a service-oriented government is to be effective.

First, conflicts between personal interests and government objectives must be resolved. The government must set several targets for the future in order to maintain the balance between various demands of the people. Effective supervision should be formed to exclude government officials who pursue personal interests at the expense of government objectives.

Second, the conflicts between the goals of interest groups and society's long-term development must be resolved. The differences between the interests of certain members of society foster the development of specific interest groups. In the future, specific reform methods will probably address these vested interests, promoting social equality. The realization of society's long-term objectives is beneficial to all members of society. However, in the short term, some methods of reform may harm or be considered harmful by certain groups, who may resist those changes. In that case, the formation of the consensus that society's long-term development outweighs short-term hardship and an understanding of how those long-term goals will affect society may be useful. In Chapters 3–6 we provide a theoretical basis for society's long-term development from different perspectives.

Third, the conflict between the objectives and interests of different departments and different levels of government must be resolved. The biggest challenge China faces now in the transition of government functions is preventing local governments from neglecting overall interests while they pursue local interests. Given society's long-term objectives, the integration of urban and rural areas, the integration of the interregional market and public service equalization all require coordinating actions from local governments. Thus, the conquest of localism by the central government is critical. The vertical management system should be strengthened appropriately.

Essentially, all three conflicts between local and national interests must be resolved. In order to guarantee the realization of national interests, the rules of law and democracy are of particular importance. They guarantee that public opinion will be considered in decision making and that government officials will not be captured by any specific vested interest group, thus maintaining social fairness. Equal rights are the foundation of the construction of law and democracy. However, the government has followed a system of vertical management, which usually allows certain individuals to manipulate the system and exercise powers without restraint. Combining the normative construction of a market economy system with the transition of government functions, mitigating the conflicts between system building and traditional systems, and strengthening government behavioral norms are all problems that China must solve. The timing of the system change is extremely important. Appropriate institutions should be created to meet the demands of economic development during each stage in order to foster sustainable economic growth. During the transition, no simple transplantation of institutions can solve the problems faced by any specific country during any specific period (Djankov et al., 2002; Acemoglu et al., 2006).

2.2 RELATIONSHIP-BASED SOCIAL STRUCTURES AND ECONOMIC TRANSITION AND DEVELOPMENT

China's governance is politically centralized but economically decentralized. This is well suited to the needs of a large country. However, many of the social structures are based on relationships. This is a distinctive feature of China as a developing country.

The transition from a planned to a market economy is a phased process. During the early stages of economic transition and development, a social structure based on relationships emerged as an informal institution, compensating for some of the flaws in the market and formal institutions. This may partially explain a phenomenon that has confused many economists: the near-miraculous growth of China's economy despite unsound formal institutions related to property rights, finance and law.

However, as economic development continues, the cost of the relationship-based society increases. For example, the scope of relationship-based transactions is usually too small to realize scale economy. The society is usually divided into insiders and outsiders, and this can artificially increase inequality. Moreover, the effects of the income gap become enlarged when social relationships are combined with political or economic power. This then causes the misallocation of resources and social inequality. The relationships might distort the new-born market mechanisms and hinder the further development of the economy. Either market power will be strong enough to dissolve the bonds of social relationships, allowing sound marketization, or it will be overwhelmed by stronger social relationships.

This section first reviews the historical origins of China's relationship-based society and its role in the economic transition. Then, we analyze the functions and costs of relationship-based transactions in economic transition and development and the challenges imposed by economic development in a relationship-based society. Finally, we analyze possible means of realizing fair and sound marketization.

Historical Foundations of the Relationship-based Society

China's relationship-based society (also called an 'acquaintance society') has deep historical roots. In terms of economic structure, China has been a settlement-oriented agricultural society with little mobility and a lower level of social division of labor for much of its history. Low mobility led to the formation of long-term relationships among people living in each community, and the low level of social division of labor promoted relationship-based transactions that crossed many markets. The historical relationship between landlords and tenants is a good example of this. In the absence of specialized markets, the transactions between landlords and tenants usually crossed several markets at once: they took place not only in the product market (landlords buying food from tenants), but also in the labor market (landlords hiring tenants), credit market (landlords lending to tenants), and the insurance market (sharecropping tenancy system). In economies with higher levels of social division of labor, people transact with different entities in different specialized markets. For example, in rural areas with low levels of division of labor and no specialized markets for commodities and services, rural residents transact not with money but with mutual aid: you help me to build a house (in the absence of a specialized construction labor market) and I will help you gather crops (in the absence of a specialized harvesting labor market).

This kind of relationship-based transaction has two dimensions, one is vertical – relations across time – and the other is horizontal – geographical. To parties on both sides of each transaction, various transactions are bound together. This makes it hard to define success and failure, and disinterested transactions become available in a single market (Yongqin Wang, 2005, 2006a, 2006b, 2007a). In a society with little division of labor, the costs of relationship-based transactions are low, and this can make up for market deficiencies. Historically, China's relationship-based society has had three aspects.

Family-based social bonds
In terms of social economy, traditional Chinese society has had two important characteristics: the economic structure of an agricultural society and governance at the level of small communities (such as villages and small towns). In particular, production, consumption, and transactions have taken place based on family or extended family connections, which were commonly relationship based and interlinked. Individuals behaved in certain ways in the context of social relationships. At the same time, because of the small scope of transactions within an agricultural society, undeveloped social division of labor and low mobility allowed these rela-

tionships to endure and self-perpetuate over long periods. Historically, production, consumption, and social interactions, which are rural-family based, were established after the foundation of the PRC, when rural production was constantly promoted. Subsequently, agricultural production advanced the formation of agricultural producers' cooperatives and then the people's commune (*Renmin Gongshe*) deprived the rural family of its function. For a long time these families lived through a period of crisis. However, following the implementation of the household contract responsibility system and reestablishment of family status, rural areas developed greatly. In a sense, the history of rural development was one of how to reestablish and improve rural-family-based production, consumption, and social interactions.

Centralized and hierarchical political structure
In terms of political structure, Chinese society has been based on a centralized hierarchy. Ever since the establishment of the system of prefectures and counties during the ancient Qin Dynasty, the political structure has always been a centralized, top-down bureaucratic organization. This kind of centralized hierarchical political structure has continued through to the present. After the foundation of the PRC in 1949, democratic centralism was adopted as a general organizational principle, but the hierarchical management of territory and a system of occupational officers were retained. Because the new China adopted a planned economy system characterized by quantity allocation, shortages of commodities and services became normal. When price mechanisms did not work, the role of relationships in resource allocation increased.

Low mobility
Long-term lack of mobility across regions has supported the relationship-based social structure. Since the Qin Dynasty, the mobility of the population has been extremely low except during times of war and great social upheaval. After the PRC was founded, the household registration system (*hukou*) constrained the movement of the population, which strengthened the relationship-based nature of society. China's limited mobility has two main causes.

As part of the catching-up strategy of promoting heavy industrialization, China gave priority to the development of urban areas, which demanded resources from rural areas. In order to reduce the negative impact of production on urban sectors and collect agricultural resources, in 1958 the government issued the Registration of Residence of the People's Republic of China, which required household registration of all residents and limited the migration of peasants to cities. The government also promoted the formation of people's communes after the completion of the socialist transformation of agriculture. Household registration for the purpose of residency not only hindered the migration of peasants to cities but also strictly constrained migration across different parts of the countryside. This situation was not altered until the 1980s.

The second reason for the lack of mobility is the work unit system (*danwei*) which was implemented in urban sectors. During the planned economy period, the work unit system became widespread in urban areas. The primary objective of cities was production; accordingly, the primary work units were production units; each unit had to provide services to workers, such as housing, medical care, training, children's education, and jobs for the spouses of staff members. The unit was both an economic organization and a political and social structure. In units, which were the basic form of social organization in cities, interactions and transactions among the people within each unit, between unit staff and unit members, between units and the government, and among different markets were long term and linked.

Role of the Relationship-based Society in Economic Transition and Development

During the early stages of the transition from a planned to a market economy, most markets were either deficient or unsound, and relationship-based transactions helped to compensate for this. Early reform preserved original political and social structures, which helped ease economic transition.

Current role of family-centered bonds

Unlike the previous rural system, which involved people's communes, the family-based contract responsibility system gave individuals in rural areas few incentives to be lazy or seek a free ride. Under the contract responsibility system, land and other means of production were family used or family occupied, and labor was input by family groups. With respect to consumption, products were shared among family members. With respect to social interactions, individuals did not have complete personal independence and undertook joint liability for one another. This type of organization not only rendered production more efficient but also served as an effective risk-sharing mechanism.

With the family as the basic unit, production, consumption, and social interactions also became a form of intra- and intergenerational risk sharing. The family bond served as an insurance mechanism, especially as a form of old-age support. Specifically, children provide certain income and care for their parents. The proportion of aged people cared for by their children is high in all parts of China: 60.8 percent in the countryside and 53.3 percent in cities and towns. The proportion of financial support given to parents in urban areas is lower than in rural areas: 43.8 percent in the countryside and 33.5 percent in cities and towns. This is because city and town residents have higher incomes and social security (Zimmer and Kwong, 2003). Raising children to provide against old age and the education of children are two key characteristics of the Chinese model of providing for the aged. Although expenditures for children (especially investments in education) are considered as consumption, they can also be considered investments in eventual old-age care. Ever since the one-child policy came into effect, parents have paid more attention to their children's education (Liu and Lu, 2008).

Community-level bonds (towns, subdistricts, villages)

Single family units can only mitigate risk to a certain degree. In rural areas, which feature the residency-based household registration system and a system of work units implemented during the early stage of transition, an individual's scope of interaction and transaction can extend beyond family to the entire local community, such as the village, town, or subdistrict. Morduch and Sicular (2001) studied the situation of risk sharing in a county in Shandong Province. To a self-sufficient family, the coefficient of variation of consumption indicates that the fluctuation of consumption is high. If mutual insurance can be arranged in countryside communities, the fluctuation of consumption can be reduced. If mutual insurance is arranged in county communities, the coefficient of variation of consumption will be decreased further.

In addition to informal forms of insurance, informal financial systems based on relationships play another important role. During the 1980s and 1990s, it was very difficult for individuals and private enterprises to borrow from banks. Informal finance involves the exchange of credit among relatives, friends, or acquaintances. Tsai (2002) studied the conditions of informal finance in some sample cities in southern and northern China. According to her research, a large proportion of people (43.6 percent in the south and 59 percent in the north) had borrowed money through informal channels, and most people were quite satisfied with the experience. During this period, informal finance accounted for three-quarters of the total credit in the private sector.

Because developing enterprises were able to rely on bonds centered around family to solve such problems as financing and staffing, the development of both individuals and private enterprises took place along family lines. The use of resources organized by family networks during the development process has in fact broken the scope of the family and extended family.

Social interactions among families, communities, and (grassroots) government

During China's economic transition, families, communities, and the government would interact in various ways, not always based on the rule of law. Early during the transition, capital and land markets were insufficient or incomplete, and township enterprises engaged in cross-market inter-linked contract arrangements between entrepreneurs and local governments in the countryside (Wang and Li, 2008). Entrepreneurs needed to establish sound relationships with the local governments that controlled the factors of production and issued property rights. Local governments also need to develop local economies in order to meet their financial requirements and find qualified workers to fill positions.

Due to the deficiencies in the financial market, financing from state-owned banks was not able to satisfy the township enterprises' demand for capital. Among capital contributions to township enterprises, sums given to or lent from members of the original communities accounted for 28.17 percent of the total; bank loans guaranteed by towns or countryside assets about 17 percent; loans guaranteed by cadres about 11 percent; and loans guaranteed by government institutions about 20.5 percent. A national research group studying private enterprises has indicated that during the seventh five-year plan, 15 percent of the funds of private enterprises (mainly township enterprises) came from money borrowed from relatives and friends, and 1.9 percent came from the workers themselves (Chen, 1995).

Township enterprises help local governments meet employment demands. Township enterprises' labor needs can be met through inter-cooperation. Once the household contract responsibility system became widespread, it created a large amount of surplus labor. The limitations placed on workers' mobility put pressure on local governments to create jobs, which is an important motivating force behind township enterprises. About 40.5 percent of the employees of township enterprises are hired by grassroots leaders. Town, village, and countryside CPC committees appoint about 75 percent of the factory directors and managers of township enterprises (ibid.).

The township enterprise is an interlinked arrangement between entrepreneurs and governments. The rights to control such enterprises and take possession of their earnings are split between the government and the enterprises themselves. For example, most of the 33 percent of the decisions regarding the day-to-day operation of any given enterprise are made by town governments, 33 percent are made by both the town government and the enterprise, and the remaining 34 percent are made independently by the enterprise (ibid.). In terms of income distribution, the government's share is much higher than what can be collected through taxation, but a certain proportion of these funds is usually reinvested in the community in the form of public goods and services. Township enterprises usually take on some social responsibilities, such as the support of compulsory education and public health.

Entirely private enterprises that operate under the shadow of collectively owned companies can also be found in some coastal areas. Their pretense to collective ownership gives them access to resources otherwise unavailable to private enterprises (such as financial resources and export rights). It also affords them government protection in terms of property rights. Local governments and relevant institutions also draw some administration fees. Some employees in SOEs can be transferred to enterprises linked to government to relieve unemployment. The number of enterprises following this model was quite large during the early 1990s. A sample study conducted in 1994 indicated that 83 percent of township enterprises were actually private enterprises. According to the statistics provided by relevant departments in Dongyang, Zhejiang Province the same year, private enterprises belonging to fake collectivities made up over 70 percent of the total number of nominally collective enterprises (Dai, 2005). Like township enterprises, these false-collective, or 'red hat', companies were part of a transitional arrangement. The red hat system made up in part for the incomplete factor market and insufficient protection of private property rights during the transition process. In the late 1990s, the factor market became more developed, and a clearer definition of private property was written into the constitution. These changes and other laws led to the transition from township to private enterprises. The red hat phenomenon almost completely disappeared.

This analysis indicates that relationships have played and continue to play an important part in society and economy, both before and after the transition. This can be shown in three prominent aspects:

1. *Role of relationship-based transactions in deficient and otherwise imperfect markets* The transition has caused a shift from plan- to market-based allocation of resources and goods. It was carried out using collective systems in the countryside, work unit systems in cities, and the abolition of market transactions. During the initial stage of the transition, there were hardly any specialized product or factor markets, not even in their simplest forms. Under these conditions, the presence of effective substitutes was essential to the success of the

transition. Coordinating the transition across different departments was also critical.

Because the social bonds and networks of rural residents are much stronger than those found in urban areas, certain reforms may be more successful in the countryside. If marketization reform occurs in urban areas first, the weaker social bonds among residents in urban areas may not be able to mitigate the risks inherent in the project. This may lead to deficiencies in both formal and informal institutions. In rural areas, marketization does not destroy existing family-based social bonds.

It is easier to implement reforms in urban areas if rural areas are reformed first. The reforms implemented in urban areas in 1984 and afterward did not immediately break unit-based social links. Units maintained close relationships with employees in terms of highly incomplete systems of labor, housing, health care, and finance until the mid-1990s. By then, various kinds of specialized markets had gradually formed, and market-oriented reforms of the pension, employment, health, and housing systems were in full swing.

2. *Relationship-based transactions as self-enforced substitute mechanisms*   During economic transitions, radical reforms, like those seen in Russia, can break down a society's previous organizational framework very quickly, causing an institutional vacuum in which social disorder, chaos, and undesirable social organizations, such as the Russian mafia, emerge. Sometimes these organizations begin to fill society's needs for contract enforcement. China promotes marketization in the context of its original political and social structure. Thus, marketization is always supported by various informal institutions, and institutional vacuum and social chaos have not resulted.

The function of formal law is severely restricted during economic transition. China's transition has taken place mainly within the framework of relationship-based social structures, such as the informal loan market. The lending rate and nature of the loan agreement differ from community to community and from person to person within the same community (Tsai, 2002). This is because the loan is usually linked to other transactions, and different interest rates reflect different transaction structures and levels of interconnectivity, which are highly dependent on specific situations.

Unlike mature market economies, whose specialized markets are fully developed and whose formal institutions, such as the law, are sound, the implementation of relationship-based transactions usually cannot be guaranteed by formal law. For example, Zhu (2000) found that providing legal services to rural areas in an attempt to solve disputes in grassroots societies did not work. People preferred to solve problems by themselves rather than seek legal help. Even in urban areas, the courts are usually not a disputing party's first choice. This is because transactions based on interlinked relationships tend to be long term and cross-market. However, law judgments are mainly based on single transactions, and this does not always suit people's long-term interests. A 2002 survey indicated that even in the Yangtze River Delta, which has a sound market, mature institutions, and a developed economy, a great number of businesses choose to negotiate directly with their opponents, to request administrative intervention from local government, or to resolve disputes through personal channels (Yujian Wang et al., 2007, Table 6.14, p. 154).

3. *Effects of relationship-based social structures on transaction costs in the context of small markets*   Relationship-based transactions are well suited to small markets, and formal institutions based on third parties (such as the courts) are better suited to wider markets. Relationship-based transactions are self-perpetuated by long-term relationships among fixed entities. The only requirement is that both parties to the transaction have the same expectations regarding its result. However, transactions based on formal institutions (such as laws) require that the relevant transaction information be verified by a third party (such as the courts). This poses set-up costs (such as legislation and the establishment of courts) and requires investments in institutional infrastructure. During the early stages of economic development, therefore, the relationship-based transactions offer substantial savings (John Shuhe Li, 2003).

These three points indicate that the social foundation of a country's economic transition is very important.[8] The radical liberalization reform that has taken place in some countries, like Russia, destroyed the relationships and interconnectivity maintained by traditional systems almost overnight, and effective formal institutions were not immediately able to fill the gap. Because the society's ability to govern itself was broken and no alternative system was available, the country faced an administration crisis. In contrast, China's more gradual transition preserved a great deal of the relationships and interconnections of the traditional social system, providing an institutional foundation for China's expanding economy (Yongqin Wang, 2005, 2006a, 2006b, 2007a).

Dissolution of the Relationship-based Society

So far, China has deliberately preserved the relationship-based social structure as it has promoted marketization and economic development.

This has revealed the foundation of the relationship-based society. Both of the main economic functions originally performed by families and communities are gradually being replaced by specialized markets.

Transition and dissolution of the bonds between families and government and between communities and government

Along with the promotion of marketization and the implementation of social policies (such as the one-child policy), the relationships and interconnection that occur at the level of family, community, and local government have been weakened to various degrees. The nuclear family composed of parents and children is the primary family form, and this is true in cities, towns, and rural areas, though there is a higher proportion of nuclear households in cities than in towns or in the countryside. Historically, the nuclear families of the 1960s have slight advantages over other types of households, but they currently have pronounced advantages over compound families, the number of which is gradually decreasing (Yuesheng Wang, 2006a). Among nuclear families, the proportion composed solely of a husband and wife has gradually increased relative to that of families composed of parents and children, especially after the late marriage, late birth, and one-child policies were implemented. The number of families with exactly one child has also increased progressively. Increases in the number of people enrolled in higher education have been found to be correlated to smaller family size. The average number of people in families has decreased from 4.41 in 1982 to 3.96 in 1990 and 3.44 in 2000 (Yuesheng Wang, 2006b).

The effects of shrinking family size on China's economic life will probably be revealed in time. Decreased family size has already been shown to weaken social bonds at the family level. Even among nuclear families, mutual supportability can decrease. Shrinking family size may weaken the capability of aging families to take care of older members (ibid.). Its implications for specialized insurance markets, credit markets, and social security are not entirely clear. Weakening bonds at the family level may intensify the risks taken by individuals.

At the community and government levels, the development of specialized markets can be said to have weakened the advantages of township enterprises. This leaves entrepreneurs less dependent on communities and local governments. The strengthening of the development and mobility of the labor market has allowed people to leave their communities to work in other regions. This caused the disintegration of many enterprises in the mid-1990s (Wang and Li, 2008). After the mid-1990s, governments extensively promoted privatization and marketization reform in employment, medical care, education, and housing. This destroyed the urban sector's traditional unit system. Following the dissolution of the unit system, unit-centered social relationships slowly disintegrated, and the cities gradually transitioned from an acquaintance- to a stranger-based world.

Labor flow and dissolution of the relationship-based society

During the early stages of transition, villages and towns were the main destinations of migrant workers, primarily because of the growth of township enterprises. However, after the mid-1980s, labor flow toward villages and towns slowed down in favor of labor movement toward cities (Shi, 2006). Migration within villages and towns was usually related to the development of township enterprises, and the period from 1990 to 1995 saw intense growth among township enterprises. The proportion of the rural labor force dedicated to township enterprises grew from 9.4 percent in 1980 to 26 percent in 1995. After that, very little progress was made (Brooks and Tao, 2003). The figure is still around 27–29 percent even now (see Chapter 3). In contrast, the growth rate of employment had been kept at an average of 3 percent since 1990 (Shi, 2006). China's labor force experienced a large-scale flow in terms of total volume and a strong tendency to move toward cities.

The large scale of the movement of the labor force during the transition period not only weakened the original bonds of the relationship-based society but also decreased the degree of social trust. This is because the formation of trust requires both the long-term cultivation of personal and family relationships and expectations of future interactions. Empirical research based on the US indicated that, although the movement of individuals did not affect trust in any obvious way, the high mobility of communities significantly decreased trust (Alesina and Ferrara, 2000). In Indonesia, the outflow of the labor force during the process of industrialization also decreased mutual cooperation and trust in local areas (Miguel et al., 2006). A special feature of China's labor market is that migrant workers who leave their home towns to work in cities are confronted with seriously discriminatory social policies from every angle and are not able to integrate into city society. Because of this, the majority of them return home. Increased movement of laborers from rural to urban areas may therefore strengthen people's trust in public organizations based in the home counties (Lu and Zhang, 2008). However, this takes place in the context of urban–rural segmentation. If such segmentation could be eliminated, labor mobility may still dissolve the relationship bond in the rural society.

Economic development and dynamic changes in the relationship-based society

As China's economic transition and development continue, the relationship-based society may well continue to disintegrate. Economic development can be expected to affect the structure of the relationship-based society in the two following ways.

The first is the specialization effect. This occurs when the scope of a market expands and specialization deepens and becomes the norm. Transactions which were previously dependent on interlinked relationships can now be carried out in specialized markets. For example, in rural areas, services that used to be performed by villagers can now be purchased in specialized markets. If the specialized markets are efficient enough, economies of scale will be realized, reducing the cost of every transaction for both customer and provider. Under these conditions, personalized, interlinked relationship-based transactions will be overwhelmed and replaced by market-based transactions, which are not personalized (Yongqin Wang, 2005, 2006a, 2006b, 2007a).

The second is the thickness effect. Along with the expansion of market scope and the deepening of specialization, the frequency and volume of transactions in specialized markets will increase continuously. These thicker markets decrease the expense of market transactions by lowering the search costs of buyers and sellers. More buyers and sellers will then be drawn to specialized market transactions. The attractiveness of relationship-based transactions will decline and may eventually disappear (Kranton, 1996).

From the point of view of the stages of economic development, relationship-based transactions are relatively cost-effective when markets are small and specialization is limited. This is because this type of transaction is self-enforced by all participants and it incurs far lower costs than the establishment of formal institutions and regulations. However, as economic development continues and markets expand in scope, relationship-based transactions offer less and less in the way of cost savings, yielding their advantage to rule-based transactions. This is because in relationship-based transactions, the addition of any participant outside the social network increases costs, and this increase is cumulative. However, in rule-based transactions, more participants mean lower per capita costs of establishing regulations. In other words, the fixed-cost investments of setting up rules eventually allow rule-based transactions to take advantage of economies of scale and reduce the cost per transaction. The optimal system for any society depends on that society's stage of economic development and the scope of the market. When the economy is underdeveloped, informal institutions relying on relationship-based transactions are more important. Once the economy has developed to a certain degree and the scope of the market is large enough, rule-based transactions relying on formal institutions and legislation become more important. Scale economies and improvements in technology can then be realized.

Generally, economic development promotes the transition from a relationship-based society to a rule-based one through the specialization and market thickness effects. This in turn promotes further economic development. According to Polanyi (1957), this transition includes a shift in the economic relationships embedded in social relationships to social relationships embedded in economic relationships. Thus, limited economic relationships become subordinate to wider and deeper economic relationships.

Challenges of the Transition from a Relationship- to a Rule-based Society

Successful realization of this structural transition depends on whether the specialization and market thickness effects occur. China's current political and social structures contain some factors that may prevent these two effects from being fully realized. We shall discuss these obstacles from three directions.

Conflict between the demands of specialization and market integration and current political structure

As discussed in Section 2.1, both decentralization reform and methods of assessment are based on relative GDP performance. Those mechanisms have fueled economic growth, but they have also led to fierce competition among regions (including duplicate facilities and industrial structures) and to the segmentation of product markets, factor markets, and public services.

The segmentation of the product and factor markets impedes the realization of economies of scale and limits specialized division of labor and expansion of the scope of the market. Thus, it can hinder the transition from a relationship- to a rule-based society. Regional segmentation of public services not only restricts interregional migration but also reduces social trust and integration. For example, local governments welcome migrant workers because they contribute to the local economy, but they take no initiative to provide the workers and their children with public services such as health care or education because these services add to the cost of local government. This makes it difficult for migrant workers to integrate themselves into local society, impeding social integration (see Chapter 3). This creates a conflict between the needs of the economy and the needs of the administration. The core issue of the contradiction lies in the discrepancy between the localism of local governments and the demand for unification and specialization of the Chinese market as a whole. This conflict may cause social disorder and chaos as the transition continues. This may be considered a consequence of the disintegration of the relationship-based society accompanied by failure to establish a rule-based society. In other words, the advancing economy and increasing levels of worker mobility are affecting the current relationship-based society, but the administrative segmentation of the market does not currently favor social integration or the establishment of a unified norm or social system.

Embedding of marketization in the current political power and social relationship

The economic history of economic development in every nation in the world tells us that there are two types of marketization. The first is incomplete marketization, which is penetrated and controlled by power structures and social relationships. The second is fully developed marketization, which overcomes the restrictions of existing power structures and social relationships, becoming equitable and efficient. The first type of marketization is especially vulnerable during transitions, when power structures and social relationships continuously assert themselves. These forces can obtain market value through marketization and become capitalized. The capitalization of power and social relationships further enhances the market's strength, giving the people in power who participate in those relationships greater negotiating power. In this way, people in advantageous power structures and social relationships can take control of market mechanisms.

Some studies have analyzed the impact of power and relationship on income. Favorable political status and social networking have indeed been found to elevate income. Research has shown that social networking in the private sector can increase personal income and that social networking in the public sector cannot. If the degree of marketization is believed to be higher in the private sector, then the positive influence of social networking on one's income level may increase alongside marketization (Knight and Yueh, 2002; Li et al., 2009).

When existing political and social powers become involved in the process of marketization, the distribution of income becomes skewed. The degree of political and social power varies among different individuals. In this way, inequity of power can increase the income gap with respect to both finances and public services. This inequality first appears in the form of differences in access to opportunities. A rift forms between insiders and outsiders with the insiders enjoying more power, participating in resource allocation, and having a greater voice in policy making. For example, the controversy surrounding the loss of capital during the transition from state-owned to privately owned enterprises is essentially that the people in power under the existing administrative system of SOEs controlled the transition process in such a way that they provided a disproportionate number of opportunities for other powerful people to take control of formerly state-owned assets (Lu et al., 2009).

If the inequity in power does indeed cause the inequity in opportunities, the conditions of society may change for the worse, including declining income mobility. In some studies, the flow of household income in China is measured using income data from 1989, 1991, 1993, 1997, and 2000. The conclusion was that household income mobility in China had remained at a high level and was greater than that of the US, Western Germany, and Belgium in terms of changes in income distribution during the same period (Ding and Wang, 2005). However, we should be very cautious when examining these results because these developed countries are already relatively stable, while China is still in transition. This does not allow for a great deal of comparison between China and these developed countries, so the results of these studies must be viewed with caution. Other research indicates that the income mobility in China has tended to decrease (Wang, 2005). During China's economic transition, if the wealthy and those empowered by the original political and social structures take advantage of the unsound markets to increase their income and then invest those funds in the pursuit of further power, income mobility in China will decrease.

The marketization controlled by power and social relationships could also interfere with the transition from a relationship- to a rule-based society by impeding the market thickness and specialization effects. If relationship-based transactions make up the majority of economic transitions in the society, then specialized markets will remain thin and search costs will remain high. People will therefore remain dependent on relationship-based interactions (Kranton, 1996). In the case of the labor market, if people rely on social relationships to find a job, then the labor market will become very thin and search costs will be high.

In those regions where a large number of businesses are privately owned, relationships between private enterprises and the government tend to be good, and mutually beneficial arrangements are common. Because of this, however, investment seeking has become a serious problem. The World Bank conducted a survey of investment environments in 23 Chinese cities and compared the amount of money devoted to gifts and bribes to government officials and supervision departments to sales revenues. In Shenzhen and Wenzhou, where private enterprises make up a large proportion of the economy, abnormal expenditures are very high (World Bank, 2003). Economists have conducted a great deal of research into political connections in China, and the fundamental conclusion is that the relationship between enterprises and governments is beneficial to the development of private enterprise. However, these benefits come at the cost of the entrepreneurs' dissatisfaction and a high cost to the public.[9]

It is dangerous to allow power structures and social relationships to control marketization. In Latin America, interest groups distorted the process of resource allocation, which was detrimental not only to equity and economic efficiency but also to social innovation. If China is to avoid this trap, then it must decouple the sociopolitical power structure from the economy. Under the current administrative system, lower-ranking government officials in reality undertake more responsibility than their superiors, and accountability measures are insufficient. Thus, local government officials can easily be corrupted by special interest groups.

Institutional mismatching and institutional vacuum during the transition

We have analyzed the scenario in which marketization might cause the relationship-based society to unravel. We have also discussed some obstacles to the transition from a relationship- to a rule-based society. In reality, when the economy has developed to a certain stage and the markets have become large enough, formal rule-based institutions may take a larger role in economic development. However, if formal institutions are not in place and relationship-based transactions still prevail, social and economic development may become mismatched. The country is especially vulnerable during the transition from a relationship- to a rule-based society, and institutional vacuums may form. There may be an economic and political crisis.[10] Once the economy has reached a certain stage, the timing of system formation, both democratization and the development of relevant laws, will be critical. However, before the economy reaches the stage when formal institutions have taken a large role, construction of a democratic, law-based system would cause a mismatch between system and economy and impede economic development. Such problems have been observed in some countries.

The importance of the timing of institutionalization becomes clearer if we analyze the transition and development in China under the East Asian model. The East Asian model has five characteristics:

1. During the early stages of economic development (such as those of Japan, Hong Kong, Singapore, South Korea, Taiwan, and modern China), strong government plays an important role in economic development.
2. All these countries experience transition from a centralized to a decentralized economy.
3. Dominant rules and legislation have a more limited effect on individuals' social and economic lives than in Western countries, but the

relationship dependent on a long-term game is embedded in many aspects.

4. Extended family enterprises play an important role in economic organization.

5. In terms of financial systems, the direct function of the capital market in East Asia has been smaller than in English-speaking American countries, but financing mediated by banks has also been prevalent. In reality, the early stages of economic development have been very successful in these countries. It is sometimes called the 'Asian Miracle'. However, in 1997, many countries fell into in a severe recession. Japan has been experiencing long-term economic stagnation since the early 1990s.

The experiences described in the East Asian model can foster understanding of the following phenomena:

1. *The role of government in economic development*   The reason why government played such an important role during the early stages of economic development was that division of labor was limited and markets were small, deficient, and unsound. Government intervention was an effective means of reducing transaction costs.

2. *The transition of economic structure from monopoly to competition*   During the early stages described in the East Asian model, the economy was usually monopolized by several large financial groups and powerful extended families, and the market structure was non-competitive. At that time, relationship-based transactions were effective, but this system was only advantageous when long-term relationships could be formed among a small number of fixed entities. During the early stages of development, this monopolistic structure did not allow other enterprises free access to resources or customers. This favored the stability and longevity of existing social relationships. However, as the economy developed, the problems caused by the inefficiency of this monopolistic system became more and more harmful to sustainable economic development.

3. *The role of legislation and democracy in the economy*   During the first stage described in the East Asian model, self-enforced, relationship-based transactions facilitated people's social and economic lives, and the situation did not yet require formal institutions enforced by any third party. However, as division of labor became more pronounced and markets expanded, the limitations of relationship-based transactions became more visible, and, after a point, formal institutions enforced by a third party, the government, became advantageous.

China is not only a large, developing country. It is also a large country in transition. The path of its 30 years of reform and opening-up dovetails nicely with the five characteristics of the East Asian model. However, the government has played a greater role in China's transition than the countries discussed in the East Asian model. The sharp reduction in production and social chaos observed in Russia and other Eastern European transitional economies have not appeared in China. This is due to China's gradual approach to transition, its cultivation of formal institutions during the early stages of economic development, the maintenance of political centralization alongside economic decentralization in terms of political governance, and the preservation of the relationship-based nature of society in terms of social governance. However, the transition and development of China requires further widening of the scope of the market, an increase in division of labor, and more economies of scale. Thus, the market segmentation caused by decentralization, constraints on the scope of the market imposed by the relationship-based nature of society, and unequal access to opportunities fostered by those in charge of current power systems and social relationships becomes increasingly harmful to China's development. Therefore, in the interests of sustainable development, the government must make the transition from an administration- to a service-oriented system and society must make the transition from a relationship- to a rule-based model.

NOTES

1. Xu (2011) shares our view that economic decentralization and political centralization are fundamental to China's economy.
2. A construction project that involved building factories in inland areas to promote national security and interregional economic balance.
3. In recent years, the relative decline in the local tax refund has raised increasingly louder voices from local governments calling for the adjustment to the proportion of tax refund. This shows that local governments consider tax refunds to be under their own purview. In undeveloped regions, overevaluation may take place when the fiscal decentralization is measured by fiscal expenditures at local levels, especially in regions heavily populated by ethnic minorities such as Qinghai and Ningxia. A large proportion of the aid from central government is used to make up for the fiscal gap and promote the normal operation of government agencies. Expenditures at local levels are not sufficient to indicate the financial ability of local governments.
4. Fiscal operation in China has unique features. Bargaining between the central and local governments is one element in the decisions regarding the amounts of central transfer payments. These payments, which involve the transfer of power of expenditure, could be said to increase the disposable financial resources of local governments. They can also indicate the bargaining power and actual level of expenditure of local governments. In this sense, the degree of fiscal decentralization is very high, and the system of fiscal decentralization has not yet undergone any fundamental change.
5. The issue of soft budget constraint involves government aid to troubled SOEs through

direct appropriation or interference with bank loans, and relieving the enterprises of some of the responsibility for their operation. This can decrease the efficiency of these enterprises.

6. Jin et al. (2005) proved that fiscal incentives of provincial governments promoted the development of the market before the reform of the tax-sharing system using the data from 1982 to 1992. Lin and Liu (2000) as well as Zhang and Zou (1998) drew the opposite conclusion through testing the relationship between China's fiscal decentralization and economic growth before 1992.

7. Cai and Treisman (2005) pointed out that, because of the interregional discrepancy, competition for capital among regions weakened them and rendered no inherent advantage.

8. Stiglitz (1999) also emphasized the functions of social foundation in economic transitions.

9. See Lu and Pan (2009) and their summary of existing research.

10. John Shuhe Li (2003) believed that, the root of the Eastern Asian financial crisis of 1997 was the transition from a relationship- to a rule-based system.

3. Urban and rural economic development during the process of urbanization and industrialization

As depicted in the painting of the Qingming Festival Riverside, China's ancient streets and metropolises have always been crowded with people. According to the historical record, ancient China's urban development was ahead of Europe's. The handicraft industry in the cities of Hangzhou, Suzhou, and Chengdu thrived during the Song Dynasty. Hangzhou, the capital of the Southern Song, had 1.5 million people, and the service industry was very important. At the end of the thirteenth century, Marco Polo came to China, and he was astonished at Suzhou's large size – the city then covered an area of 4 square miles and was densely populated – and at Hangzhou's beauty and prosperity. In modern times, China has been relatively undeveloped with respect to urbanization and urban development.

Since the beginning of China's reform and opening-up in 1978, its economic development has taken the form of urbanization and industrialization, which are important indicators of the efficiency of modern social and economic development. Ancient people gathered in cities and participated in the handicraft and service industries, where the urban layout allowed them to work more efficiently through an agglomeration effect. For a long time, China relied on Lewis's (1954) dual economy theory to direct its urban and rural economic development. The theory stated that industry was the foundation of urbanization and that the development of modern industry freed the labor force from traditional agricultural production in favor of the manufacturing and service industries found in cities. However, the traditional dual economy theory does not adequately explain urban and rural economic development or China's current urbanization process. On one hand, China has a long history of an urban–rural divide, and one of the important decisive factors in China's urbanization has been the change in the policy toward integration of urban and rural areas. On the other hand, the dual economy theory does not incorporate spatial factors and therefore cannot take into account the effects of economic agglomeration on economic development and the accompanying urbanization process. The urbanization process should not progress identically through different regions.

Over the past 30 years, China has evolved from a poor and old-fashioned agricultural country to a large, industrial country, and it plays an important role in the international production chain. However, urbanization has lagged behind industrialization, and problems such as the small scale of cities and minor differences in that scale have implications for its continued growth. Over the past 30 years, China has not fully promoted integration between urban and rural areas and has not paid enough attention to the spatial agglomeration inherent in the urbanization process in inland and coastal areas. In this chapter, we analyze the existence and influence of the urban–rural divide policies on the unique urbanization and industrialization processes that have been observed in China. In the next chapter, we shall also use spatial angles to discuss the issues of urbanization and regional economic development.

The urbanization and industrialization that have taken place since the reform have been heavily influenced by the country's history, which can be traced back to a specific starting point and the political objective of that time. After the founding of modern China, the development of industry, particularly with an eye toward surpassing Britain and the US, received a great deal of attention. A series of policies were implemented that involved the urban–rural divide. These policies were the fundamental reason why urbanization lagged behind industrialization during this period. Under the policies of the urban–rural divide, even if the transfer of the rural labor force is realized, this may not result in a unified society. A new, dual society separated along the lines of urban residents possessing *hukou* and migrant workers lacking the *hukou*. This type of stratification has already appeared in some cities, where it poses a potential threat to harmonious development. The urban–rural divide and the blocking of interregional labor mobility are connected to economic decentralization. Incentives to developing local economies currently give local governments little reason to want migrant workers from other provinces to become permanent residents.

China's objectives must shift from simple economic growth to comprehensive social development. The report of the 17th CPC National Congress pointed out that the important relationships within the project of Chinese socialism should be recognized and properly handled. Of these, the overall planning of urban and rural development takes priority, indicating that the government has already placed importance on the adjustment of urban-biased policies.

3.1   CHINA'S ECONOMY DURING THE PROCESS OF URBANIZATION AND INDUSTRIALIZATION

Many of China's cities are almost unrecognizable from their counterparts in 1978 or even 1998. Since the 1990s, labor mobility from rural to urban areas has taken place on a prodigious scale. Every year, enough migrant workers to populate a medium-sized country travel via planes, trains, and automobiles to return home in preparation for the spring festival. Migrant workers move but they do not settle where they work. Thus, the gap between urbanization and industrialization has become a serious problem. Against this backdrop, agricultural price reform and the household responsibility system have promoted agricultural growth. Township and village enterprises have made rapid progress thanks to a surplus of the labor force in rural areas. However, nothing has closed the increasingly pronounced urban–rural gap.

Achievements and Challenges of Urbanization and Industrialization

The advances in industrialization and urbanization that have been made over the past 30 years can be observed directly. By proportion of GDP, the industrial (including the service industry) and urban sectors have taken an increasingly important position. China has not only ended a period of comprehensive shortage of industrial products; it has also become the world's factory.

The movement of labor from rural to urban areas has played an important role in the urbanization process. Migrant workers have become an irreplaceable part of non-agricultural industries in cities. The geographical distribution of the flow of migrant workers is highly consistent with the industry agglomeration illustrated in Chapter 4. This indicates that the process of industrialization has changed the layout of the regional economy, and it affirms the economic rule of the agglomeration of economy toward coastal areas.

Until the early 1990s, labor mobility between regions and between urban and rural areas was relatively small. Today, however, this type of mobility takes place on a huge scale. China's second agriculture census indicated that the number of migrant workers moving away from agricultural work had already reached 132 million in 2006, accounting for 25 percent of the total rural labor force. If the 80–90 million rural laborers participating in non-agricultural industries locally are included, then the number of rural laborers who have moved into non-agricultural industries is closer to 210–220 million, over 40 percent of the total rural labor force.[1] Based on the investigation of the State Statistics Bureau, Sheng (2008) provided the times-series estimation of the scale of rural migrant laborers (Table 3.1).

Table 3.1 Migrant laborers in rural areas (1985–2005)

	Total number of rural laborers (10,000)	Non-agricultural labor force in local rural areas (10,000)	Rural non-agricultural labor force (%)	Number of outside laborers in rural areas (10,000)	Amount of outside labor in the total rural labor force (%)	Number of people immigrating from rural to urban areas* (10,000)	Urbanization rate calculated by population with urban hukou (%)
1985	37,065	6,233	16.8	800	2.2	260	20.2
1986	37,990	6,682	17.6	900	2.4	248	20.9
1987	39,000	7,050	18.1	1,050	2.7	235	21.6
1988	40,076	7,361	18.4	1,250	3.1	290	21.9
1989	40,939	7,558	18.5	1,500	3.7	212	22.1
1990	42,010	7,694	18.3	1,800	4.3	198	21.6
1991	43,093	7,916	18.4	2,140	5.0	228	21.8
1992	43,802	8,380	19.1	2,592	5.9	221	22.2
1993	44,256	9,209	20.8	2,752	6.2	222	22.9
1994	44,654	9,798	21.9	2,888	6.5	223	23.6
1995	45,042	10,257	22.8	3,000	6.7	254	24.3
1996	45,288	10,378	22.9	3,400	7.5	257	24.9

Table 3.1 (continued)

	Total number of rural laborers (10,000)	Non-agricultural labor force in local rural areas (10,000)	Rural non-agricultural labor force (%)	Number of outside laborers in rural areas (10,000)	Amount of outside labor in the total rural labor force (%)	Number of people immigrating from rural to urban areas* (10,000)	Urbanization rate calculated by population with urban *hukou* (%)
1997	45,962	10,610	23.1	3,890	8.5	299	26.0
1998	46,432	10,804	23.3	4,936	10.6	339	26.3
1999	46,897	10,955	23.4	5,240	11.1	377	26.7
2000	47,962	11,224	23.4	7,600	15.8	507	26.8
2001	48,229	11,532	23.9	9,050	18.8	258	26.8
2002	48,472	11,873	24.5	10,470	21.6	780	27.2
2003	48,884	12,080	24.7	11,390	23.3	694	27.5
2004	49,676	12,753	25.6	11,823	23.8	520	27.5
2005	50,387	13,480	26.7	12,578	24.2	600	27.7

Note: * Rural individuals who have obtained registered urban *hukou*. This number is much smaller than that of the actual migrant labor force. The urbanization rate calculated by population possessing urban *hukou* is much lower than that calculated by permanent urban residency.

Source: Sheng (2008, Table 1-4, p. 9 and Table 4-1, p. 72).

Rural laborers flock into cities in order to have a better life. This begs the question of how a city fosters a better life. During the agglomeration of economic activity and population in cities, economic development became intense due to the expansion of city scales. The scale effect comes from at least three contributing factors: sharing, matching, and learning. By sharing infrastructure and facilities, producers in cities can obtain a comprehensive supply of input on a wide range of topics. This allows them to realize scale economies, decreasing average production costs while producing more. The sharing of input allows suppliers to provide highly specialized products and services according to customer demand. Matching occurs when the wide range of market and production factors allows better matches to be found. Cities offer enterprises a better choice of the necessary inputs and laborers with special skills to meet specific market demands. In a place with many enterprises, the demand for a variety of inputs can be satisfied much more easily, and it becomes easier for employees to find suitable employers. Learning occurs when the spatial agglomeration accelerates the spread of knowledge and allows a convenient information exchange between employees and employers and among different industries (Gill et al., 2007).

With continued promotion of industrial development, the agglomeration effect of cities will become more and more important. First, globalization will increase the importance of the geographical advantage of the coastal regions, and the agglomeration effect of eastern coastal regions will become more pronounced. In China, coastal regions and areas near big ports are more open, which further promotes the agglomeration of industries toward eastern coastal regions (Lu and Chen, 2006b). Second, since the second half of the twentieth century, many of the characteristics of a knowledge economy have gradually appeared. The functions of knowledge related to economic development are becoming more and more evident. These differ from the traditional pattern of economic growth, which is mainly dependent on the accumulation of physical capital and commodities. The generation and spread of knowledge requires more interpersonal interactions, and it allows the learning effect to be applied to scale economy. Currently, cities are usually sources of skilled, talented people, which is one reason why high-tech and creative industries usually develop better in big cities. When cities finally enter the post-industrialization phase, the proportion of employees working in the service industry increases. The settled, minimally mobile nature of many of the service industries highlights the need for spatial agglomeration in cities. Although the service industry's share of the economy is constantly growing, after the industrial agglomeration in large cities reaches a certain point and those cities enter the post-industrialization phase, the absolute scale of manufacturing in big cities will decline. The development of the service industry at this time promotes the scale effect in cities, attracting more industries with higher value.

Because urbanization and industrialization promote and reinforce each other, China's cities are currently experiencing rapid growth. Under the system of economic decentralization, local governments become actively engaged in urban construction, especially in the construction of urban infrastructure, which plays an important role in attracting foreign capital. Table 3.2 shows the achievements in the municipal constructions of China's urban development with a series of total volume indicators. As shown in Table 3.3, many people's living conditions improved rapidly, as shown by both relative and per capita indicators. It can be seen that the speed of improvement in living conditions increased between 1990 and 2009, and the total volume of all indicators from 2001 to 2009 outnumbered that from 1990 to 2000.

These figures make it clear that, in cities, the standard of living is improving. Various per capita indicators are rising rapidly. This raises the question, however, of whether enough people are enjoying these improvements. Considering the industrialization growth rates that have been observed since 1978, the urbanization level is still quite low, and rural populations still account for half of the total population. Figure 3.1 depicts the changes in industrialization and urbanization levels that have occurred since the beginning of reform and opening-up. Here, the industrialization level is measured using the proportion of GDP made up by secondary industries, and the level of urbanization is indicated by the proportion of the total population that comprises urban residents. The level of industrialization is always higher than the level of urbanization, indicating that the urbanization process is lagging behind the industrialization process. Here we use secondary industries as a means of measuring the industrialization process and facilitating comparisons between China and other countries. The difference between urbanization and industrialization in China appears even greater if the contribution of tertiary industries is taken into account.

As shown, the industrialization level has declined gradually. This was a structural correction for the excessive heavy industrialization that took place during the pre-reform era. Heavy industry was prioritized during the planned economy period, leaving China with a disproportionate amount of heavy industry. In 1978, the contribution of such industry to the total volume of industry was as high as 56.9 percent. Subsequently, with the development of the more consumer-oriented light industries, the structure within the industry experienced adjustments. Up until the 1990s, the upgrading of the consumption structure and China's new role as a global

Table 3.2 Indicators of total volume of urban municipal constructions (1978–2009)

Indicators \ Year & growth rate	1978	1990	2000	2005	2006	2007	2008	2009	Average growth rate, 1979–2006 (%)	Average growth rate, 1979–2009 (%)
Total volume of annual water supply (100 million tons)	78.8	382.3	469.0	502.1	540.5	502.0	500.1	496	7.1	5.7
Volume of artificial gas supply (100 million cubic meters)	–	174.7	152.4	255.8	296.5				–	–
Volume of natural gas supply (100 million cubic meters)	–	64.2	82.1	210.5	244.8				–	–
Length of roads (10 thousand kilometers)	2.7	9.5	16.0	24.7	24.1	24.6	26.0	26.9	8.1	7.6
Length of draining pipes (10 thousand kilometers)	2.0	5.8	14.2	24.1	26.1	29.2	31.5	34.4	9.7	9.7
Number of public transportation buses in operation (10 thousand)	2.6	6.2	22.6	31.3	31.6				9.4	–
Area of green spaces in gardens (10 thousand hectares)	8.2	47.5	86.5	146.8	132.1				10.4	–

Source: *China Statistical Yearbook 2010* (China Statistics Press).

Table 3.3   Urban municipal construction in China (1990–2009)

Year / Indicators	1990	2000	2006	2007	2008	2009
Water use rate (%)	48.0	63.9	86.67	93.83	94.73	96.12
Gas use rate (%)	19.1	45.4	79.11	87.40	89.55	91.41
Green space in parks per capita (m²)	1.8	3.7	8.30	8.98	9.71	10.66

Source: *China Statistical Yearbook 2010* (China Statistics Press).

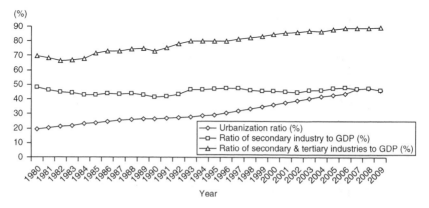

Source: *China Statistical Yearbook 2010* (China Statistics Press).

*Figure 3.1   Industrialization and urbanization levels in China
              (1980–2009)*

base of manufacturing caused the level of the industrialization to increase
to some extent, as indicated in Figure 3.1.

Since the beginning of reform and opening-up, the level of urbanization
has risen steadily. As shown in Figure 3.1, the gap between industrialization and urbanization has decreased over time. When the tertiary industry
is included in these calculations, the difference between urbanization and
industrialization can be said to have decreased rather slowly. The difference between the urbanization and industrialization ratios was about 53.9
percent in 1978 and 42.95 percent in 2009. China's urbanization has been
more complicated than its industrialization. Due to the strict limitations
imposed by the household registration system (*hukou*), a small portion of
migrants from rural areas had some access to urban residency and were
able to obtain urban *hukou*, but most of them could not, even once they
had become regular residents of cities. The *China Statistical Yearbook*
published by the government currently includes rural-to-urban migrants

Table 3.4　Number and proportion of big cities grouped by population in municipal districts (1991–2009)

Year	Total number of cities	Number of big cities		Relative number of cities with a population over 2 million (%)
		Population of more than 4 million	Population of 2–4 million	
1991	479	9		1.88
1993	570	10		1.75
1996	666	11		1.65
1997	668	12		1.80
1998	668	13		1.95
1999	667	13		1.95
2000	663	13		1.96
2001	662	8	17	3.78
2002	660	10	23	5.00
2003	660	11	22	5.00
2005	286*	13	25	13.29
2006	286*	13	24	12.94
2007	286*	13	26	13.64
2008	287*	13	28	14.29
2009	287*	14	28	14.63

Note:　* The statistics for 2005–09 only include cities at the prefecture level, and the statistics regarding the total number of cities and the relative number of cities with a populations over 2 million were not comparable to those recorded in earlier years.

Source:　*China Statistical Yearbook* (China Statistics Press).

living in cities for more than six months per year as part of the urban population. This shows the real urbanization process more objectively.

The rapid development of the urbanization process is also indicated by prominent changes in the size and number of cities. Although the changes in administrative regions and statistical criteria regarding whether prefecture-level cities should be included makes it difficult to compare the number of cities from year to year, the number of big cities, especially cities with a population of over 2 million, was not greatly affected. As shown in Table 3.4, large cities make up more and more of the total number of urban areas.

The increase in the number of big cities indicates the power of economic agglomeration. However, under the current urbanization mechanism, which is sometimes promoted by changes in the geographical division of administrative regions, the increase in urban regions may be disconnected from the development of local industry because of the active pursuit of urbanization by the local governments. The State Council relaxed the standards required for the establishment of cities and towns in the mid-1990s. Later, many counties in almost every region decided to convert to cities and towns, which increased the number of cities and towns all over the country and led to a decline in the density of urban populations. This model of urban construction is one important reason for the low efficiency of land utilization. According to statistics, in the decade following the mid-1990s, the area of 338 cities had increased 60 percent from 16,000 square kilometers to 25,000 square kilometers. Concurrently, the population (including migrant workers) of these cities increased by only about 10 percent, from 270 million to around 300 million. The speed of increase in city area was six times that of the increase in the population (Yan and Jiang, 2007). Under the system of economic decentralization, local governments pursued levels of local urbanization, especially in the sense of land area, but the agglomeration of the labor force toward cities (especially big cities) is insufficient. This caused a rapid decline in urban population density, mitigating many of the benefits of the agglomeration effect.

Characteristics and Influence of the Gap between Urbanization and Industrialization

Urbanization has facilitated the development of industry in the years since the beginning of opening-up. However, further comparisons of the levels of urbanization and industrialization show that the level of urbanization has long lagged behind that of industrialization (Figure 3.2). In countries such as Russia, Brazil, Mexico, and South Korea, the level of urbanization has surpassed the level of industrialization; only in Bangladesh, whose economy is relatively undeveloped, is the level of urbanization close to the level of industrialization. India saw its urbanization overtake industrialization in 1997. By comparison, China's less-developed urbanization process is very visible, and this prevents many of its people from enjoying the benefits of industrialization.

If the comparative analysis given above has a defect, it is that these different countries are in different developmental phases, and the levels of urbanization and industrialization among different countries may not be very comparable. We must view the data from another angle. As shown in Figure 3.3, GDP per capita is shown along the horizontal axis, and the proportion of urban population is shown along the vertical axis. The figure displays the correlation between the level of economic development and the level of urbanization in several countries in 2008. China's position shows that its urbanization level remains very lower considering its

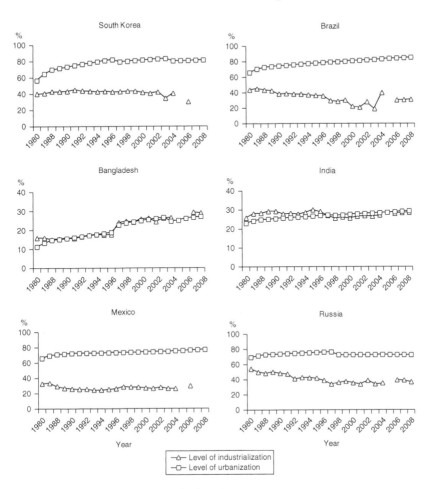

Source: *International Statistics Yearbook 2009.*

Figure 3.2   *Industrialization and urbanization levels in various countries over time (1980–2008)*

per capita GDP. If China were consistent with the international average, then its urbanization level would have been about 50.5 percent, but it was in fact only 43.1 percent, a difference of about 7.4 percent. Considering that China's GDP per capita itself would be much higher if it were calculated using purchasing power parity, China's urbanization should be even higher.

The crude levels of urbanization have a few direct consequences. One is that it makes it difficult for cities to fully utilize economies of scale in

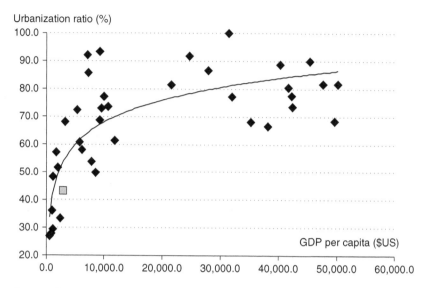

Source: See www.stats.gov.cn.

*Figure 3.3   Levels of economic development relative to urbanization
          (2008)*

the process of development, which may cause a loss in production. The
empirical research performed by Au and Henderson indicates that many
of China's cities have suffered from a loss of production efficiency due to
the small scale at which they must operate, and there is far less industrial
agglomeration than there should be. One important reason for this is the
limitations on cross-regional labor mobility. Au and Henderson's research
indicates that about 51–62 percent of cities in China are relatively small.
Typically, this accounts for a loss of an average of 17 percent of labor
productivity. The cities that suffered production losses of 25–70 percent
per employee were found to account for one-quarter of the total number
of cities sampled (Au and Henderson, 2006a, 2006b).

   From the comparison of the Gini coefficient of city scale, internationally speaking, China's cities differ little from each other in terms of scale.[2]
The Gini coefficient in China was 0.43 in 2000, much lower than that of
many large countries, including Brazil (0.65), Japan (0.65), Indonesia
(0.61), the UK (0.60), Mexico (0.60), Nigeria (0.60), France (0.59), India
(0.58), Germany (0.56), the US (0.54), and Spain (0.52). Only a few countries in the former Soviet Union had city scale indexes close to China's.
These included Russia (0.45) and Ukraine (0.40).[3]

   The next questions are why China's urbanization has lagged behind the international average and why its difference in the scale of urban development is so small. The so-called lag in urbanization and the small differences in city scales indicate both that urban development in China diminishes efficiency, and that there are definitely some factors that hinder the effects of market power. Because the urbanization process involves the agglomeration of various economic activities as well as the production of elements toward cities, it may be that the agglomeration of elements toward cities has been hindered. This has been found to be true. The policy of the urban–rural divide that has long constrained the process of urbanization and the layout of cities is the primary culprit.

Development of Agriculture and Township Enterprises

The development of agriculture must be analyzed against the background of urbanization and industrialization. Food security is highly relevant to the stability of any country, so agricultural reform is always connected to stability. From the land-system reform to reforms targeting the prices of agricultural products, the country has fostered the enthusiasm of the peasants and has improved food security. Reforms of the rural land system involved the household responsibility system. These reforms achieved great success in the 1980s. However, against the background of the urban–rural divide, the agricultural development that has taken place since the reform and opening-up has differed wildly from that of traditional developed economies.

In classical dual economy theory, with the help of the continuous outflow of a surplus labor force, agricultural development may be realized under perfect market conditions. In China, the continuous development of industry caused a labor shortage within the cities. Because of increasing salaries and wages, the industrial sector in cities draws laborers away from the agricultural sector. At the same time, the continuous outflow of the rural labor force can increase capital and land per capita and also the revenues of the agricultural sector. Because the policies surrounding the urban–rural divide make it difficult for laborers to move freely, the process of urbanization in China has lagged behind the international average, and the development of the agricultural sector has slowed. This has increased the income gap between urban and rural areas, and it may continue to do so (Chen and Lu, 2008b). When agricultural laborers cannot move to cities and other industrial sectors, agricultural reform is mostly restricted to land-system reform on the basis of the household contract responsibility system and the market-oriented price reform of agricultural products.

Before the reform and opening-up, there was a fear of land contract systems in regions such as Anhui. For a long time, the people's public community system was considered the ideal pattern of socialist ownership in rural areas, and land contract systems were always considered illegal. Despite this, a land contract system was quietly implemented in Fengyang County's Xiaogang Village in Anhui Province, with peasants signing a letter of commitment. Starting in 1978, the household responsibility system gradually replaced the public community system, and nuclear families once again became the most fundamental unit of rural production. In the first few years after the Third Plenary Session of the Eleventh Central Committee, the household responsibility system was gradually popularized and extended throughout the country. Subsequently, the Law of the People's Republic of China on Land Contracts in Rural Areas officially took effect on March 1, 2003. It not only clarified the right to use agricultural land and established the portion of revenue due to the collective but also provided peasants with the right to transfer their land-use rights. The government also raised the purchase price of several types of grain. This allowed market incentives to push the development of the agricultural economy, and peasant income increased by a factor of 2.69 (Xu, 2008). From 1978 to 1984, grain production increased by 100 million tons, from 305 million tons in 1978 to 407 million tons in 1984. According to research carried out by Lin (1992), the contribution of the household responsibility system to the rapid growth of agricultural production during this period was 46.89 percent, much higher than the contribution of other factors such as increased prices of agricultural products or decreased prices of agricultural supplies.

In order to stabilize the living standards of urban residents, the government elected not to raise the retail price of food when it increased the purchase price of food. This put pressure on the central government's financial budget. To compensate for that, the central government reformed the system by which food was purchased and sold in 1985 and re-established a unified purchase price for grains. The direct consequence of this was that when peasants were faced with the decision of whether to increase production, they did not consider market prices but rather the purchase price of grain. In 1985, the purchase price was lower than the market price. This decreased peasants' enthusiasm for farming. In 1986, the original grain-purchasing pattern was restored, but the production of grain did not return to 1984 levels until 1989. The rising price of grain seen in 1994 and 1995 and the complete marketization of the national grain purchasing and selling system effected in April 2002 each caused surges in grain production. Figure 3.4 shows the changes in the level of grain production since 1978, and the effects of each of these policies on the grain production are clearly visible.

The growth of peasants' per capita income has not matched grain pro-

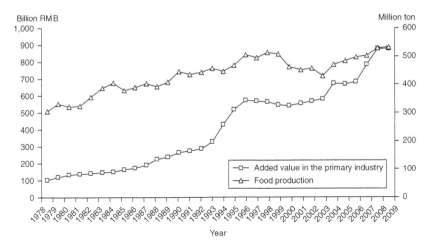

Note: The value added in the primary industry has been adjusted to the comparable 1978 prices according to the indicator of gross domestic production of the first industry

Source: *China Statistical Yearbook* (China Statistics Press).

Figure 3.4   *Changes in the grain production and value added since the reform (1978–2009)*

duction or agricultural added value. The system limits income in part by limiting outflow of surplus agricultural labor. As shown in Figure 3.5, aside from the promotion of agricultural development that can be attributed to implementation of the household responsibility system and the increased purchase price, the increase in the net income per capita in rural areas has always lagged behind that seen in cities. In 2010 and 2011, the urban–rural income gap narrowed, but it is not yet clear whether this is a turning point.

A certain phenomenon has been observed in the urbanization and industrialization process: the emergence of township enterprises. From a mainstream economic viewpoint, the unclear property rights of township enterprises decrease the efficiency of enterprises. Despite this conventional understanding, township enterprises developed rapidly during the early stages of reform, especially during the 1980s. This was especially true of rural township enterprises, which generated many jobs. From Figure 3.6, we see that the number of employees in township enterprises showed a period of rapid growth in the 1980s, but after the 1990s, especially in 1993, the number of employees in township enterprises, both absolute and as a proportion of rural employment, increased more slowly. After the mid-1990s, labor mobility increased. The departure of rural workers to

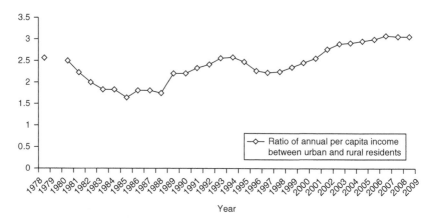

Source: The data collected between 1980 and 1987 are from a study by Ravallion and Chen (2007); the rest of the data were calculated from the *China Statistical Yearbook* (China Statistics Press) for each year. The urban–rural income per capita has been deflated using CPI.

Figure 3.5   Annual per capita income of urban and rural residents (1981–2009)

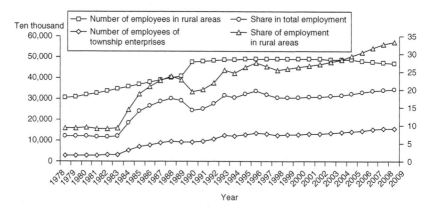

Source: China Statistical Yearbook (China Statistics Press).

Figure 3.6   Number of employees in township enterprises (1978–2009)

cities may account for this decrease in the growth of township enterprise employment.

Economists have put forward many explanations for the success of the township enterprises. At first, explanations tended to consider township enterprises as modified versions of conventional enterprises. However, if we consider that their success during the 1980s was based on those specialties, then it becomes difficult to explain the relative backwardness after the 1990s.

There were both economic and ideological reasons behind the emergence of the township enterprises. In the economic aspect, much of the surplus labor force had accumulated in the rural areas. At first, the restrictions on labor mobility were not relaxed, so township enterprises could employ laborers at extremely low wages; unlike SOEs, they did not need to provide pensions or medical care. This cost advantage in addition to market opportunities brought by the reform led to the rapid development of township enterprises. The kinship network played a very important part in this development, giving them more solidarity, interreliance, and opportunities than they would otherwise have had. In regions with stronger kinship networks, private township enterprises became more developed (Peng, 2004). Ideologically, private enterprises faced resistance for quite some time.[4] However, in this kind of environment, many entrepreneurial start-ups chose to set up private enterprises but register them as collective enterprises. This phenomenon is called 'wearing a red hat'. After Deng Xiaoping's Southern Tour speeches and the announcement of the CPC decision to promote a non-public economy as a component of the socialist market economy, many of these private enterprises in every region began to get rid of their red hats.

As pointed out previously in this chapter, the institutional obstacles of limited labor mobility and lack of access to the efficiency that can be caused by agglomeration affected the development of township enterprises in rural areas. The 1990s brought a free flow of labor, reducing the advantages of such enterprises. Furthermore, the small scale of township enterprises and the lack of industrial agglomeration were also detrimental.

3.2 FORMATION AND INFLUENCE OF THE URBAN–RURAL DIVIDE

The urban–rural divide was an important means of promoting urban development and the industrialization process during the planned economy period. In the 30 years since the reform and opening-up, the urban–rural divide continued to affect the processes of urbanization and industrialization. Today, however, China finds itself at a crossroads. If urban–rural integration is not realized, then the consequent slow urbanization will become unfavorable to the full utilization of the urban agglomeration effect. A long-term urban–rural divide may affect the future of urban development. Today, China is facing a challenge. The urban–rural divide was once an obstacle to rural development and a danger to the interests of rural residents, but a continued urban–rural divide would hurt both rural and urban residents.

Reasons for the Industrialization Strategy and Urban–Rural Divide

Historically, the government's strategy of catching up to other countries has been an important reason behind policies related to the urban–rural divide (Yang and Cai, 2000). During the early stages of the foundation of the new China, in order to surpass developed countries such as Britain and the US, the development of industry, especially heavy industry, became the country's priority. Under conditions of capital constraint, many developing countries try to adopt economic and social policies favorable to the urban sector in order to promote capital-intensified heavy industries and accelerate the industrialization process. This involves investing profits from agriculture in the industrial sector, creating conditions for a booming economy (Krueger et al., 1991). During the planned economy period, with its weak economic foundation, transferring resources from agriculture to industry required creating a price gap between industrial and agricultural products. The industrial sector's profits were raised artificially, and the sector was expanded through national investment. The implementation of a price scissors between industrial and agricultural products was normal for the formation of policies favorable to cities. This method was designed to create agricultural surplus through the distortion of product prices and production factors to compensate for industrialization (Schultz, 1978). This distorted price system required the agricultural sector to make great sacrifices in favor of industry. According to research by Li (1993), from 1955 to 1985 the government transferred an agricultural surplus worth a total of 543 billion RMB to the industrial sector by lowering the price of agricultural products. Because China's industries were mainly concentrated in cities, urban residents saw more of the benefits of industrialization than their rural counterparts did. This model cannot be sustained over the long term. Under this system, it became necessary to prevent the labor force from moving freely from rural to urban areas. The *hukou* system was managed very strictly, restricting peasants to rural areas. From the foundation of new China through 1958, *hukou* management required little from immigrants. However, around 1956, the government sensed the pressure of arranging employment within cities. The government then tightened the restrictions on peasant migration, and methods of dealing with people entering cities suddenly changed from advising first and often accepting, to refusal of entry.

The issues of large populations and limited public service resources gave urban residents an incentive to support policies exacerbating the urban–rural divide. Urban residents believed that defending the divide would prevent the exacerbation of existing unemployment problems caused by the huge influx of laborers into cities, where they consume public services. Similar policies in favor of cities have been enacted in other developing countries. It is not easy for the relatively dispersed peasant population to resort to collective action in order to influence policy, but urban populations are usually close to political centers and thus able to attract more attention from decision makers (Lipton, 1977). Along with the transition from a planned to a market economy, the people's public community system had already been abolished; the price system was no longer controlled by the government; and China's goal has changed from surpassing other countries to focusing on addressing its own problems. However, the *hukou* system has not yet been abolished. One possible reason for this may be that the urban sector formed its own special group under the previous system. The maintenance of this group would have relied greatly on the existence of the urban–rural divide policy. Urban residents continue to put pressure on the government to prevent their benefits from decreasing. For example, in 1978, the price compensation for urban residents was 1.1 billion RMB, and it rose quickly to 7.9 billion RMB in 1979. From 1979 on, the food compensation for urban residents continued to rise. In 1985, when restrictions on meat prices were relaxed, there was also compensation for meat. Total government price compensation reached 26.2 billion RMB in 1985 and 71.2 billion in 1998, accounting for 7.6 percent of the total government budget (Yang and Cai, 2000).

The economic decentralization pattern implemented during the process of reform and opening-up was also an important reason for the urban–rural divide. Under the system of decentralization, local governments promoted fast, short-term economic growth that could be expressed as part of GDP. For this reason, they paid more attention to industrial development than to agriculture or construction. During a considerably long period prior to 2001, the proportion of the fiscal expenditure used to support agricultural development in each province decreased remarkably (Lu and Chen, 2006a). Second, under the current system of decentralization, local interests are more in line with local economic development, so local governments have paid more attention to local than to national interests. Although the urban–rural divide may have done some harm to China's overall economic development, it has had benefits for urban residents, and this made it easy for local governments to adopt the system (Chen and Lu, 2008b). Third, with economic decentralization, local governments are more likely to protect the interests of individuals with capital who make investments locally, and common workers can be neglected. Currently, migrant workers lacking local *hukou* are a major at-risk group.

History and Current Status of the Urban–Rural Divide

At the very beginning of the implementation of the *hukou* system, the rural population was expected to provide food to the cities at set, low prices. At the same time, the quota of various coupons also controlled the provision of commodities in cities connected to the *hukou* system. Peasants were required to first obtain food coupons before entering cities. To leave their home province, they required national food coupons. Because rural residents could not obtain housing, non-staple foods, or fuel supplies, they could not stay long, even if they were granted entry into the cities. Until 1977, the Ministry of Public Security's regulations on handling the *hukou* transfer clearly stated that the transition from agricultural *hukou* to non-agricultural *hukou* and transferring to Beijing, Shanghai, or Tianjin from other cities had to be strictly controlled. It was also important to control the transfers from towns to cities, from small cities to big cities, and from ordinary rural areas to the outskirts of cities.

After the reform and opening-up, the people's public community system was abolished, and coupons were no longer an obstacle to labor mobility. The manufacturing, construction, and food industries in cities began to generate demand for cheap labor from rural areas. From the mid-1980s, along with the successful implementation of the household responsibility system in rural areas and relief of the pressure of urban employment, the government began to allow peasants to enter cities and towns for work and business on a conditional basis.

Because the *hukou* system is still in force, limitations on labor mobility still exist. Urban centers still exert strict control over the migrant workers in their jurisdiction. People without a certificate for temporary residence used to be sent back to their home region by the urban administrative sector. Even when free inflow of the rural labor force into the cities was allowed, similar limitations appeared in other forms. The most common of these was that employees lacking local urban *hukou* could not enjoy equal social security benefits or public services with local people. During the early stages of the period in which migrant workers were permitted to enter cities, the urban development planning did not include the migrant workers' demands for housing, children's education, and social security in the provision of urban public goods. In fact, there existed systematic discrimination regarding children's education, health care for women and children, and social security in each region. For a long time, public schools either charged higher fees for the children of migrant workers at the age of compulsory education or simply pushed them out of the schools or into private schools, which have categorically poorer conditions than the public schools. As a result, many of the children of migrant workers must be left behind to attend schools in their home town while their parents work in the city. In recent years, local governments have begun to include compulsory education for the children of migrant workers in the local budget. Migrant workers are usually overrepresented in jobs associated with difficult working conditions, but only a few types of industrial injury are covered by medical insurance. According to a survey by the State Statistics Bureau, migrant workers whose employers provide them with a pension and insurance for medical care, industrial injuries, and unemployment account for only 5.9, 9.7, 20.7, and 1.8 percent, respectively, of the total (Sheng et al., 2009). The *hukou* system prevents migrant workers from spending their old age in cities, and most must return to rural areas. Much empirical research on labor mobility has shown that old and married migrant workers are less likely to move to cities (Zhao, 1997, 1999a, 1999b). Our own research has shown that laborers with children aged 6–12 were less willing to move to urban areas for work (Chen et al., 2010).

The urban–rural divide also involves huge differences in access to social services, most notably education and medical care. The educational and medical facilities enjoyed by urban residents are of higher quality than those available to rural residents (Zhang, 2003). Due to the insufficient input in education, the facilities in rural areas are extremely weak, and only a small number of rural children can attend university. These lucky students usually remain in the cities. Medical conditions in rural areas also fall far behind those of the cities. Due to the narrow coverage of the social health-care system, there is high illness-related unemployment in rural areas (Sun and Yao, 2006; Zhang et al., 2006). These inequalities will be discussed further in Chapter 5.

Economic and Social Consequences of the Urban–Rural Divide

The economic consequences of the urban–rural divide are highly visible. The income gap is probably its most tangible characteristic. Changes in the ratio of annual income per capita among urban and rural residents were depicted in Figure 3.5, where we see that the annual disposable income per capita in cities is far greater than that of rural areas. The income gap between urban and rural areas was at its lowest in 1984, almost certainly because of rural reform and the implementation of the household responsibility system. Subsequently, differences between urban and rural income increased until 1994, when the government raised the purchase price of agricultural products. After 1997, which saw a decline in the purchase price of agricultural products and marketization of the retail price, the income gap once again increased. In 2005, the actual ratio of urban–rural income per capita reached 2.95. If factors such as medical and education subsidies given to urban residents are taken into account, the actual difference in income is much greater (Shi Li, 2003).

Urban-biased economic policies are an important cause of the urban–rural income gap (for example, Yang, 1999; Chen, 2002; Lu and Chen, 2006a). Shi Li (2003) thought that the following factors were important for the formation of a large urban–rural income gap: governmental control of agricultural and sideline product prices; rural residents' high tax burden and expenses; the physical separation of the urban and rural labor markets and the reduction in the size of the urban labor market; and discrimination from social welfare and social security systems. These factors are all specific characteristics of economic policies that work in favor of cities. Urban residents are also offered inflation subsidies and investment credits not available to rural residents (Yang, 1999; Yang and Zhou, 1999; Tian, 2001).[5]

Urban-biased economic policies have a direct connection with the fiscal decentralization system, as indicated by fiscal expenditures in cities. Fiscal expenditures are the main source of economic growth in the urban sector, and the proportion of such expenditures of each provincial government used to support agricultural production decreased sharply during the 1990s. This widened the urban–rural income gap (Lu and Chen, 2006a). Under the current system of fiscal transfer, rural areas with less fiscal revenue can obtain supportive transfer payments. Undeveloped rural areas weaken attempts to increase the tax base, so this type of transfer payment has significant implications for the future of these areas. The transfer payments given to rich urban areas are mainly used to support economic development, giving cities incentives to pursue economic development. The joint effect of the two aspects of the system is intensification of the inequities between urban and rural areas (Yao, 2006).

From the point of view of the labor market, poverty in China is mainly a rural problem (Knight and Song, 1993). Economic policies that favor cities have caused pronounced urban–rural disparities in terms of the availability of public services. The *hukou* system provides urban residents with housing, medical care, pensions, and education, but it exacerbates the urban–rural income gap. Even if all limitations on labor mobility are lifted, the *hukou* system will still mean higher living costs for rural residents who move to cities. Labor mobility alone cannot reduce the urban–rural income gap (Yang, 1999; Yao, 2000).

In fact, the urban–rural income gap has already become the main type of income gap in China. The less-developed central and western regions have a high proportion of rural residents. If the urban–rural income gap increases, then regions with a higher proportion of peasants will undergo slower per capita income growth. The contribution of urban–rural differences to the cross-regional income gap began to increase at the end of the 1990s, and it now accounts for about 70–80 percent of the income gap across regions. This means that if the government is able to eliminate the urban–rural income gap, the difference among regions will decline by 70–80 percent automatically. Among the factors that caused the differences in regional development, the importance of the urban–rural income gap is much greater than the importance of the differences between eastern, central, and western regions (Wan, 2007).

Although the urban–rural divide helped to foster urban development in the earlier stages of China's development, it is also responsible for the unfavorable aspects of city development. Due to the political restrictions on the free flow of the labor force, the development level of cities is generally poor, and the difference among the scale of cities is not big enough. In the current period when the agglomeration effect of cities is becoming more and more important, the loss of diseconomies of scale is serious.

More and more rural residents have become regular city residents. The urban–rural divide is pushing the cities toward a dualistic society made up of people with and without *hukou*. This separation is particularly visible in the labor market, where *hukou*-based discrimination is rampant. Only 24 percent of the salary differences between migrant and local urban laborers can be explained by differences in personal characteristics. The remaining 76 percent can be attributed to discrimination (Cai et al., 2003). This indicates that, under the current system, increases in the level of education of migrant workers would not completely eliminate the salary differences. Segmentation in the labor market may continue to enlarge despite education reforms. In Guangdong, the 2000–04 payroll statistics of seven enterprises showed increasingly wide differences between the salaries of migrant workers and the average salary of employees from Guangdong Province. During that period, increases in the salaries of migrant workers were not evident (Meng and Bai, 2007). In Shanghai, four large-scale surveys have indicated that, from 1995 to 2003, the speed of the increase in returns from human capital differed significantly between migrant laborers and local residents, and the difference between the two has been increasing (Yan, 2007). There has also been research comparing statistics collected between 1999 and 2002. Results indicate that salary differences between rural migrants and urban residents have increased. The main reason for this is the relative decline in the returns to migrant workers' education (Zhang and Meng, 2007).

Once a dualistic society has formed within cities, it can threaten the future of harmonious urban development. If migrant laborers cannot enjoy equal access to public services such as education and medical care, then social segmentation will be handed down from generation to generation. If the majority of the rural population cannot meet the country's requirements for a highly skilled labor force through the accumulation of human capital, then the unequal access to educational opportunities will have serious long-term consequences.

Because migrant workers in cities belong to low-income groups, they tend to move into suburban areas and low-cost communities with bad environments. The phenomenon of residential segregation within cities will remain intense for a long time to come. Residential segregation, particularly in low-income areas, may lead to various social problems, such as serious unemployment, poverty, and crime. Such segregation has economic, social, and psychological roots. The economic cause is the high cost of housing and services in high-level communities, and many ordinary people cannot enter this market. Among all the adequate and systematic services around high-level communities, the most important ones are schools, hospitals, and security. Only those on a high income can afford the high costs of these services. Socially and psychologically, living in high-level communities makes people feel superior to others. The people in these neighborhoods also tend to form advantageous social networks. During China's urban development, the higher the income level of the community, the better the residential environment. High housing prices force those on a low income to move toward remote and suburban districts. Residential segregation by income has significant overlap with residential segregation by *hukou* identity.

Dualistic social separation within cities prevents migrant workers from setting up new social networks, especially networks that cross urban–rural lines. It can even cause mutual mistrust between urban residents and new migrants. Normally, peasants entering cities for work depend on relationships with relatives when selecting a destination for relocation and to obtain employment information (Zhao, 2003; Bao et al., 2007). This kind of social relationship network is formed in rural areas and can be transplanted into the cities, where it strengthens migrant workers' ability to absorb risks by promoting mutual assistance among individuals. By comparison, the existence of the *hukou* system usually prevents social organization, activities, and services already present in urban communities from absorbing migrant workers. As a result, people entering cities for work have limited social capital within the groups of migrant workers. The dualistic social separation within cities makes migrant workers distrust urban residents and municipal governments (Wang et al., 2009). This increases the difficulties in the administration within cities and the implementation of public policies, causing huge social losses.

Another result of restrictions on labor mobility is that they do not favor economic growth driven by consumption. Statistics show that consumption makes up only a small part of China's GDP, and it is still decreasing. The *hukou* system has played a role in this. We should consider what is likely to happen if migrant workers gain an urban *hukou*. First, they will consider purchasing durable goods. If they, like many other migrants, plan to return home after several years, they will avoid buying unnecessary goods, given the high cost of transport. Second, they may borrow from banks to consume. Without a local urban *hukou*, their consumption credit is limited because financial institutions will require formal income information and work certificates before consumption loans are issued. Because many people without local *hukou* do not have a stable job or a formal labor contract, this type of loan is usually beyond their reach. Compared to local urban residents, migrant workers consume far less and take on less debt. Third, migrant workers who obtain a *hukou* may be absorbed into the urban social security system, which will allow them to reduce the portion of their own savings that they set aside for old age and medical expenses. The limitations of the *hukou* system have a significant impact in terms of consumption. Research by Binkai Chen et al. (2010) showed that the marginal propensity of consumption of urban migrants was about 14 percent lower than that of urban residents – if an urban resident is given an additional 100 RMB, he or she will spend 51 RMB, but if that additional 100 RMB is given to an urban migrant, he or she will only spend 37 RMB. This difference of 14 percent takes into consideration difference in terms of income and education and remittances sent back to the migrants' home towns (ibid.). Relaxing the restrictions of the *hukou* system may stimulate China's domestic demand.

3.3   FROM URBAN–RURAL DIVIDE TO INTEGRATION

There are currently at least 150 million rural residents working and living in cities. These people have supported the urbanization and industrialization process by providing the low-cost labor that has allowed China to become an industrial country. We can conclude without any exaggeration that allowing these 150 million rural residents to enter the cities was the most important economic event to occur in the past 30 years. China's next challenge is to fully integrate this large number of rural-to-urban migrants into its cities.

There is some question of whether the influence of the urban–rural divide will gradually disappear or remain indefinitely throughout the process of globalization, marketization, and modernization. In order to answer this question, we must determine what would promote the transition towards integration and discuss the meaning of urban–rural integration from the perspectives of spatial, social, and political integration.

Causes of Urban–Rural Integration

Urban–rural integration may at first come from a city's need to continue developing. Continuing industrialization, urbanization, and economic agglomeration will increase the demand for migrant workers. Migrant workers and original urban residents are usually in different labor markets, but they act cooperatively in the city's development. The more developed the city is, the more capital it accumulates, and the higher the skill level of the original urban residents. This also increases the demand for migrant workers with relatively low skill levels to fill positions that the urban residents have exited.

Changes in the supply and demand of the labor force also promote urban–rural integration in the labor market. If a rural surplus labor force were to be completely absorbed into the urban sector at a time of rising agricultural production, then the incomes of the remaining peasants would increase. Currently, competition within the labor force is intense in cities and among enterprises within cities; the system will probably eventually favor urban–rural integration. In 2004, the coastal regions experienced a shortage of migrant workers, which appeared again after the onset of the global economic crisis. Given that the urban population, including migrants, accounts for about 50 percent of the total population, a shortage of migrant workers might not indicate a general labor shortage, but it would indicate competition for migrant workers among different parts of the country. This competition will gradually grow in strength. Salaries and welfare levels in the Pearl River Delta region have gradually become less competitive than those in the Yangtze River Delta region. For this reason, more people are relocating to the Yangtze River Delta.

The urban–rural divide harms sustainable economic and social development. Sustainable development can also motivate urban–rural integration. Our research has shown that the widening of the urban–rural income gap will harm economic growth. Over the long term, if the ratio of urban–rural per capita income increases by 1 percent, the rate of economic growth will decrease by about 3.8 percent. This is because investment is still an important factor in the economy, and the income gap decreases investment. We also found that economic growth helped to narrow the urban–rural income gap. In other words, continued narrowing of the gap will promote economic growth, which will in turn lead to a further narrowing. Ignoring the urban–rural income gap will negatively affect economic growth, cre-

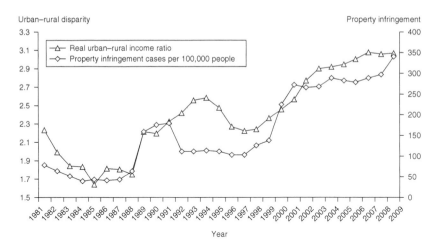

Source: *China Statistical Yearbook 2010* (China Statistics Press), and calculation by the authors; the data source of the ratio of urban-to-rural income is the same as in Figure 3.5.

Figure 3.7 *Urban–rural income gap and cases of property infringement (1981–2009)*

ating a cycle of exacerbated urban–rural differences and unsustainable economic growth (Wan et al., 2006).

Theoretically, there are many ways in which income can affect investment. The widening income gap may lead to social and political instability, worsening the social investment environment. Under these conditions, more resources are used for the protection of property rights (for example, safeguards, courts, and the police), and the accumulation of productive physical capital decreases (for example, Benhabib and Rustichini, 1996). Figure 3.7 depicts the urban–rural income gap and the rate of property infringement. These two issues tend to be correlated, though no direct causal relationship has ever been found between the two. The income gap and consequent social instability negatively influence investment and economic growth, which merits attention.

From 2004 to 2008, the government emphasized the importance of issues related to agriculture, rural areas, and peasants in the form of the No. 1 Document. In 2000, the government decided to conduct trials on reforming rural taxes and expenses in Anhui Province. In 2002, this program was extended to 16 provinces, cities, and autonomous regions. The main purpose of this reform was to reduce the peasants' tax burden. In 2004, the government announced that it would gradually decrease agricultural taxes and abolish them within five years. In 2006, the agricultural tax was completely abolished. In 2004, the government indirectly changed its method of compensating peasants by providing huge amounts of compensation funds to state-owned food suppliers and sellers, but it sent farming compensation directly to peasants. This stabilized grain production somewhat and raised peasants' income. In the meantime, in the fields of education and medical care, the government began to push forward policies favorable to rural areas. In 2006, the government announced that it would exempt all miscellaneous fees for students in the compulsory education system in rural areas within two years and continue to provide free textbooks and compensation for living expenses to students from poor families. This policy was gradually extended to central and eastern regions. A new type of rural cooperative medical care began a trial run in 2004. In 2010, the No. 1 Central Document affirmed that the overall planning of urban–rural development should be considered a fundamental requirement for the general construction of a moderately prosperous society; that improvement in living conditions in rural areas is an important part of the national income structure; that the stimulation of rural demand should be considered a key method of increasing domestic demand; that the development of modern agriculture should be considered an important mission to economic development; and that new construction in rural areas and the promotion of urbanization should be considered a permanent reason to maintain stability and promote rapid economic development.

Adjustments in governmental fiscal expenditures since 2001 show the attention paid to the issues of agriculture, rural areas, and peasants. Figure 3.8 depicts the changes in the proportion of total government expenditures relevant to agriculture.[6] The proportion of agriculture-related expenditures has experienced a reversal, a decrease until 2002 followed by an increase.

In summary, transition from an urban–rural divide to integration would favor economic and social development. Because marginal production of the labor force is far lower in rural than in urban areas, urban–rural integration would allow more peasants who have moved to cities to find employment and increase total production. When cities receive a sufficient number of laborers, the agglomeration effect is enhanced. The advantages indicated in economic development will favor further narrowing of the urban–rural income gap, relieving the urban–rural social conflicts, promoting social harmony, and facilitating economic growth.

Policy Measures for Urban–Rural Integration

This subsection will discuss the spatial, social, and political integration of urban and rural areas.

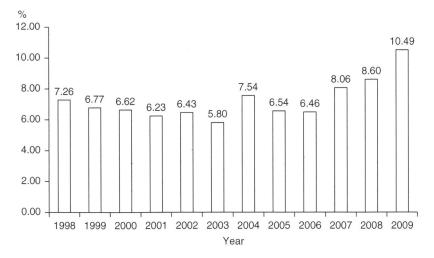

Source: *China Statistical Yearbook 2010* (China Statistics Press), and calculation by the authors.

Figure 3.8 Changes in the proportion of agriculture-related payments (1990–2009)

After the disintegration of the people's public community system and the gradual abolition of the coupon system in the mid- and late 1980s, migrant workers began to enter cities to look for work. This heralded the beginning of spatial integration between urban and rural areas. Spatial integration is also necessary for urban development. As the accumulated capital increases, so does the demand for labor. In 20–30 years, China may reach 75 percent urbanization or more. Along with the constant rise of urbanization, the bi-directional flow of residents between urban and rural areas will be freer. This type of spatial integration is a preliminary form of urban–rural integration, and the easiest to realize.

Even when laborers are allowed to move from rural to urban areas at will, current conditions prevent peasants in cities from enjoying equal rights with registered urban residents. Social security and children's education are key areas of inequality. In this way, even though migrant workers make substantial contributions to cities during their best working years, they do not receive a pension or medical care commensurate with these contributions. Even if their children accompany them to urban areas, they cannot enjoy equal opportunities for education. The current proto-dualistic society must be replaced by a socially integrated model.

In 2000, the central government made active adjustments to policies affecting migrant workers. In the Outline of the 10th Five-Year Plan for National Economic and Social Development, the government announced that it would break the urban–rural divide by reforming the *hukou* system, encouraging orderly migration, and abolishing the unreasonable restrictions placed on the movements of rural laborers so that they may enter urban areas to work. At the end of March 2001, the Opinions on the Promotion of the Reform of the System of Residence Management in Small Cities and Towns was approved by the State Council and transferred to the Ministry of Public Security. This document stipulated that in counties, cities, and towns, people with legal fixed living places, stable jobs, or financial resources and any immediate relatives living with them are all allowed to apply for regular permanent urban residency. It also stipulated that people who have settled in small cities and towns should be guaranteed equal rights and should undertake equal obligations to the original urban residents in terms of access to schools, joining the army, and employment; discriminative policies are banned. Although the above-mentioned active adjustments to policies have not yet been popularized in big cities, it is an important step that may enable migrant workers to enjoy public services and realize urban–rural social integration.

The inception of a policy by the central government is only the first step. That policy must be implemented by local governments. Under current conditions, the implementation of equal public services between people with and without *hukou* may superficially harm the interests of people with urban *hukou*. This policy will therefore be difficult to implement smoothly at the local level.

The matter of greatest interest to rural residents is whether peasants can enjoy the same benefits as urban residents. Urban residents have already enjoyed the benefits of increased value of land during the urban development in the forms of the revaluation of housing prices and compensation for demolition. In comparison, when rural lands are expropriated, peasants are usually only compensated for the value of the land as calculated by potential agricultural production. Land and *hukou* reform were recently carried out in Chongqing in an attempt to induce peasants to voluntarily give up their rights to use non-agricultural lands of their housing sites, which will then be used for the development of suburban housing. At the same time, peasants would receive *hukou*, social security, and public services in cities, and compensation would be based on market prices. Correspondingly, their housing land will be re-cultivated as agricultural land. Thus, the total amount of agricultural land can be kept constant. This may be a suitable model for land and *hukou* reform in the future.

The term 'political urban–rural integration' refers to giving rural residents the right to influence policy alongside urban residents. In this system, peasant groups are allowed equal opportunities to participate in policy making. We have mentioned before that the political structures of many developing countries can lead to a serious inequity between urban and rural residents in terms of political negotiation and political influence. Governments therefore usually adopt policies in favor of cities (Lipton, 1977; Bates, 1981). If the municipal governments representing the interests of cities make these policies unilaterally, then they tend to be biased in favor of cities. Even when urban and rural laborers are allowed to move at will, the urban–rural income gap is still considerable, and it continues to grow (Chen and Lu, 2008b). Equalizing the political power between urban and rural groups is the most important means of reversing the policy of urban–rural divide.

Under China's current political system, one way to politically integrate urban and rural areas would be to provide equal opportunities for residents to send representatives to the People's Congress, which is the supreme body of state power. In 2007, the 17th CPC National Congress proposed to implement a new voting process in which deputies of the People's Congress would be sent according to the population ratio between urban and rural areas. The Decisions on the Amendment of the Law on Voting for the National People's Congress and the Local People's Congress at All Levels was approved by the third session of the 11th National People's Congress on March 14, 2010. It stipulates in its 16th article that the deputies of the NPC must be distributed by the NPC standing committee according to the population of each province. Each deputy must represent the same number of urban and rural residents, ensuring that each region, ethnic group, and socioeconomic group receives the appropriate number of deputies.

Nobel economics laureate Joseph Stiglitz has cited urbanization in China, along with technological developments in the United States, as the two most important issues that will shape world development in the twenty-first century. The analysis provided in this chapter indicates that the urbanization and industrialization process in China should be considered within the systematic background of urban–rural integration. The construction of new socialist rural areas requires that the government not directly increase the input in the construction of rural areas and activities of agricultural production but rather indirectly promote agricultural development, raise peasants' income, and improve conditions in rural areas through the development of integrated cities.

NOTES

1. Data source: the announcement of the main statistics of the 2nd census in agriculture (No. 5).
2. The Gini coefficient was used to measure inequality. Possible values range between 0 and 1. The closer to 1, the bigger the difference.
3. See Fujita et al. (2004) for details.
4. In October 1987, the report of the 13th CPC National Congress pointed out, 'the development of private economy to some degree is a necessary and beneficial complement to the public-owned economy', and the status of the private economy was recognized. Subsequently, the proposal of an amendment in the constitution approved in April 1988 provided the private economy with legal and social status accordingly. However, the disturbance in the domestic and foreign circumstances around 1990 led to a discussion on the choice of capitalism or socialism, which seriously undermined the development of the private economy.
5. Yang (1999) also thought that an important reason for the intense inequity and rapid economic growth that has taken place since the reform and opening-up in 1978 was the urban-biased policies implemented by the government, including restrictions on labor mobility and aspects of the welfare system that favor urban residents.
6. In the budget and financial statements for each province, there are three items related to rural areas: payment in support of production in rural areas, payment for synthesized agricultural development, and operating expenses such as agriculture, forestry, water conservancy, and meteorology. The names of the items in 2003 and 2004 were agricultural payment, forestry, water conservancy, and meteorology.

4. Industrial agglomeration in the process of globalization and regional economic development

As early as the Tang Dynasty, China had expanded its power into western Asia and Europe. At that time, because people usually traded by land, Chang'An was not only the ancient capital of the Tang Dynasty but also the communications hub of the Silk Road. China's economic center moved from the north to the south during the Song Dynasty, and this pattern remains in place today. In the Ming Dynasty, Zheng He started his voyage to the West from China's southeastern coastal areas, which could have helped China take the lead in the history of marine navigation in the world. However, a few years later, a blanket ban on maritime voyages subsequently hindered China's naval progress. In 1978, after years of isolated and semi-isolated development, China reopened its doors. By then the pattern of international trade had already changed from land transportation to shipping by sea, which made China's southeast coastal areas key to China's economic opening-up.

China's economic development over the past 30 years has been a process of integration into the global system while making the most of its advantages, and constantly learning from the experiences of more-developed countries, and adopting useful technology. China's experience indicates once again that in the era of economic globalization, pursuing economic development by maximizing global division of labor can facilitate economic take-off. Over the past 30 years, China has successfully transformed itself from a rudimentary agrarian country into the world's manufacturing base. It transports commodities at all levels to every corner of the world. Most of these commodities are shipped by sea.

However, China's economic opening-up is only a part of its economic globalization, and one driving source of that globalization is the world-wide manufacturing market. In order to analyze the changes brought about by China's economic opening-up, we should start by studying the map of China to examine the relationship between economic globalization and Chinese regional economic development. Differences in geography, history, and policies across different parts of China have created regional differences in the degree of globalization, and income and development. Many industries are agglomerating in the eastern coastal areas (particularly the Yangtze River Delta, the Pearl River Delta and the Bohai Rim). After 30 years of rapid development, the economic aggregate of Guangdong Province has surpassed Singapore, Hong Kong, and Taiwan, which are three of the four 'Asian dragons'. A 2005 Human Development Report issued by the UNDP pointed out that, in terms of the Human Development Index, Shanghai approaches Portugal, a developed country, but Guizhou was similar to Namibia. China's process of integrating into the global economy is related to its unbalanced strategy of regional economic development. However, the ultimate goal of this unbalanced strategy is to promote the development of the nation as a whole. In 1986, the architect of China's reform, Deng Xiaoping, said, 'The purpose of allowing some regions and some people to become prosperous before others is to enable all of them to prosper eventually. We have to make sure that there is no polarization of society – that's what socialism means' (Deng Xiaoping, Vol. III, 1993, p. 195). At the beginning of reform and opening-up, the demands of economic development required that China abandon its previous strategy of balanced development in favor of investing in its coastal areas. Thus, the policy of opening-up has exacerbated the cross-regional income and development gaps.

The widening regional development gap presents a puzzling problem for China. However, the interregional imbalance that has appeared in its economy is not a special case. Economic activities often agglomerate towards the geographical areas that can best engage in economic interactions with other countries. For example, after the implementation of the North American Free Trade Agreement (NAFTA), certain economic activities in Canada and Mexico agglomerated in their US borders. Nonetheless, the widening development gap is still a serious problem in China. The development gap is detrimental to social harmony, and the interregional income gap increases tendencies toward local protectionism. This causes serious interregional duplication of construction and market segmentation. Thus, China's economic decentralization can promote localism in local governments.

The government is aware of the necessity of adjusting regional economic development policies. During his inspection tour of southern China in 1992, Deng Xiaoping (Vol. III, 1993, p. 374) commented,

> The socialist system must and can avoid polarization. One of the solutions is that the areas that have become prosperous first must support the poor ones by paying more taxes or turning in more profits to the state. Of course, this should

not be carried out too hastily. . . . I can imagine that the right time might be the end of this century, when our people are living fairly comfortable lives.

Everything that was happening in China was as Deng Xiaoping expected. At the end of the twentieth century, the government considered balancing regional and urban–rural development to be a significant objective, as evidenced by the launching of strategies for the large-scale development of the western region, revitalization of the old northeast industrial base, and development of the central regions, among others. The 17th CPC National Congress pointed out that coordinating regional development had to be one of the objectives of Chinese socialism.

There are two main ways in which China could balance interregional development. The first is to make fiscal transfer payments to less-developed areas via the central government. However, using fiscal transfer payments alone may reduce economic efficiency. The other option is to continue promoting economic agglomeration in the coastal areas, which will at least temporarily widen the development gap, given that interregional labor mobility is still constrained by the *hukou* system. The question of how to effect coordinated interregional development in the future while maintaining sustainable economic growth, and whether a compromise strategy would be effective, must be answered in the context of globalization.

4.1 CHINA'S ECONOMY IN THE ERA OF GLOBALIZATION

As a positive participant in the third wave of globalization, the speed of China's integration into the world economy is as dramatic as the speed of its economic growth. China has become an important participant in the process of globalization in terms of both international trade and international flow of capital. In this section, we follow the traditional understanding of China's transition from an isolated country to a large, developing country with an open economy.

Expansion of Special Economic Zones and Economic Opening-up Zones

After nearly 30 years of isolated and semi-isolated development, China instituted a strategy of economic opening-up. This immediately led to discussions of the merits of socialism versus capitalism. At this time, China's economy lacked confidence, and there were many uncertainties regarding the possible outcomes of the economic opening-up. The government took advantage of Guangdong Province's and Fujian Province's position as neighbors to Hong Kong and Macao in order to create special export zones. Also in the early stages of launching China's opening-up policy, the government founded special economic zones in Shenzhen, Zhuhai, Shantou, and Xiamen. Thus, China's reform was characterized by experimentalism from the very beginning, and the process of economic opening-up was not promoted comprehensively at the beginning but rather took place in different ways in different areas.

From the point of view of regional development, the policy of economic opening-up was carried out first in eastern coastal regions because of their favorable location. This mainly took the form of the founding of economic special zones and economic development zones, which enjoyed preferential policies. For example, these economic zones were endowed with more power of economic self-management, and were allowed to use foreign capital for joint ventures, cooperative enterprises, and individual proprietorship. Businesses operating in special zones enjoyed management autonomy and preferential tax rates. In 1984, in light of the achievements of existing special economic zones, the government decided to open up 14 more coastal cities. It announced that it would offer preferential treatment to foreign businessmen who invested and provided advanced technologies. It also gave those cities more rights to self-management to promote their foreign economic activities. In 1985, the Yangtze River Delta, the Pearl River Delta, and the Xiamen-Zhangzhou-Quanzhou Delta, and Shanghai started to enjoy the same preferential policies as the coastal economic open zones. In 1988, Hainan was established as the fifth special economic zone, and the government further enlarged existing coastal economic open zones until they finally included 153 cities and counties in eight provinces and municipalities in eastern China. The first 14 national-level economic and technological development zones were all located in eastern coastal areas. The fact that opening-up to the outside world took place exclusively in eastern coastal regions in the 1980s not only promoted economic development in these areas but also pushed forward the process of nationwide economic opening-up, especially with respect to active foreign trade and attracting foreign investment. This unbalanced development strategy, while interregional migration was still constrained, led to much of the development gap that was growing between coastal areas and the interior.

Growth and Structure Upgrading of International Trade

Trade with the outside world was the first step in China's economic opening-up. China's imports and exports have realized rapid growth, which persisted through Asia's 1997 financial crisis. The volume of inter-

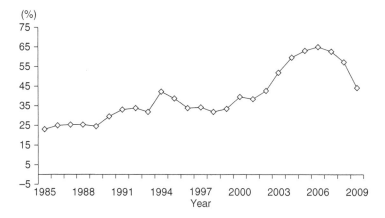

Sources: *China Statistical Yearbook* (various years) (China Statistics Press).

Figure 4.1 *China's trade dependency ratio (1985–2009)*

national trade placed China 32nd in the world in 1978, and it moved up to 15th, 10th, and sixth in 1989, 1997, and 2001, respectively. The ratio of international trade to GDP rose from 9.85 percent in 1978 to 42.78 percent in 2001. In 2002, China's trade volume exceeded US$600 billion, which accounted for over half of its GDP in 2002.[1] This placed China fifth in international trade in the world. The import and export trade volume in 2005 was US$1,421.9 billion, which was 1.8 times the 2001 figure. At this time, China ranked third in the world, behind only the US and Germany. The ratio of China's import and export trade volume increased to 6.7 percent in 2005 from 4 percent in 2001.[2] In 2006, the import and export volume increased to US$1,760.397 billion, and the ratio of import and export volume to GDP (trade dependency ratio) reached 65.66 percent (Figure 4.1).

China's trade structure changed gradually throughout its globalization process. In 1980, manufactured goods made up 49.7 percent of total exports, and the ratio reached 76 percent in 1992. In 2006, 92.8 percent of total exports were manufactured goods, 22.5 percent of which were high-tech products. Manufactured goods accounted for 94.7 percent of total exports in 2009. Fossil fuels, lubricating oil, and other raw materials made up the largest portion of the total exports by volume. The export of textiles and other light industrial products, rubber products, mining products, and processed ores ranked second until 1985. Subsequently, the export of textiles and other light industrial products, rubber products, mining products, and processed ores took over first place, and remained there until

1995. The volume of the export of fossil fuels, lubricating oil, other raw materials, and food and live animals moved down to second place from 1988 to 1995. Machinery and transport equipment leaped into first place during the period from 1995 to 2009, and textiles and other light industrial products, rubber products, mining products, and processed ores moved down to second place (see Chapter 6, Section 6.2). In the international market, products made in China continued to become cheaper. However, the complexity of these products increased, which has kept them competitive in the international market (Xu, 2007).

Along with expansion and opening-up to the outside world, China's foreign exchange reserves have grown by leaps and bounds. In 1990, foreign exchange reserves exceeded US$10 billion for the first time, reaching US$11.1 billion by the end of 1990, US$105.1 billion in 1996, US$212.1 billion in 2001, and US$818.9 billion in 2005. By the end of February 2006, China's foreign exchange reserves had increased to US$853.6 billion, surpassing Japan as the country with the largest foreign exchange reserves. By the end of 2011, China's foreign exchange reserves had reached US$3.18 trillion.[3]

Large-scale Floating of Foreign Capital and Other Factors of Production

The rapid growth of the export trade is related to both the comparative advantages of its labor force – low prices and high-quality work – and the influx of FDI. The contributions of international industrial capital have helped China become an important manufacturing base, and a great number of foreign-invested enterprises in China have themselves become exporters. Over the past decade, export of foreign capital enterprises has accounted for about half of the total exports (Chapter 6). At the beginning of reform and opening-up, FDI was rare in China. In 1979, China founded special economic zones to attract FDI, but large amounts of FDI did not begin to have an effect until 1984. The second wave of FDI took place after Deng Xiaoping's 1992 Southern Tour. For over ten years, China has attracted the most FDI of any developing country. In 2005, FDI continued to grow steadily, reaching a volume of US$63.8 billion for the whole year. The FDI utilized by China accounted for one-third of the total volume of developing countries, ranking third in the world.[4] In 2006, the foreign investment in actual use in China amounted to US$63.021 billion, and the ratio of foreign investment to GDP was 2.64 percent. In 2009, the foreign investment in actual use was US$90.033 billion with a foreign-investment-to-GDP ratio of 1.8 percent (exchange rate calculated by annual average value). In recent years, due to the rapid development of domestic enterprises, there is also some capital outflow. In 2001, over-

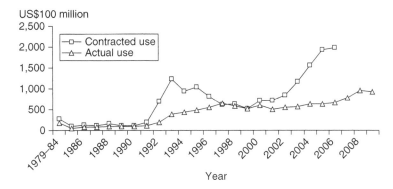

US$100 million

Sources: *China Statistical Yearbook* (various years) (China Statistics Press).

Figure 4.2   China's FDI flow (1979–2009)

seas investment was triple that of 1997, rising from US$2.562 billion to US$6.885 billion. In 2006, overseas non-financial investment reached the equivalent of US$17.6 billion. In 2009, it reached US$47.8 billion dollars (Figure 4.2).[5]

Entering the WTO

Entering the WTO further accelerated China's globalization. Before joining the WTO, China's opening-up involved mostly quantitative growth. After joining, China amended many of the internal systems and rules that affected international trade to accommodate the international economic order and structure of the WTO. On January 1, 2005, five years after entering the WTO, China had achieved its promised goals of abolishing all non-tariff measures, such as import quotas and permission requirements. By July 1, 2004, China had fulfilled its promise of giving businesses the power to engage in foreign trade, half a year ahead of schedule. The approval system for engagement in foreign trade, which had been in place for 50 years, was abolished.

4.2   GLOBALIZATION AND INDUSTRIAL AGGLOMERATION

When China opened its doors and returned to an international division of labor, different regions showed different advantages. Deng Xiaoping (Vol. III, 1993) commented,

> If a few regions develop a little faster, they will spur the others to catch up. This is a shortcut we can take to speed up development and attain common prosperity. (p. 166)

> [A]s we develop the coastal areas successfully, we shall be able to increase people's incomes, which accordingly will lead to higher consumption. This is in conformity with the laws of development. We shall allow some areas to become rich first; egalitarianism will not work. (p. 52)

Under this overall policy, China implemented the strategy that set the development of coastal regions as its first priority, starting with the establishment of four special economic zones. Although the new economic map of the country, which was mainly concerned with economic agglomeration, emerged formally after the 1990s, the regional development strategies selected by China's leaders were largely consistent with Deng Xiaoping's vision.

As mentioned in Chapter 3, the agglomeration of economic activities has a scale effect, which is an important motivator of economic growth. Specifically, it includes the sharing, matching, and learning effects realized by agglomeration among the various economic activities. This idea has been neglected by traditional economic theories, and the new economic geography has increased the importance of space. The positive effects of economic agglomeration have been confirmed by relevant research in various countries. In China, the tendency toward agglomeration is highly visible (Fan, 2004, 2006, 2008; Wen, 2004; Chen et al., 2006; Jin et al., 2006; Lu and Chen, 2006b; Lu and Tao, 2006).

The positive effects of industrial agglomeration and division of labor can be seen through some specific cases. For example, the Frontier Hotel, located in Urumqi, the capital city of Xinjiang, a western province bordering Russian and Central Asian countries, began to entertain businessmen from the Commonwealth of Independent States in 1991. These visitors were purchasing commodities in Urumqi after the disintegration of the Soviet Union. Subsequently, as cross-border business developed, this hotel developed into an all-in-one enterprise that provided services such as accommodation, trade, storage, and ports for international commerce. It also promoted the development of related services, such as food and entertainment. This is one example of agglomeration in the service industry. This case has also provided evidence of industrial agglomeration:

> The international trade in Frontier Hotel was mainly clothes, shoes, and hats, 95 percent of which came from the interior and coastal provinces, and also included special products for specific ethnic groups. The reason why inland companies did not transfer their workshops to Xinjiang was that it lacked the

advantage of industrial division of labor and agglomeration in local areas. Although the parts needed for the processing of clothes, shoes, and hats were not complicated, the industrial linkage with specific division of labor had already developed in the Jiangsu and Zhejiang coastal areas, which optimized the cost of manufacture, types for selection, and speed of supply, and the cost of products plus long-distance freight was even lower than producing locally in Xinjiang. (Zhu, 2007, pp. 48–9)

This raises the question of what form the industrial agglomeration took in Zhejiang, a coastal province. In a 2006 report on the Zhejiang economy it was stated that economic clustering is a major pillar of Zhejiang's leading industries and regional economy (Economic and Trade Committee of Zhejiang Province, 2006). Currently, industries and regions that show specific advantages are mostly those with developed economic clusters. The effects of these are evident in the development of industry clusters with international competitiveness. The first of these is the effective competition effect. The high concentration of enterprises of the same industry in the same geographical space increases market competition. This motivates enterprises to respond quickly to changes in the market, establish marketing strategies, and promote progress in technology and management. The second is the production specialization effect. The enterprises adopt a flexible specialized (professional plus flexible) means of production, promoting the formation of local networks based on specialized participation and cooperation, which can bring pronounced collective benefits. These tend to be more flexible than large, vertically integrated enterprises, and the costs of manufacturing and transaction are decreased. Operation efficiency and competitiveness increase as well. The third effect of clustering is positive externalities. Through local networks, enterprises that are embedded in industrial clusters, especially small and medium-sized enterprises, create production and operating conditions beyond the reach of single firms, and the scale of regional industry can be adjusted to favor large enterprises. Industrial clusters can lead to the agglomeration of various production elements and relevant organizations, giving enterprises easy access to information, resources, experienced staff, and professional personnel from the outside and also provides external support services such as design, training, logistics, financing, and technical support. The fourth effect is the interactive learning effect. The high agglomeration of enterprises of the same type allows them to learn from one another. This promotes knowledge spillover, technique expansion, and advantage integration, which increases competitive advantages and promotes increases in the value chain.

Changes in the structure of regional economic development show the importance of location. Before the economic reforms of 1978, for both

security reasons and the sake of balancing regional economic development, many industries were situated in inland provinces. Since 1978,
however, the market has come to dominate economic development, and
industry has become concentrated in coastal regions in the east (especially
the Yangtze River Delta, the Pearl River Delta, and the Bohai Rim). The
importance of traditional industrial bases in the northeast is decreasing.
This provides raw data for the analysis of economic growth, industrial
agglomeration, and city development. Because the main channel of
modern international trade is shipping by sea, coastal regions are better
situated for the international market. Shanghai, Hong Kong, and neigh-
boring Shenzhen are China's most important port cities. The Yangtze
River Delta and the Pearl River Delta enjoy great geographical advantages
as coastal regions because they are situated close to large ports. In inland
cities far from the coast, the cost of transporting goods is higher, but the
cost of labor is lower. In these areas, it is therefore more appropriate to
produce large quantities of commodities that can be transported easily by
train or boat, such as coal, and products with high added value that are
suitable for air transportation, such as computer chips (Gill et al., 2007).

Industrial Agglomeration during Globalization and Urbanization

The layout of the industrial complex has been transformed from a relative dispersion to agglomeration in the coastal areas of the southeast.
Before 1978, the geographical layout of industry still showed some signs
of dispersion. Specifically, (i) many provinces in eastern and central China
accounted for a small proportion of the country's industrial volume,
less than 4 percent for each; (ii) the importance of industry in the three
provinces of northeastern China was very evident, especially in Liaoning,
which housed a disproportionate amount of the country's total industry; (iii) Gansu and Shaanxi each housed over 2 percent of the country's
total industry, which, once adjusted for the size of the province, was
higher than that of some provinces in central and eastern China; and (iv)
although the geographical areas of three municipalities – Beijing, Tianjin,
and Shanghai – were relatively small, their industrial volumes were moderate to high, exceeding many other provinces (Chen et al., 2006; Lu and
Chen, 2006b).

If we separate China's provinces into two regions, coastal and inland,
and consider the contribution of each to the country's total industrial
GDP from 1987 to 2009, then it becomes clear that industry has tended to
move toward coastal regions (Figure 4.3). The specific features of industrial agglomeration appear to be as follows: (i) considerable increase in the
proportion of industry in coastal areas, and the contributions of the top

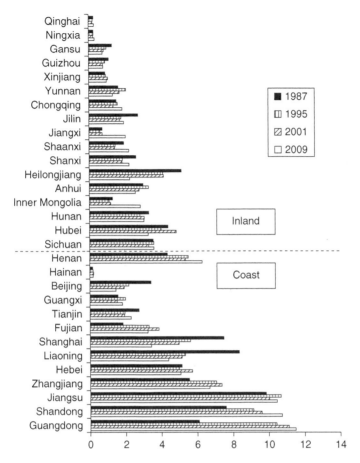

Note: Beijing is here considered a coastal area. Data are ordered according to relative contribution of industry by coastal and inland areas in 2009.

Sources: *China Statistical Yearbook* (China Statistics Press), and calculation by the authors.

Figure 4.3   Industry share (%) for each provincial administrative unit

four provinces, namely Guangdong, Shandong, Jiangsu, and Zhejiang, were 11.4 percent, 10.73 percent, 10.46 percent, and 6.68 percent, respectively, in 2009; (ii) the importance of industry in the three provinces in the northeast decreased markedly. The proportion of industry in Liaoning fell to 4.4 percent; and that in Heilongjiang and Jilin to 1.94 percent and 2.25 percent, respectively; (iii) the proportion of industry in western provinces tended to decrease; and (iv) the proportion of industry in the four municipalities of Shanghai, Tianjin, Beijing, and Chongqing fell markedly to 3.43 percent, 2.3 percent, 1.46 percent, and 1.85 percent, respectively.

The tendency toward industrial agglomeration is visible at the industrial level. The degree of regional agglomeration of the manufacturing industry tended to increase between 1998 and 2003 (Lu and Tao, 2006). For 29 double-digit-level industries (relatively grossly divided industry types), agglomeration tended to appear among provinces between 1981 and 2001. The Gini coefficient of provincial regional layout decreased in only two of these 29 categories. The CR3 (the proportion of the top three provinces) decreased in seven categories (Fan, 2008).

This change in the relative contributions of inland and coastal areas to industry was in accordance with the movement of laborers from the countryside toward coastal areas in the southeast. Jiangsu, Zhejiang, Shanghai, and Guangdong became the main destinations of cross-regional flow of labor. Thus, the change in the proportion of industry was in accordance with the direction of labor mobility. This is especially true of agglomeration in the Yangtze River Delta and the Pearl River Delta.

The question of whether industrial growth is related to each region's process of globalization and urbanization can be answered by the fact that both the opening-up of ports and urbanization promoted industrial agglomeration. Provinces close to the two biggest ports, Shanghai and Hong Kong, experienced more economic opening-up, and regions that experienced relatively high degrees of opening-up early during the reform period maintained these subsequently, giving them pronounced advantages with respect to industrial agglomeration. In addition, improvements in provincial market capacity (economic development level), transportation, and communications infrastructure, and decreases in government interference have favored industrial agglomeration (Chen et al., 2006).

Globalization opened up both the product and capital markets. Both FDI per capita and the degree of opening-up of the product market as measured by the trade dependency ratio indicate that coastal regions in the east had a much higher degree of opening-up and that globalization had become the most important cause of the increasingly large cross-regional income gap (Wan et al., 2007).

Regional Imbalances during Globalization, Industrialization, and Urbanization

Industrial agglomeration is increasing cross-regional differences in development. In the context of globalization, China's regional imbalances must be evaluated with respect to global division of labor. Considering that shipping by sea is the main method of transportation in international

*Table 4.1   FDI shares of eastern, central, and western areas (1983–2009)
(%)*

	1983–2001	2002–2004	1983–2004	2006	2009
Eastern area	87.76	86.83	87.50	86.45	84.69
Central area	8.98	10.91	9.51	9.47	9.17
Western area	3.26	2.26	2.99	4.07	6.14

Sources: Data from 1983 to 2004 are drawn from Chen (2007), which includes Guangxi in eastern areas. Data from 2006 and 2009 were calculated by the authors using the *China Statistical Yearbook* from 2007 and 2010 (China Statistics Press). For comparison, Guangxi is counted as part of the eastern area.

trade, coastal regions have a strong advantage. Multinational companies have made China their manufacturing base, concentrating large amounts of FDI in coastal regions. This facilitates transport of the resulting products to other parts of the world.

The geographical distribution of FDI highlights the relationship between globalization and regional imbalance. As shown in Table 4.1, since the 1980s, provinces in the east have taken up the largest proportion of FDI. After China's entry into the WTO, there were small changes in the distribution of FDI across eastern, central, and western areas. Eastern China's lead seems to have been reduced somewhat in favor of central and western provinces between 2002 and 2004. According to 2009 figures, the FDI received by western regions has increased considerably. However, central and western provinces are still at a disadvantage relative to eastern provinces with respect to attracting FDI. Under the system of economic decentralization, outside investment became one of the methods used to assess the performance of local officials at all levels, so attracting investments became an important objective of local governments. In order to attract investments, regions engaged in fierce competition, each trying to provide the most favorable conditions, even at the cost of counteracting each other's efforts or diminishing the welfare of local residents (Zhang, 2007).

The differences in globalization across eastern, central, and western China are also clear in urbanization. This indicates that agglomeration mainly occurred in big cities and in the east. After 1992, China saw both rapid urbanization and rapid economic growth. One outstanding feature of this dual transformation is that the number of cities with a population of over one million increased sharply all over the country, from 32 to 117 between 1993 and 2006. The regional distribution of these large cities also changed. The proportion of big cities in eastern regions decreased somewhat, mainly because of the decline in the number of cities in

Table 4.2 Cities with a population of over one million in eastern, central, and western China (1982–2009)

Year	1982		1993		2006		2009	
	No. of cities	%	No. of cities	%	No. of cities	%	No. of cities	%
Total number	20	100.0	31	100.0	117	100.0	124	100.0
Eastern area	11	55.0	15	48.4	54	46.2	56	45.2
Shanghai, Jiangsu, and Zhejiang	2	10.0	3	9.7	16	13.7	17	13.7
Guangdong (including Hainan)	1	5.0	1	3.2	11	9.4	12	9.7
Fujian	0	0.0	0	0.0	4	3.4	4	3.2
Beijing, Tianjin, Liaoning, Shandong, and Hebei	8	40.0	11	35.5	23	19.7	23	18.5
Central China	4	20.0	9	29.0	36	30.8	38	30.6
Western China	5	25.0	7	22.6	27	23.1	30	24.2

Source: Data for 1982, 1993, 2006, and 2009 are from *China Statistical Yearbook* (China Statistics Press), 1983, 1994, 2007, and 2010, respectively.

provinces surrounding the Bohai Rim. Jiangsu, Zhejiang, and Shanghai, which are located in the Yangtze River Delta, and Guangdong, which is located in the Pearl River Delta, gained more big cities after 1993. This was in accordance with industrial agglomeration. Across the entire assessment period, the number of big cities in central provinces increased by 13.3 percent, but the number of big cities in western provinces decreased by 4.5 percent (Table 4.2).

4.3 FROM REGIONAL IMBALANCE TO REGIONAL BALANCE

The early stages of China's pre-designed development path involved establishing good conditions in eastern areas with the expectation that these areas would later promote the development of the entire country. This strategy was considered suitable for a poor, developing country, like a lifeboat escaping from a desert island. If the boat cannot carry everyone without sinking, then the best course of action is to allow strong individuals to leave first and find reinforcements to come and rescue the rest.

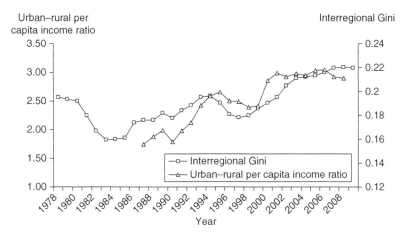

Note and sources: Regarding the urban-rural per capita income ratio, urban and rural incomes have been deflated by the urban and rural CPIs, respectively, except for 1978–84 and 1988–89 due to lack of indices for these years. The interregional Gini coefficient was used to determine per capita income across different provinces, and the original data are from the *55-year Statistical Series of New China* and *China Statistical Yearbook*. We deflated the provincial-level per capita disposable income of urban residents and the rural net per capita income using the urban and rural CPIs of each province. These values were weighted by the proportion of the population involved in farming to calculate the per capita income of each province.

Figure 4.4   Income disparity between urban and rural areas and among provincial administrative areas (1978–2009)

However, this scenario requires those left behind to trust that the individuals leaving in the boat will successfully bring about their rescue.

Mechanisms Underlying Regional Balance

China's economic growth was brought about by globalization, but cross-regional differences in economic development emerged and became enlarged. This trend can be summarized as follows:

1. The cross-regional income gap has been increasing gradually. The Gini coefficient of interregional per capita income has increased gradually, rising to 0.238 in 2005 (Figure 4.4). The average income of urban employees and the per capita income of urban households also indicate that the cross-provincial gap is increasing (Knight et al., 2006).
2. The income gap between coastal areas in the east and central and western regions is increasing, but the income gap within the three

economic zones has narrowed to some extent (Yao and Zhang, 2001; Zhang et al., 2001).

3. Data regarding the average income of urban employees and the per capita household income indicate that the income gap within each province is increasing, but the provinces are coming to resemble each other more closely, experiencing income gaps of similar size (Knight et al., 2006).

4. Cross-regional economic differences have tended to increase, and cross-regional variations in the income gap resemble those in the gap between urban and rural areas (Figure 4.4). Cross-regional differences may be largely due to the greater rural population of inland provinces and increases in the urban–rural difference (Wan, 2006).[6]

These regional differences developed for complicated reasons, and scholars have studied those reasons from many angles. Regional differences can mainly be summarized as follows:

1. Various favorable policies (especially those promoting economic opening-up and marketization) have allowed eastern coastal areas to integrate themselves into the global economy to a greater degree than other areas (Démurger et al., 2002). Eastern areas have received more direct international investment than other areas, which have allowed them to develop rapidly (Wan et al., 2007).

2. Unbalanced development of privately owned businesses and township enterprises have also driven regional imbalances (Rozzelle, 1994; Wan, 1998; Wan et al., 2007).

3. Fiscal transfers from the central to local governments were disproportionately allocated to eastern areas for many years (Raiser, 1998; Ma and Yu, 2003).

4. Differences in terms of infrastructure laid different foundations for economic development (Démurger, 2001).

Among all the factors that affect regional disparity, geographical and political differences are the most fundamental; the rest are merely the manifestations of these regional differences. Coastal areas are much closer to international markets and they have significant advantages that allow them greater participation in globalization and international division of labor. The influence of geographical location on regional differences also manifested itself in differences among cities. In 2000, differences in GDP per capita of 53 large cities were analyzed, and a single factor, the distance to the port, was found to explain 58 percent of the average GDP per capita among cities (Leman, 2005). During the process of economic opening-up, geographical location became a decisive element in economic growth. Generally speaking, places more distant from Hong Kong and Shanghai developed more slowly (Xu et al., 2010). Under the development strategy of regional imbalance, coastal regions also benefited from favorable policies. These geographical and political advantages became the fundamental reasons behind industrial agglomeration toward the Yangtze River Delta, the Pearl River Delta, and the Bohai Rim. A report from the World Bank stated that the enlargement of the cross-regional income gap was partially caused by favorable trade and investment policies, but a more fundamental reason is that the comparative advantages of different regions were restrained before the reform. The favorable policies implemented in coastal areas after the reform were designed to give these areas comparative advantages. The World Bank stated that these policies were reasonable (World Bank, 1997b).

During the process of opening-up, the inflow of foreign capital and the development of an export-oriented economy allowed certain regions advantages over others, but there is some question regarding the extent to which economic opening-up can explain regional differences. Our research indicates that cross-regional differences in terms of FDI per capita and trade dependency ratio have already become the most significant contributors to the income gap among provincial administrative regions. We found that the degree to which certain factors could explain the overall income gap among regions was relevant:

1. FDI per capita and the ratio of trade to GDP, both of which are used to represent the economic opening-up, tended to account for much of the cross-regional income gap, and this effect became more pronounced over time. In 2001, the two indexes accounted for 21.66 percent of the overall income gap, placing them first among all possible causes and contributing factors.
2. Capital accumulation is the major factor that leads to a cross-regional income gap. In 2001, capital accumulation was able to explain 19.11 percent of the overall cross-regional income gap.
3. Economic reform characterized by privatization and diminished government interference progressed differently in different regions, and this tended to intensify the income gap. In 2001, these factors accounted for 14.26 percent and 14.07 percent, respectively, of the overall difference among regions.
4. Differences in geographical location, education, urbanization, and population dependency ratio also enlarged the cross-regional income gap, but the contributions of these factors are growing weaker (Wan et al., 2007).

Differences in economic development and income level across regions also influenced cross-regional inequality in other ways. Under the system of fiscal decentralization, local governments were obliged to finance local public services such as education and medical care. Differences in economic development and income led to differences in the quantity and quality of public services in different regions. A detailed analysis is given in Chapter 5.

The enlargement of the cross-regional income gap was accompanied by market segmentation and local protectionism, which do not favor sustainable economic growth or the utilization of economies of scale. Before 1978, for the purpose of balancing regional development and increasing military security, the central government made large industrial investments in inland provinces and actively balanced development across regions. After the economic reform, fiscal transfers from the central government become more concentrated in economically developed regions. Meanwhile, local governments at all levels were given the right to make local economic policies. Local governments then had an incentive to segment markets, protect weak local enterprises from competition, and in this way increase local fiscal revenue and employment in the short term. However, in recent years, a large amount of empirical research has shown that serious market segmentation existed even after the reform and opening-up (for example, Young, 2000; Zheng and Li, 2003). However, other studies have suggested that markets are becoming more integrated and specialized (Naughton, 2000; Xu, 2002; Bai et al. 2004; Gui et al., 2006; Lu et al., 2006; Lu and Chen, 2006b). Some researchers have argued that the degree of market segmentation among provinces in China is increasing to the point at which it is even greater than among European countries (Poncet, 2002, 2003).

The local government's support of market segmentation has a strategic aspect. Undeveloped regions are investing in emerging industries and then providing protection in order to create leverage that they can use to obtain central transfer payments. Thus, these regions may catch up with developed regions. In the context of imbalanced regional development, the strategies of undeveloped regions can benefit those regions under certain conditions. However, they may also lead to a duplication of resources and inefficient resource allocation.[7] This can be harmful to economic agglomeration and sustainable growth (Lu et al., 2004, 2007; Lu and Chen, 2006b).

There have been three rounds of duplications. The first occurred during the 1980s, mainly in the household appliance industry (especially color TV sets). The second, which occurred during the 1990s, mainly involved the automobile industry. In the third, during the first years of the twenty-first century, duplications were more concentrated in the field of high and new technology; many areas supported opto-electronics, biographic medicine, and software industries. Duplication is a double-edged sword. It can encourage competition among regions. However, scholars have also argued that excessive duplications have been harmful because they have prevented each region from specializing and cooperating with other regions. During the formation of cross-regional market segmentation, government intervention took on a very important role. Our own research shows that domestic product markets have gradually moved toward integration. The tax-sharing reform implemented in the mid-1990s increased the total amount of central fiscal revenue. Local governments have exerted greater efforts in taxation, and the degree of government intervention measured by the ratio of local governmental expenditure to local GDP has tended to increase. Local protectionism has become a direct means of ensuring local fiscal revenue, which does not favor long-lasting economies of scale (Lu and Chen, 2006b; Chen et al., 2007a). Less government intervention in the adoption of appropriate central fiscal transfer policies, and balanced development may foster interregional specialization, market integration, and economic growth (Fan and Zhang, 2010a).

Policy of Balanced Development and its Effects

The enlargement of the cross-regional income gap has been accompanied by increased efficiency in the allocation of economic resources. However, exceedingly large income gaps can cause regions to adopt policies that favor market segmentation, preventing China from benefiting from its advantages of scale. Unbalanced development may also cause regions to develop different long-term goals, which may involve political risks and negatively affect democratization (Shah et al., 2006).

In response to the increasingly serious problem of regional imbalance, the country has adjusted its regional development strategy, adopting policies in favor of economically backward regions. One of these policies involved increasing fiscal transfers to undeveloped regions. Since the 1990s, the government has gradually focused more on balanced development across regions. In 1992, the government approved 15 new ports and 26 counties for opening-up. The total number has since reached 167 and 825, respectively. During this period, the opening-up policy was extended to inland areas. In March 1992, the government allowed four border cities in the northeast and Inner Mongolia to establish national-level frontier economic cooperation zones. The total number of newly established national-level frontier economic cooperation zones reached 14 in 1992, most of them in central and western areas (Table 4.3). In August, the government continued to announce policies that would extend the policies

Table 4.3 Evolution of opening-up areas

Year	Opening-up types	Location
1978–1988	Special economic zones	Shenzhen, Zhuhai, Shantou, Xiamen (1980), Hainan (1988)
	Open coastal cities	Dalian, Qinhuangdao, Tianjin, Yantai, Qingdao, Lianyungang, Nantong, Shanghai, Ningbo, Wenzhou, Fuzhou, Guangzhou, Zhanjiang, Beihai (1984)
	National-level economic and technological development zones	Dalian, Qinhuangdao, Yantai, Qingdao, Ningbo, Zhanjiang, Tianjin, Lianyungang, Nantong, Guangzhou, Fuzhou, Shanghai Minhang, Shanghai Hongqiao, Shanghai Caohejing (1984–86)
	Coastal economic open zones	Guangdong, Fujian, Zhejiang, Jiangsu, Shanghai, Shandong, Tianjin, Hebei, Liaoning, Guangxi (1985–88)
1988–1998	Provincial capitals, cities along the Yangtze River	Urumqi, Nanning, Kunming, Harbin, Changchun, Hohhot, Shijiazhuang, Taiyuan, Hefei, Nanchang, Zhengzhou, Changsha, Chengdu, Guiyang, Xi'an, Lanzhou, Xining, Yinchuan, Chongqin, Yueyang, Wuhan, Jiujiang, Wuhu (1992)
	National-level frontier economic cooperation zones	Heihe, Suifenhe, Huichun, Manzhouli, Dandong, Erlianhaote, Yining, Tacheng, Bole, Pingxiang, Wanding, Hekou, Ruili, Dongxing (1992)
	National-level economic and technological development zones	Wenzhou, Kunshan, Yingkou, Weihai, Fujian Rongqiao, Fujian Dongshan (1992), Shenyang, Hangzhou, Wuhan, Wuhu, Changchun, Harbin, Chongqin, Xiaoshan, Nansha, Daya Bay (1993), Urumqi, Beijing (1994)
	National-level high-tech industrial development zones	Zhongguancun Science and Technology Park (1988), Wuhan Donghu, Nanjing, Shenyang, Tianjin, Xi'an, Chengdu, Weihai Huoju, Zhongshan Huoju, Changchun, Harbin, Changsha, Fuzhou, Guangzhou, Hefei, Chongqin,

Year	Category	Locations
		Hangzhou, Guilin, Zhengzhou, Lanzhou, Shijiazhuang, Ji'nan, Dalian, Xiamen Huoju, Haihou (1991), Suzhou, Wuxi, Changzhou, Foshan, Huizhou, Zhuhai, Qingdao, Weifang, Zibo, Kunming, Guiyang, Nanchang, Taiyuan, Nanning, Urumqi, Baotou Xitu, Xiangfan, Zhuzhou, Luoyang, Daqin, Baoji, Jilin, Mianyang, Baoding, Anshan, Shanghai Zhangjiang (1992), Shenzhen (1996), Yangling Agriculture (1997)
	National-level industrial parks	Xiamen Haicang Taiwanese Investment Zone (1989), Shanghai Jinqiao Export Processing Zone (1990), Hainan Yangpu Economic Development Zone (1992), Ningbo Daxie Development Zone (1993), Suzhou Industrial Park (1994)
	National-level bonded areas	Shanghai Waigaoqiao (1990), Tianjin Port (1991), Shenzhen (1991–96), Xiamen Xiangyu, Haikou, Qingdao, Zhangjiagang, Ningbo, Fuzhou, Guangzhou (1992), Dalian (1992/2000), Shantou (1993), Zhuhai (1996)
1998–2008	National-level economic and technological development zones	Hefei, Zhengzhou, Chengdu, Changsha, Xi'an, Kunming, Guiyang, Shihezi, Nanchang, Xining, Hohhot (2000), Nanning, Taiyuan, Yinchuan, Lhasa (2001), Lanzhou, Nanjing (2002)
	National-level high-tech industrial development zones	Ningbo (2007)

Note: Hainan Yangpu economic open zone simultaneously enjoys the policies in bonded areas.

Source: See www.cadz.org.cn.

implemented in coastal cities to five cities along the Yangtze River, four capital cities in border areas, and 11 capital cities in inland areas. The specific policies included extending the rights of cities to engage in foreign economic cooperation, supporting the import of advanced foreign technologies and managerial staff, implementing policies favorable to foreign investment, and allowing the establishment of appropriate economic and technological development zones. A considerable number of economic and technological development zones and high-tech industrial development zones are located in central and western areas (Table 4.3).

In recent years, along with the continuous enlargement of interregional disparity, balanced cross-regional development has received much attention from the government. The strategy of developing the western regions, of reviving old industrial bases in the northeast, and the rise of central China came into being. All of these phenomena can be attributed to the attitude and resolution of the government. In 2000, the government started the strategy of developing the western regions and announced that it would accelerate the development of infrastructure, increase protection of the environment, actively adjust industrial structures, speed up the cultivation of talented people, and strengthen the degree of reform and opening-up in western regions. Subsequently, financial investment from the central government increased yearly. In 2005, the central construction fund invested about 460 billion RMB in western regions. Fiscal transfer payments and specialized aid amounted to more than 500 billion RMB, and more than a third of long-term treasury bonds for construction were used in western regions. The country had supported the construction of 60 important projects in western areas, with a total investment of 850 billion RMB. Treasury bonds alone accounted for over 270 billion RMB. During the same period, western regions attracted FDI of more than US$9 billion in addition to loans from international organizations and foreign governments, which brought the actual figure up to nearly US$15 billion. Over 10 thousand companies moved to western regions bringing in a total of over 300 billion RMB.[8] The government redoubled its efforts to construct rural infrastructure and social programs in western regions. In 2003, the government began to revive old industrial bases, such as those in the northeast, strengthened economic reform, and provided favorable policies regarding taxation, national financial investment, and the attraction of foreign investment for the three northeastern provinces and some areas in Inner Mongolia. In 2004, the government reiterated the importance of promoting the development of central regions and issued programmatic documents in 2006. Since 2000, economic and technological development zones and national-level high-tech industrial development zones have tended to favor central and western regions (Table 4.3).

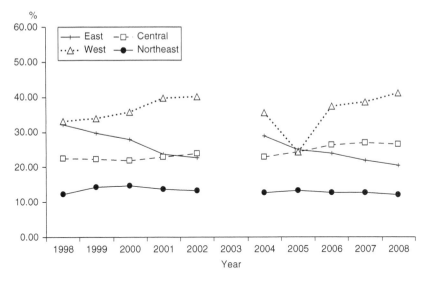

Note: Lack of data for Chongqing in 2000. Data for 2003 is not included in the figure, because it shows an abrupt growth in the east.

Source: *China Fiscal Yearbook* (China Finance Press, various years) and calculation by the authors.

Figure 4.5 *Four regions' proportion in the net central fiscal transfer (1998–2008)*

The adjustment of regional development policies is indicated by the central fiscal transfer payments. For a long period following reform and opening-up, more such payments were distributed to eastern coastal regions than to other areas. This accelerated the development of the east but intensified imbalance among regions (Ma and Yu, 2003; Raiser, 1998). This has changed in recent years. Figure 4.5 shows the changes in distribution of fiscal transfers to eastern, central, western, and northeastern provinces.[9] As shown, the relative size of the total amount of money transferred to eastern regions has declined. After the implementation of the western region development strategy in 2000, the relative amount of money transferred to western regions increased from 2000 to 2002. Examinations of the strategies of reviving old industrial bases in the northeast (implemented in 2003) and of developing central China (implemented in 2004) are marred by abnormal figures for 2003. Figure 4.5 does not show any marked increase in the proportion of these two regions with respect to fiscal transfers.

Due to the huge differences in the level of development among

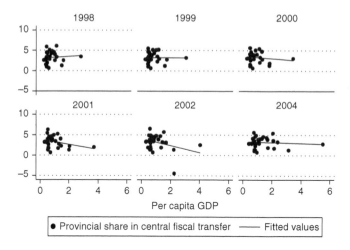

Note: The only location with negative net transfer payments in 2002 was Beijing. Excluding this observation, there was no fundamental change in the slope of the fitted line that year.

Source: *China Fiscal Yearbook* (various years) (China Finance Press) and calculation by the authors.

Figure 4.6   Economic development level and share of net central fiscal transfer (%) (1998–2004)

provinces in eastern, central, western, and northeastern China, it is not enough to analyze the changes in the distribution of central fiscal transfer payments across these four regions. In recent years, the government has put more emphasis on balancing development across regions. We found that this was reflected in the proportion of central fiscal transfer payments awarded to each province. As shown in Figure 4.6, the proportion of payments given to each province is linked to its per capita GDP. Relatively rich provinces continued to receive more payments than other provinces until 1998. In 1999, this disparity had largely disappeared. Since 2000, more payments have been awarded to relatively undeveloped provinces.

The central government's fiscal transfer system is intended to balance development across regions. This raises the question of whether it has worked – whether the provinces that received more fiscal transfer saw more growth. Data have shown that, generally speaking, the larger the proportion of central transfer payments, the slower the growth (Chen and Lu, 2008a). Fan and Zhang (2010b) found that in the short term, transfer payments had a positive effect on local economic growth by allowing the expenditures of local governments to increase, contributing to GDP growth. However, in the long run, such payments had a negative effect on economic growth. For every additional percentage point in the proportion of transfer payments, long-term growth decreased by 0.03 percentage points. This figure ran as high as 0.37 percent in western regions.

Realization of Regional Balance and Economic Growth

The first stage of the reform and opening-up was a planned economy whose system and policies supported balanced development across regions. This made China an excellent model for the study of industrial agglomeration and regional economic development. The changes that accompanied regional development have become an important aspect of development as a large country.

Under the combined actions of globalization, urbanization, and favorable economic policies for coastal areas, industries have shown a tendency toward agglomeration, and coastal areas (especially the Yangtze River Delta, the Pearl River Delta, and the Bohai Rim) have become centers of industrial agglomeration. The metropolitan areas in the Yangtze River Delta have taken the lead and become the world's sixth largest city cluster and an international manufacturing base. Guangdong Province, which is located in the Pearl River Delta, has also seen strong development. It ranks first among all provincial administrative regions within the country in terms of industry. Besides three major metropolitan areas, China also plans to create several regional economic and industrial centers in Wuhan, Chongqing, and Xi'an to promote gradual regional development. As mentioned in Chapter 3, China is entering into an era of rapid urbanization, and the degree of urbanization is increasing by 1 percentage point annually. In two decades, over 70 percent of the population may be living in cities, and more than half may be concentrated in the three major economic zones. The country may then be better able to take advantage of the agglomeration effect. The burden of population on the land will be greatly relieved, and the efficiency of land use may be increased. This may significantly motivate sustainable economic growth.

Two forces are still hindering industrial agglomeration. The first is the local governments' behavior toward market segmentation. The other is restrictions placed on cross-regional labor mobility by the system of household registration (*hukou*) combined with the vaguely defined property rights of rural landowners. Because of minimally integrated markets and restricted labor mobility, industrial agglomeration and urbanization have been constrained, and the cities have remained relatively small with little difference in scale among cities. Thus, economic growth has suffered (Chapter 3). For China, industrial agglomeration is an indispensable stage of economic development. If it tries to pursue regional balance solely through decentralized economic development under the condition that economic agglomeration has not achieved its expected level, there will be a loss of driving forces and international competitiveness.

Industrial agglomeration greatly promotes economic growth. However, it is also accompanied by an enlarged cross-regional and urban–rural income gap. This has certain undesirable effects on sustainable economic growth. One of the main difficulties in regional economic development is the realization of coordinated development between urban and rural areas and across regions while maintaining high levels of economic growth. The government has already realized the importance of coordinating urban and rural development and of developing different regions. It has already awarded more funding to relatively undeveloped inland and rural regions than it did in the past. However, there is no evidence to show that central fiscal transfer payments have promoted faster economic growth in undeveloped regions. This may be because the effect of market power is stronger than the effect of straight funding, or that transfer payments serve only to shrink the short-term income gap rather than to increase economic development.

This raises the question of whether economic agglomeration and the interregional income gap really conflict with each other. Our answer is no. While we do not deny that economic agglomeration has widened the cross-regional income gap, we also note that the agglomeration effect is not endless. Along with the agglomeration of people and economic activities, a congestion effect that offsets agglomeration has also appeared. This effect includes traffic jams, environmental pollution, and higher prices of land and labor. These agglomeration and congestion effects will cause the scale of cities to reach a certain optimal level (Au and Henderson, 2006b). Reasonable amounts of labor mobility favor the full utilization of the scale effect of urban economic development. It also favors increases in per capita ownership of resources in relatively undeveloped rural regions, thus having a positive effect on narrowing the income gap among regions as well as between urban and rural areas. According to a World Bank study (2008), cross-regional income convergence took place in the US, Chile, and Pakistan because of sufficient factor mobility rather than because of special policies in regional development. In the history of developed countries, such as the US and France, regional income gaps have once been observed. However, these gaps have narrowed later on. This was attributed to factor mobility and sustainable development. Globally, the richer a country is, the smaller the regional gap (ibid.). If the agglomeration and congestion effects occur simultaneously, the increases in residents' quality of life lag behind economic development. Put simply, high income requires sacrifices in other aspects of quality of life, such as living in a congested city rather than in a small city or in the countryside. Only through agglomeration can China realize constant development and obtain the fiscal revenue to redistribute among regions such as in the equalization of public services. If agglomeration is abandoned, development will slow down, and the entire country will suffer. Thus, the central government will lack the financial strength to carry out cross-regional balanced development policies.

For the sake of stability, China must prevent the income gap from becoming excessively wide, and its main means of doing so is through transfer payments. Balanced development across regions cannot rely too much on fiscal transfer payments, and transfer payments should not be used solely as compensatory income. Balancing development among regions and between urban and rural areas should not be realized at the cost of economic efficiency. If the government does not wish to sacrifice growth to control the cross-regional and urban–rural income gap, then it should adopt the following policies:

1. To take advantage of scale economy and promote economic growth, the government should reduce market segmentation, reform the *hukou* system, and affirm the property rights of rural landowners, promote cross-regional mobility of laborers, promote urbanization and economic agglomeration, and promote the appropriate expansion of urban populations in the Yangtze River Delta, the Pearl River Delta, and the Bohai Rim regions.
2. To promote equal access to public services in urban and rural areas and across regions and to narrow the cross-regional salary gap among civil servants and personnel of public services (such as teachers in middle and primary schools), transfer payments should be used to equalize access to public services rather than for direct investment in inland industries that have no comparative advantages.
3. Under conditions in which labor mobility is restricted, infrastructure and human capital in undeveloped regions and rural areas should be strengthened, in order to foster long-term economic growth and further agglomeration in coastal areas.
4. China should adjust its balanced development policies to integrate urban and rural economies and narrow the urban–rural income gap (especially in inland provinces). This policy will also narrow the income gap among regions.

The central government serves an irreplaceable purpose with respect to coordinated development, the most important aspects of which are:

1. *Sustaining a unified large domestic market*   In the current world, it is particularly important for China to maintain a large, unified market. This allows it to take advantage of economies of scale. For example, China relies on the large scale of its market to develop industries such as large passenger and freight airplanes and satellite GPS. China should pass legislation to prevent local governments from segmenting the market.

2. *Promoting trans-provincial cooperation*   China is a large country, so a unified market must be established in stages. It must first promote cooperation within the Yangtze River Delta, the Pearl River Delta, and the Bohai Rim. Interregional cooperation can counteract the market segmentation policies carried out by local governments. One realistic obstacle to this comes from the restrictions on labor mobility due to the social security system, which is segmented among regions. Eliminating market segmentation may promote regional integration of social security. However, free labor mobility may enlarge the developmental differences across cities in the short run. The central government should consider establishing coordinating mechanisms favorable to a unified market.

3. *Mitigating the power of local governments*   This allows society to rely more on civil forces to promote economic development. Over the past 30 years, China has developed rapidly and most of this development has been driven by the government. China will only be able to realize sustainable economic growth by diminishing interference from local governments. First, it is necessary to weaken the power of local governments in order to create conditions suitable to the establishment of a unified market. The central government is currently trying to develop undeveloped regions through the cross-regional rotation of government officials, which prevents local forces from becoming overly strong. However, the short tenures of these local officials gives them an incentive to pursue short-term objectives at the expense of long-term sustainable development. Second, the current stage of economic development has far less need for government-led economic development than in the past. China's infrastructure has developed considerably, especially in coastal areas, so the relative importance of infrastructure constructed through government programs has become smaller and smaller. Meanwhile, the private sector has become stronger. The capital market has become established as a source of financing, diminishing

the importance of the government as a source of capital. As China has developed, information requirements have become more complicated, putting the government at a disadvantage. A detailed discussion of the timing of the transition of the government's role is given in Chapter 6.

4. *Promoting the appropriate equalization of local public services based on property tax* 'To narrow development difference between regions, it is necessary to emphasize the equalization of basic public services and guide reasonable cross-regional mobility of production factors'.[10] Local governments provide many services, including basic education. Economic theory indicates that the most effective mechanism of financing public services is property taxation, which links payments directly to consumption of services. This technique should be popularized in China. The future of China's coordinated regional development requires appropriate equalization of public services and quality of life alongside economic differentiation across regions. Appropriate equalization of public services across regions should involve not only direct input in infrastructure construction, but also appropriate equalization in the salaries of civil servants and other public sector personnel (such as teachers). This requires that the central government retain some of the proceeds from property taxes so that the funds can be used to equalize the income of these civil servants and other public sector personnel.

NOTES

1. The data quoted in this section are drawn from State Statistics Bureau, *55-year Statistical Series of New China* and *China Statistical Yearbook* (various years), if there is no special note.
2. See WTO Database; Chinese data are drawn from *China Statistical Yearbook*.
3. See website of State Administration of Foreign Exchange.
4. See *World Investment Report 2006*. Data about China are drawn from *China Statistical Yearbook*.
5. Data for 2006 were drawn from *Statistics Bulletin of the National Economic and Social Development of the People's Republic of China (2006)*, see http://www.stats.gov.cn/tjgb/ndtjgb/qgndtjgb/t20070228_402387821.htm.
6. Some early research showed that, after 1978, unbalanced development decreased among coastal provinces, which tended to narrow the development difference among regions nationwide. However, there was no significant narrowing of imbalance in the development between coastal and inland provinces, or among inland provinces (Jian et al., 1996; Raiser, 1998).
7. Wei (2001) provides a large amount of evidence regarding duplications.
8. See http://www.chinawest.gov.cn.
9. Central net transfer payments are here equal to transfers from the central government minus transfers to the central government. Traditionally, China is divided into

eastern, central, and western areas. Here we treat the three northeastern provinces as a separate region in order to assess the influence of the strategy of reviving old industrial bases. Among the three northeastern provinces, Liaoning is usually included in the eastern region, while Heilong Jiang and Jilin are usually considered part of the central region. In order to be in accordance with the policy of great development of western regions, we have treated Guangxi and Inner Mongolia as part of western China in Figure 4.5.

10.   Quoted from the report of the 17th CPC National Congress.

5. Transitions of public services and government responsibilities during the marketization process

Since the foundation of the new China, an overwhelming majority of urban residents have been covered by a welfare network that includes pensions, medical care, education, and housing, all supported by state-owned and collective enterprises. In rural areas, health care was provided through cooperative medical-care organizations within the scope of the collective economy. Since the beginning of China's reform and opening-up, the power of marketization has had a pronounced impact on the social welfare system. In the cities, as early as the mid-1980s, state-owned and collective enterprises had already felt the pressure of competition from non-public enterprises, which carried a much lighter welfare burden. At that time, the reform of marketization and the socialization of the welfare system began to take effect. Since the mid-1990s, marketization reform has caused substantial changes in pensions, medical care, education, and housing. The system that has customarily been used to assess political achievements is heavily based on GDP growth. This gives local governments an incentive to invest local funds in areas that can promote GDP growth directly, while the funding of public services is more often left to the market. The dismantling of people's public communities has caused a serious lack of medical care in rural areas.

The reform of marketization has inspired the development of new pension, medical-care, education, and housing systems. The average quantity, quality, and efficiency of medical care, education, and housing have all increased. However, because local governments have pursued short-term objectives, particularly short-term economic growth, reforms relevant to public service have tended toward marketization and privatization. In terms of financing, the relative amount of government expenditures used for public services has declined. A large number of privately owned institutions have entered public service, providing services such as education and medical care in competition with public institutions. Market pricing has gradually replaced government pricing and regulation, and this has caused a certain degree of disorder, which has created problems such as inconvenient access to hospitals and high medical costs. Because the capital in the public service field comes mostly from local financing, and because these fiscal expenditures are concentrated in urban areas, serious levels of regional and urban–rural inequality have emerged with respect to access to public services. Factors such as income, profession, and social status have exerted great influence on the level of public service accessible by different groups of individuals. The upgrading and equalization of access to quality public services are relevant to the long-term sustainable development of the country. However, in China short-term economic growth is placed first, while the long-term objectives of development and the sustainability of economic growth are neglected.

Most people in China attribute the inequality of public services to marketization reform. In fact, to introduce market mechanisms into the public services field is acceptable to most. The key point is not whether marketization is necessary but what kind of marketization is necessary. In a market economy, the government should undertake the financing of public service with emphasis on fairness, and the private sector should undertake the provision of public services with emphasis on efficiency. In the future, China should shift policies underlying the distribution of public services away from efficiency and toward fairness. In recent years, all levels of government have injected additional fiscal revenue to improve people's living conditions. This is part of the transition of the government's role away from administration- to service-oriented government.

Reform of the financing and the delivery of public services has been an important issue over the past 30 years of marketization reform. To evaluate this problem further, we must first define public service and identify the fields that are most significant in the history of the economic reform.

The scope of public service is not defined solely by whether a service qualifies as a public good. First, some things that are of value to the community are not necessarily services but may be to a large number of services. For example, roads, running water, and natural gas are not services, but they are generally considered public goods. The government provides a large number of goods and services of this nature by maintaining roads, water systems and gas pipes. Second, some services are not strictly public goods, but are normally considered the objectives of a public service system. For example, education can be considered a club good, only public within a class, and most medical services are typical private goods, because a consumer's acquisition of a certain medical service prevents consumption by others. Housing is another example of a private good. However, education and medical care are services related to people's livelihoods and relevant to the equalization opportunities for personal development. All over the world, the government of almost every country provides education (especially primary education) and medical care. Basic housing also qualifies as social security. Government function is very important in some fields that are seemingly private. In these cases, the government is providing a special public good, namely, fairness.

This chapter does not cover all the reforms regarding the fields of public service. It focuses instead on the four aspects of public service that have the closest relationship with people's livelihoods: education, medical care, pensions, and housing. Reform of the housing market will be a key point.

5.1   DEVELOPMENT OF PUBLIC SERVICES

When people attribute inequality and inefficiency in the field of public services to marketization reform, they typically forget that the past 30 years of reform have also brought great progress in the fields of education, medical care, pensions, and housing. This can be seen in the variations in the supply patterns and the improvement of supply efficiency. If we consider governments to be the main force supporting progress in the four areas, then following the reform and opening-up, especially after the mid-1990s, marketization reform has become one of the main causes of progress in these fields.

Development of Elementary Education

The government pays great attention to elementary education. As early as January 1956, the Ministry of Education announced a plan to popularize compulsory education across the country within seven years. Unfortunately, due to China's weak financial state, this objective was not realized at that time. Early during the reform and opening-up period, China's leaders placed more emphasis on elementary education and were resolved to popularize a nine-year compulsory education, an idea promoted by Deng Xiaoping. The first national education affairs meeting was held immediately following the Cultural Revolution, during which the nine-year target was agreed. In 1985, the CPC Central Committee published its Decision on Education System Reform, and the State Education Commission was founded in the same year. On April 12, 1986, the 'Compulsory Education Law of the People's Republic of China' was announced and implemented.

During the early stages of reform, the government tried its best to fund education well, despite the country's limited fiscal resources. In 1992, expenditure for education amounted to 86.705 billion RMB. By 2005, this

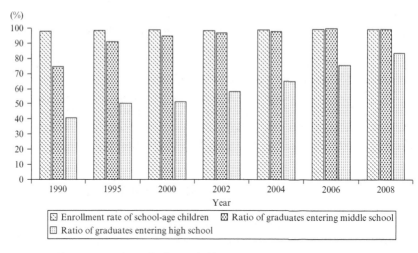

Source: *China Statistical Yearbook 2009* (China Statistics Press).

Figure 5.1 *Enrollment rate of school-age children and ratio of graduates entering schools at higher level*

figure had increased nearly ninefold, to 841.884 billion RMB. That year, education expenditure in middle schools was 259.308 billion RMB, and expenditure in primary schools was 203.152 billion RMB.[1] Elementary education absorbed over 50 percent of the government's total education budget. Improved economic conditions and increased financial input into education, meant that elementary education saw considerable improvement. The number of professional teachers in ordinary middle schools was 3.182 million in 1978; this number increased to 5.855 million in 2008. The number of professional teachers in high schools increased from 0.741 million in 1978 to 1.48 million in 2008, and the number of professional teachers in vocational middle schools increased from 23,000 in 1980 to 319,700 in 2008.

The improved teaching conditions also resulted in an increase in various rates of enrollment and admission into institutions of higher learning. Figure 5.1 shows the increase in enrollment rates of school-age children and the number of graduates entering universities and other tertiary schools.

Progress in Medical and Health Services

Ever since the founding of modern China, the government has paid a great deal of attention to medical and health services. A prevention priorities policy was announced. The collective medical communities in the rural areas were booming in the 1960s, when input in rural health care increased substantially. A large number of 'barefoot doctors'[2] were trained because of this. In 1978, there were 4.777 million barefoot doctors and 1.666 million sanitarians. Collective medical care covered over 90 percent of the population, leading to great improvements in the health of rural residents.[3] A three-tier medical-care and disease-prevention network was established, headed by county hospitals and connected by country (town) health centers. This system was based on village health centers, integrating the functions of disease prevention, medical care, and health protection. In cities, the public medical system was established. This system covered all government employees (including retirees), disabled soldiers, college teachers and students, and employees in public institutions. There was also an insurance system covering employees and some collective organizations in SOEs. The participants in public medical care were eligible to receive outpatient and inpatient services free of charge, with coverage extended to the participants' relatives. Labor insurance and medical care provided participants with a welfare program similar to public-funded medical care, with 50 percent reimbursement of the medical expenses of their family members.

The reform of the economic system started in 1978 and incorporated a demand for reform in the medical field. The level of medical care and health of residents has been promoted. Table 5.1 shows the increase in the

Table 5.1   The growth of medical and health services in China

	Year		Growth (%)
	1978	2008	
Population (10,000)	96,256	132,802	37.9
Health-care institutions (10,000)	16.97	27.83	63.9
Hospitals	9,293	19,712	112.1
Beds in health-care institutions (1,000)	204.17	403.87	97.8
Beds in hospitals (1,000)	110.00	288.29	162.1
Sanitarians (1,000)	310.56	616.91	98.6
Doctors (1,000)	103.30	208.23	101.6
	1980	2008	
Number of patients treated in hospitals (100m)	10.53	19.08	81.19
Number of patients treated in hospitals belonging to health departments (100m)	6.33	15.68	147.7

Source: China Health Statistical Yearbook 2009 (China Union Medical University Press).

number of hospitals and health-care centers and the number of hospital beds and doctors in health-care institutions, showing that China has made huge progress.

Achievements in the Pension System and Other Social Services

After the foundation of modern China, the social security system was established in urban areas through the implementation of state-owned and collective organizations, as in the then-extant Soviet Union and other socialist countries. In February 1951, the central government published 'The Regulations of the People's Republic of China on Labor Insurance', stipulating that the country would organize and enterprises would implement public benefits including pension, medical, and work-related injury insurance for employees and their family members. Thus, the foundation of social security for employees in SOEs was established. Rural areas were more traditional, relying on family in their old age and using government programs to augment this plan (Wu, 2003). Along with the continuous progression of the reform of the economic system, the disadvantages of the social security system in both rural and urban areas were gradually exposed. In 1986, the State Council published 'Temporary Regulations on the Implementation of Labor Contract System in State-owned Enterprises', announcing that pension accounts would be opened for contracted employees. In 1991, the State Council published various documents and began to socialize the pension system in urban areas. In November 1993, the Third Plenary Session of the 14th CPC Central Committee published 'The Decision of the CPC Central Committee on Several Issues Concerning the Establishment of a Socialist Market Economic Structure'. One important result of the meeting was the decision to set up a new social security system. Starting in 1995, the first priority was to set up a basic pension and medical insurance system for urban employees. Further development was made in terms of pension, medical, unemployment, and work-related injury insurance. Figure 5.2 shows the number of participants in basic pension insurance programs in recent years.

In cities, during the economic transition, some low- and medium-income families found that they could not support themselves. In September 1997, the State Council published 'Notice on the Establishment of Nationwide Urban Subsistence Security System', which required that the subsistence security system for residents be set up in urban areas to ensure basic living conditions. The recipients of this security system were urban residents with non-rural registered residences whose family income per capita was lower than the local subsistence line. Until the end of 2008, the number of urban residents receiving subsistence security was 233.48 million nationwide.

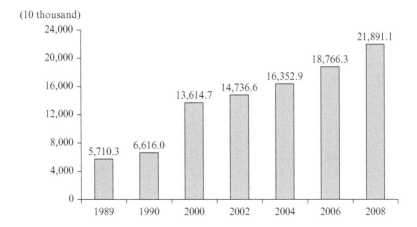

Source: China Statistical Yearbook 2009 (China Statistics Press).

Figure 5.2   Number of participants in basic pension insurance

Some regions also tried to extend the subsistence security system to rural residents. Rural areas still had many poor individuals, many of whom were unable to work. Without a source of income or relatives to rely on, they were dependent on aid from the government. In some relatively rich regions, subsistence security systems for all citizens were implemented. In Zhejiang Province, the system took effect in October 2001. By the end of June 2007, 31 provinces had set up subsistence security systems covering rural residents.

Under the system of fiscal decentralization, the urban social security system operated at the city level, and the cross-regional portability of social security accounts was very low. Along with the deepening of urbanization and the increase in labor mobility, the social security accounts of the labor force needed cross-regional portability. The new Labor Contract Law, which took effect on January 1, 2008, provided regulations for the cross-regional transfer of social insurance in Article 49, stipulating that the government would take action to set up a system of cross-regional transferable social insurance.

Growth of the Real Estate Industry and the Improvement of Housing Conditions

Two decades after the reform of the urban housing system, the housing problem has been greatly alleviated. In 1978, the total area of newly built urban housing all over the country was only 38 million square meters,

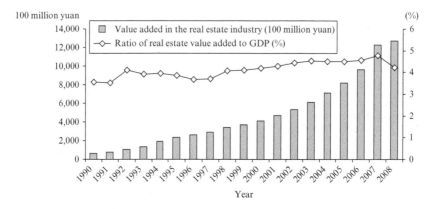

Source: *China Statistical Yearbook* (1996–2009) (China Statistics Press).

Figure 5.3 *Value added in the real estate industry and its contribution to GDP (1990–2008)*

which meant that the newly added area of housing per capita was only 0.1 square meters in that year. Statistics from 1985 show that over 27 percent of the urban residents had to share a house with others, 7.4 percent had a housing area of less than 4 square meters per capita, 37 percent had to share a kitchen with others, and 76 percent had no separate toilet (Xie, 1999). To address these multiple difficulties, Deng Xiaoping put forward the general idea of reform through selling publicly owned houses, adjusting rents, and encouraging individuals to build and purchase houses. His remarks in 1978 and 1980 initiated the government's reform of the housing system. Starting in 1998, the housing system entered a new stage of all-round marketization.

The prosperity of the real estate industry has been an important element of China's marketization reform (Figure 5.3). In 1986, there were only 1991 real estate development enterprises. That number increased to 56,290 in 2005. In 2006, the country's total investment in real estate was 2.1446 trillion yuan, taking up 23 percent of the total investment of the whole society. Commercial building investments alone amounted to 1.3612 trillion yuan, becoming an important driving force behind economic growth. The sales volume of commercial buildings nationwide increased year by year (Figure 5.4). During the 13 years from 1985 to 1997, the total area of completed urban houses was 3.516 billion square meters, with an average of 293 million square meters annually, and during the 10 years from 1998 to 2008, the total area of completed urban houses was 6.615 billion square meters, with an average of 661 million square meters annually (Figure 5.5).

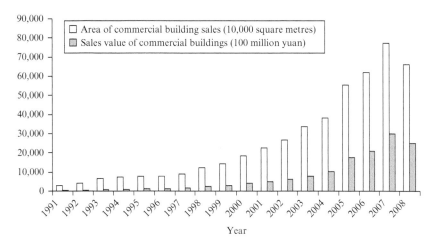

Source: *China Statistical Yearbook* (1991–2008) (China Statistics Press).

Figure 5.4   *Sales status of commercial buildings country-wide*
(1991–2008)

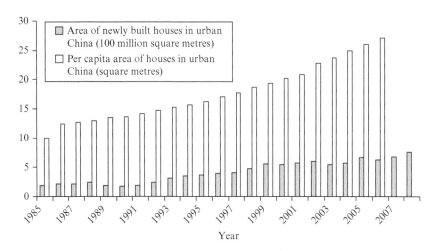

Source: *China Statistical Yearbook* (1996–2009) (China Statistics Press).

Figure 5.5   *Newly built housing and housing per capita in urban areas*
country-wide (1985–2008)

This tendency for fast growth has continued in recent years. The rapid development of the real estate industry is also indicated by the increase in the number of employees. In 1985, the number of people employed in the industry was only 360,000, taking up 0.28 percent of urban employment. In 2008, this number increased to 1.72 million, accounting for 1.42 percent of urban employment.

Once the marketization of the real estate industry was well under way, people's housing conditions improved greatly. The total area of urban housing per capita was 10.02 square meters in 1985, and 17.78 square meters in 1997. This growth has become faster since 1998.

5.2   MARKETIZATION REFORM OF PUBLIC SERVICES

One main aspect of public service reform has been the marketization of financing. The supply pattern of some types of public services has involved newly introduced market mechanisms. We shall analyze the relevant marketization reforms of four public service fields.

Process of Marketization Reform on Public Services

History of elementary educational reform

The reform of the elementary education system that has taken place since the 1990s is driven by two factors. One is the emergence of private schools. Some of the current private schools are former public schools, which were privatized during the reform process. Non-public schools enrich the supply of elementary education, challenging the belief that only the government can supply education. The other factor is the reform of the admission system. From the 1980s to the late 1990s, students took exams as part of their transition from primary school to middle school. This system has gradually been replaced by one in which children attend the school nearest to their home.

Before 1992, almost all primary and middle schools belonged to the national education system. They were controlled and financially supported by local governments and by educational administration institutions. Middle schools were divided throughout the country into key schools and normal schools. Regarding the system of admission to higher education, the middle schools in most regions required applications and a certain exam score from primary school graduates. Children attended a primary school near their home according to household registration status (*hukou*). At that time, private education was still in its exploratory stage, and it generally took the form of non-academic education, such as after-school classes and technical training institutions. Public education systems and standardized examinations were the main features of China's elementary education market during that period. Deng Xiaoping's remarks on his 1992 Southern Tour initiated the introduction of private education to common citizens. In 1993, the central government published its 'Guidelines for China's Educational Reform and Development'. A network of schools run by non-governmental organizations appeared nationwide. After the publication of the Law of Private Education Promotion in 2002, private elementary education boomed.

After 2005, elementary education policies showed a tendency toward equalization. For example, in May 2005, the Ministry of Education published documents encouraging the balanced development of compulsory education, hoping to put an end to the increasing differences in education between urban and rural areas, between regions, and between schools. This policy emphasized three issues. First was equal allocation of education resources among different schools. The new Law on Compulsory Education was amended and approved in 2006. It established the principle of balanced development of schools in the form of legislation in Article 22, stipulating that governments and education administration departments should reduce the differences in conditions between schools and forbid the separation into key schools and normal ones. Second, the public schools followed a single-fee policy, prohibiting the payment of additional fees to choose a particular school. In November 2006, the Ministry of Education clarified the timetable for free compulsory education. The policy of exempting two items and giving allowance for one item was aimed at rural students from poor families. Free compulsory education was made available throughout rural areas in 2010, and it will be made generally available nationwide in 2015. Third, partially privatized schools were required to purchase their operations outright and become true private schools or else be taken into the public school system. A large number of partially privatized schools became public ones.

The emergence of private education and the general popularization of attending nearby schools combined to create a mainstream transition in China's elementary education market. We can roughly divide the changes that have taken place over the past ten years into three stages. Stage one took place before the mid-1990s, when there were very few private schools. Elementary educational services were in general supplied solely by the government, and graduates from primary and middle schools took exams to enter into public middle schools and high schools. Stage two lasted from the mid-1990s to the early twenty-first century. Various kinds of private schools developed quickly and the policy of attending local schools was popularized within the public education system. Stage three took place after 2005. Along with the publication of a series of policies, the proportion of students attending a private as opposed to a public elementary school declined to some degree. The education administration department attempted to decrease inequality among public schools.

History of reform of the medical and health system

The economic reforms initiated in 1978 have included requirements for reform of the medical system. In urban areas, free social security and medical insurance were provided directly by the employers. In order to lessen the burden on SOEs and create an environment of fair competition between state-owned and private businesses, it was necessary to separate the provision of medical-care financing from private enterprise and gradually transfer the responsibility for medical expenses from businesses to social insurance institutions and individuals. Laid-off employees, unemployed people, and emerging, non-standard forms of employment have created huge challenges for the original, state-supported medical security system. In rural areas, the disintegration of the people's public communities and the implementation of the household responsibility system have eliminated many of the sources of funding for village-funded medical centers and barefoot doctors. The rural cooperative medical service system has started to disintegrate. In 1990, only 6.1 percent of the population was covered by rural cooperative medical systems (Zhu, 2000; Liu et al., 2002).

Fiscal decentralization reform has had a considerable influence on the funding of medical and health-care services. In 1994, tax-sharing reform increased the financial strength of the central government but weakened that of local governments. Local governments, however, continued to provide medical and health services. China's fiscal decentralization and assessment-based governmental competition caused local governments to favor public expenditures such as basic construction over human capital investments and public services. Governmental competition has intensified the uneven distribution of government expenditures already present under the fiscal decentralization system (Fu and Zhang, 2007). Governmental health-care expenditures have increased every year since the 1980s, but the amount of the total national budget taken up by medical services has declined from 2.86 percent during the sixth five-year plan to 1.66 percent in 2004. As reform has progressed, government financing has gradually been withdrawn from the medical system, increasing the autonomy of medical institutions. Hospitals have gradually become for-profit institutions. The economic reforms of the 1990s accelerated the marketization of the medical field. After that, national contributions to health care declined every year, and the majority of hospitals found their own revenue. For

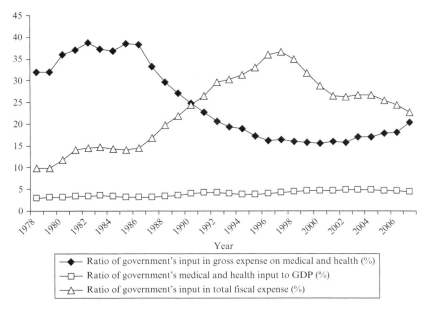

Source: *China Health Statistical Yearbook 2009* (China Union Medical University Press).

Figure 5.6   Changes in governmental contributions to medical and health services (1978–2008)

example, in the 1990s, drug revenues were used to support medical services. In 1980, government contributions to health care accounted for a third of the total national budget. This declined to a quarter in 1990 and 17 percent in 2004 (Figure 5.6).

In 1992, against a background of accelerated economic reform, further reforms of the medical and health-care system took place. This round of reforms further improved the hospital managerial systems and extended the responsibility of directors. In 2000, the State Council published documents reasserting that the main emphasis of the reform of the urban medical and health system was to establish a system suited to the requirements of the socialist market economy. Decreasing amounts of government funding lowered hospital revenue, driving up prices and increasing the burden on consumers. The difficulty of finding medical care also became more pronounced. Medical reform has become a hot topic, particularly with respect to the role of marketization reform in the medical field.

Beginning in 1985, each region began experimenting with the contract and director responsibility systems in medical institutions, in an attempt to strengthen the autonomy of local institutions in terms of personnel affairs, finance, operation, and management. The responsibility system for hospital management and operations was a departure from the previous pattern of government management of public hospitals. It was the first experiment in the separation of property and operation rights. However, the degree of autonomy in the management of public hospitals was relatively low, and administrative supervision in public hospitals tended to take the form of direct administrative interventions in which the hospital finances, assets, and personnel management were all directly decided by the relevant administrative departments. This greatly restricted hospital autonomy. The managerial tools available to hospital management for the regulation of hospital staff are relatively limited. Hospital administrators do not have the right to hire or dismiss staff, and it is difficult to punish or encourage personnel through bonuses. Under the current system, incentives for medical staff must take the form of persuasion (Anderson and Mei, 2006).

There have been some innovations in the hospital property rights structure. Private medical institutions have expanded quickly. However, the previous, public medical institutions involved comprehensive separations, and many institutions have transferred ownership from the state or collective to private individuals and organizations. After the 1990s, many regions undertook ownership reforms for professional medical institutions which were to take place through auctions and corporatization. Some state- and collectively owned medical institutions became privatized. In 2002, there were 152,826 public medical institutions (state- and collectively owned). This figure decreased to 125,746 in 2008, a drop from 49.9 to 45.2 percent. The number of non-public medical institutions (including joint and private operations) rose from 153,176 in 2002 to 152,591 in 2008. Although non-public hospitals outnumbered public hospitals, their market share was too small to be addressed. In 2008, the revenue of non-public hospitals was 90.95 billion RMB, and that of public hospitals was 868.653 billion RMB, accounting for 90.5 percent of the total revenue.[4]

Another change involved in the marketization reform of medical and health systems is the socialization of medical insurance. Participants have individual medical care accounts whose benefits are relative to personal income. This promotes unequal access to quality of medical services among urban citizens.

History of pension reform
In February 1951, the central government published 'Regulations of the People's Republic of China on Labor Insurance'. These regulations established the labor insurance system, at first in large state-owned industrial enterprises, and then gradually extended to state-owned commercial and trade industries. Social security funds were provided by private enter-

prises, which would extract a portion of each employee's salary. From 1969 on, businesses ceased to calculate payroll withdrawals using percentages of individual salaries, but rather classified funding for retirement pensions, public medical care, and other labor insurance allowances as non-operating expenditures. It was not until 1986 that the State Council published 'Provisional Regulations for the Implementation of a Labor Contract System in State-owned Enterprises', announcing that the retirement expenses of new employees who had been under the labor contract system would be socialized. However, the level of socialization of retirement expenses was always very low, and the financing and management of these systems never fully adapted to the reformed economic system (Wu, 2003).

In rural areas, the relief system focused on the 'Five Securities' – food and clothing, housing, medical care, education and funerals – for people who had lost the ability to work or had no relatives to take care of them. Later, the community cooperative medical system was established to cover rural residents. There was no formal pension system. Families provided most of the old-age care.

In urban areas, along with deepening economic reform, the disadvantages of the original social security system were exposed. In 1984, in order to resolve the huge differences in pensions between new and old enterprises, Sichuan, Guangdong, Jiangsu, and Liaoning conducted a trial socialization reform program for retirement expenses in SOEs in both cities and counties. In 1986, the State Council decreed that retirement pension fund accounts were to be established for contracted employees. Pension reform complemented medical reform, starting in the mid-1980s. In November 1993, the central government announced that corporations and individuals would jointly fund pension and medical insurance programs for urban employees. Peasants continued to depend primarily on their families, with some aid coming from the community.

Pension reform must address the aging of the population, rapid urbanization, and employment diversification. In order to deal with the challenge of aging workers and relieve the payment pressure of pension insurance, China adopted a suggestion from the World Bank, and implemented a new pension insurance system composed of three pillars: (i) social funds for subsistence allowances and social redistribution; (ii) individual accounts; and (iii) voluntary complementary pension insurance. The current social security system includes traditional financing of basic pension insurance expenses, which is provided jointly by the government, corporations, and individuals. The calculation and distribution of basic pensions, incentives, and differences in contributions are set out in individual accounts, and pension distributions were made relative to income earned during working years.

History of housing reform

In the planned economy system, employees' salaries were kept low, and the government provided security and welfare accordingly. Houses were constructed and provided by the government and by private enterprises. These were distributed to employees as welfare. This system of distribution had serious disadvantages, causing heavy financial burdens to the government and distorting supply and demand in the housing market. This can be seen in the small size of urban residences and the poor quality of many types of housing. In light of these difficulties, the government initiated the housing system reform for urban residents.

The housing reforms enacted between 1978 and 1985 allowed the sale of publicly owned houses to employees. By 1985, about 10 million square meters of publicly owned houses had been sold to urban residents (Xie, 1999). The recycling of housing investment capital accelerated, and the speed at which urban housing was constructed increased considerably. In 1985, the area of newly constructed urban houses was 188 million square meters, over four times as much as in 1978. The first meeting on the national housing system reform took place in August 1988. The participants announced that the target of the urban housing system reform would be to commercialize the housing market. The system of awarding houses would gradually be replaced by a monetary award, which individuals might use to purchase houses, starting with low-rent publicly owned houses. In July 1994, the State Council published documents establishing a housing security system, announcing that the basic premise of urban housing system reform was to build economically affordable housing for low- and medium-income families and market-price houses for high-income families. In 1997, a system of public accumulation funds for housing construction was established in every large city. From the mid-1980s to the mid-1990s, the total area of urban housing increased 30 percent annually on average, and the area of newly constructed urban houses reached 406 million square meters in 1997 (ibid.).

In July 1998, the State Council announced that the awarding of houses to individual families would stop. The monetization of housing distribution was gradually realized. This facilitated the elimination of the old housing distribution system, which greatly changed the housing supply system and structure of the housing market. During the marketization period, house prices increased dramatically, and policies were enacted to rein them in. On August 13, 2007, the office of the State Council published documents focusing on the housing security of low- and medium-income urban families and establishing low-rent housing as the heart of the housing security system. Limited property rights to economically affordable housing were established.

State of the Traditional Welfare System

China has completed the marketization of much of its public service system over the past 30 years. Before we make any evaluation of this reform, we must first establish why it was necessary. The answer comprises four components.

Improve efficiency

Under the planned economy, public services such as medical insurance, pensions, and elementary school education, which should be undertaken by government and society, were handled by businesses. This put a heavy burden on private enterprises, and inefficiency was rampant. One of the central objectives of reform of SOEs was to relieve them of those burdens and promote efficiency.

The old system was not well suited to economic reform, and that could decrease efficiency in three areas (Wu, 2003). The first is the dampening of payers' initiatives. The pension system under the planned economy was 'pay-as-you-go', and was in fact an intergenerational transfer system in which the current working generation supported the previous one. This undermined the motivation of the current working generation. The second problem is high operating costs. Funding for the planned economy social security system came directly and indirectly from fiscal capital, and payers had no relationship to the beneficiaries. Under this financing system, beneficiaries looked for higher interest rates, and corporations competed with each other by raising payment standards. No one had any incentive to supervise the revenue and payment of social security funds. The third issue is unfair competition among enterprises. Along with the aging of the population, the burden on private enterprise became heavier and heavier. This was especially true of businesses with a large number of retired employees who were due retirement pensions and medical expense. Employees in newer enterprises were younger, giving newer companies a smaller burden and an unfair edge. The different levels of social security offered by employers prevented employees from moving from one job to another. In 1986, the State Council published 'Provisional Regulations for the Implementation of Labor Contract System in State-owned Enterprises', announcing that pension accounts would be opened for contracted employees. In 1991, the State Council began to socialize the pension system in urban areas. One of the motivations behind this series of reforms was to promote efficiency in the social security system and create conditions for fair competition among businesses.

Inefficiency is also a problem in the public medical-care system. Overly strict management affects the initiative and creativity of medical personnel. Urban public medical-care and labor security medical-care systems seem to lack patient constraint and waste a great deal of resources (Development Research Center of the State Council, 2005). During the economic reforms the price of medical services increased a lot, placing heavy burdens on the country and on employers.

Generally, two important objectives of market reform are to reduce the inefficiency related to the previous system's resource allocation and to render public service expenditures more suitable to the demands of social and economic development.

Requirements of economic reform

Reform of the urban sectors started with SOEs. At first, it was not promoted nationwide. New problems emerged throughout the reform process, motivating further reform.

Reform of the old welfare system promoted fair competition among enterprises and created a private sector. As the original publicly owned enterprises provided employees with a series of welfare benefits, including pensions, medical care, children's education, and housing, different enterprises were able to compete to different degrees, and the burdens on publicly owned enterprises became excessive. In the mid-1980s, after the initiation of urban reform, these enterprises gradually formulated their own objectives for profit, necessitating welfare reform.

Risk sharing needs to be strengthened. The old welfare system included elements of pension and medical security systems. If these obligations are met by employers, then there is very little risk sharing. In rural areas, the collective community economy was dismantled after the reform, and the household responsibility system pulled the economic life of rural areas back into family and village collectives. The provision of public goods such as education and medical care in rural areas also changed accordingly.

Under the previous planned economy system, the elementary education of the children of employees of SOEs and public administrative institutions was provided by their employers. Along with strict reform of the property rights of SOEs, many businesses and other institutions began to separate from their affiliated schools, some of which were transformed into private schools. In rural areas, the funding for primary school education involved a dual-track system in three parts: the first involved paying educational expenses through financing, the second through local village collective activity, and the third by the students themselves. However, along with the reform of the rural fiscal and tax systems and the relief of the burden on peasants, the rural compulsory education system changed accordingly. A national system of education and management emerged.

The reform of the medical and pension systems was similar to education reform. SOEs under the planned economy system shouldered many social responsibilities. After the property rights of SOEs were reestablished, the original relationship between employees and employers evolved into a contract system. Under this system, medical insurance and pensions remain unaffected by changes in employees' circumstances. During the process of relieving the burden on SOEs and reform of the legal concept of ownership, the medical insurance and pension systems were transferred to the government and society. After the reform of medical insurance and pension systems, all government medical insurance systems were gradually transferred to society as a whole, and the establishment of personal accounts was in accordance with the requirements of reform. Part of the medical insurance system for rural residents was also gradually dismantled due to the implementation of the household responsibility system. At the end of the twentieth century, rural areas nationwide began to reestablish a new type of rural cooperative medical-care system undertaken jointly by county government, village government, and the peasants themselves.

Housing reform for urban residents took a similar path. Under the planned economy, houses were given to employees for free by companies and by the government as a kind of welfare. After urban reform, employees bought their own houses in the market. During the transition, low-income groups started to buy economically affordable houses or rent low-rent houses from the government.

Integration of the urban–rural dualistic economy

Another motivating force behind the marketization of elementary education, medical insurance, and pensions was the transition from a separate, dual economy to a single, integrated one. In the dual economy, the government gradually established compulsory education, medical-care, and pension systems for urban residents. In rural areas, aside from the rural cooperative medical-care and social security systems for a small number of households enjoying the five guarantees, families provided medical and elder care.

Economic activity began to agglomerate in coastal areas, causing large-scale, cross-regional labor mobility, mainly from inland rural areas. At the same time, due to the development of urbanization, newcomers to cities were unable to enjoy medical insurance, pensions, or subsidized urban housing because they were not registered as urban residents under the *hukou* system.

As the number of migrant workers in the cities increased, a problem emerged: their children had no access to the compulsory education available in cities. Many migrants left their children behind when they left for the cities. The General Office of the State Council quoted documents issued by the Ministry of Education in September 2003, requiring the local areas with an influx of peasant workers to set standard fees for the children of migrant workers who wished to attend city schools. These standard fees were required to be the same as those charged local children. 'Suggestions of the State Council on Solving the Problem of Migrant Workers', published in March 2006, promoted equal access to compulsory education for the children of migrant workers. Governments of areas with an inflow of migrant workers were charged with the responsibility of providing compulsory education for children living with migrant workers. Full-time public middle and primary schools were the main schools accepting children of migrant workers. Public funds were provided to schools according to the number of students served. Urban public schools were expected to give equal treatment to children of migrant workers in terms of fees, management and services. No additional charges were permitted.

'Suggestions of the State Council on Solving the Problem of Migrant Workers' also stipulated that migrant workers should be included in the urban public service and medical security systems for serious illnesses. Each region was allowed to choose a method by which to establish medical insurance funds for serious illnesses for migrant workers during their working years. By law, migrant workers had to be covered under work-related injury insurance. All employers were required to allow migrant workers to participate in work-related injury insurance so long as they paid their fees on time. When workers who had not participated in an insurance program sustained work-related injuries, employers were required to award compensation according to the standards stipulated by work-related injury insurance programs.

Urban–rural integration has been a major goal of the reform, and several stipulations have been implemented by the government to promote such integration. The priority placed on heavy industry under previous urban-biased policies allowed the country to accumulate capital. However, the long duration of the urban–rural divide has had negative influences on social development and sustainable economic growth. The government therefore implemented a single social security system and a single market in order to promote the free flow of production factors and efficient allocation of resources. As the number of city residents without local *hukou* continues to increase, the process of including new immigrants in the urban social security system (including the housing system) may be key to urban–rural integration.

Changes in consumer demand
Consumers have also influenced the marketization reform of government services. The education, medical-care, pension, and housing fields are closely related to residents' lives, so it is reasonable to use public funds

to provide residents with fundamental security in these areas and prevent huge inconsistencies in access. However, education, medical care, pensions, and housing usually qualify as private goods. The demand for these goods is closely connected to income. Consumer demand for products and services in these fields has changed, and the original system cannot satisfy the new demand. New suppliers must enter the market.

Consumer demand for housing and education was simpler under the planned economy system, with few differences among different consumers. Most employees lived in small houses that had been given to them by their employers. The development of the economy and increases in people's standard of living created differences in income levels among different groups of people. Higher-income groups developed new and different demands for housing and education. For example, in urban sectors, parents with high incomes were not satisfied with sending their children to understaffed schools. To meet this demand, private schools with more flexible management systems, sufficient and competent teachers, and better facilities emerged. The housing market also experienced differentiated demand.

There was also a demand for transition in health care. First, changes in age demographics rendered a larger proportion of the population liable to illness – children under the age of five and adults over 50 years old. Second, industrialization and social transition changed the human environment and people's living patterns, bringing new health problems, such as obesity, cardiovascular disease, and diabetes, which are all related to diet, and other illnesses related to smoking and drinking. Statistics showed that the bi-weekly disease rate in both urban and rural areas increased. The country's overall disease rate was 140 percent in 1993, 150 percent in 1998, and 157 percent in 2003 (Ministry of Public Health, 2004). Cross-regional and cross-income differences in quality of health have grown over time. Generally, urban residents are healthier than rural residents, high-income workers are healthier than low-income workers, and individuals with more education are healthier than those with less education (Feng and Yu, 2007). Medical technology has also changed greatly. Modern medical treatments are very different from those available in 1970. There have been pronounced breakthroughs in people's ability to control, treat, and cure illnesses.

5.3   INEQUALITIES GENERATED BY THE MARKETIZATION OF PUBLIC SERVICES

The marketization of public services has transformed certain products and services into purely private goods, separating them from the functions of the government and allowing them to be allocated by price. This created inequalities in the access to these products and services. Even though compulsory education, and medical and pension insurance are still public services, a considerable proportion of the funding now comes from personal income or local governments' fiscal revenue. Public services show cross-regional and urban–rural inequality. When people's standards of living increased, the demand for public services also increased. People naturally became dissatisfied with any inequalities in public services. We shall now discuss these inequalities from different perspectives.

Urban–Rural Inequality

In order to prioritize heavy industry, China accepted the urban–rural divide and supported urban-biased economic policies. This eventually led to differences in access to public services. From the late 1970s to the mid-1980s, urban residents enjoyed a welfare system that was still difficult for rural residents to access under the limitations of the *hukou* system. For example, SOEs and several other government institutions still controlled and supplied a considerable proportion of houses. In the meantime, only the permanent employees of SOEs and public institutions enjoyed health insurance or pensions. Middle and primary school education and child care were also provided only to residents with urban *hukou* (Yang, 1999; Kanbur and Zhang, 2005). Zhang (2003) thought that unequal access to education and medical care was increasing in pace with economic reform and attributed this largely to urban-biased policies. The education and medical-care facilities enjoyed by urban residents outnumbered rural ones, causing differences in social development.

In elementary education, the clearest bias lay in the allocation of funding. In China, the funding for compulsory education in urban areas has been taken care of mostly by businesses and public contributions. In rural areas, the fees for compulsory education were shared by the government and by village collectives and the rural students themselves. Even after the passage of the Compulsory Education Law of the People's Republic of China in April 1986, the government had still not provided funds for compulsory education in rural areas. In these rural areas, residents and enterprises had become the main sponsors of compulsory education. Local governments had incentives to invest in fields that brought short-term profits, limiting the capital available for investment in education. Under the system of fiscal decentralization, local governments still had little incentive to invest in education because it could not bring about short-term economic growth. For a long time, rural schools received very little financial investment from local governments.

After 2000, the government began to deal with the problem of irregular school fees. Rural tax reform had also begun, and the government had canceled both the additional fees that students' families had paid for education as well as education fund collections, changing the sources of funding of compulsory education. However, the education fund lacked resources. The burden on peasants was decreased, but funding for rural compulsory education became unreliable. Up until the end of 2002, there were still 431 counties where the nine-year compulsory education system was not a reality. There were also dozens of counties, mostly in rural areas and western regions, with no access to compulsory primary education. There was also a high dropout rate; in 12 western provinces, the timely completion rate of a primary school education was less than 85 percent. The completion rate of a standard nine-year compulsory education was less than 60 percent. Students from poor families were also in urgent need of financial aid. According to preliminary investigations and statistics, there were about 24 million students from poor families in poor parts of central and western regions. Of these, only a fifth received any financial aid from the national government (State Statistics Bureau, 2003).

During the process of reform, the difference between urban and rural illiteracy rates decreased somewhat before 1990. After 1990, illiteracy declined faster among urban residents than among rural residents, and the difference in illiteracy rates between urban and rural areas increased (Zhang, 2003). This indirectly shows that inequalities still exist between urban and rural areas in terms of governmental provision of elementary education.

Urban–rural inequalities in access to governmental-supplied medical services are also visible. During the early stages of marketization reform, government contributions to medical and health services were low. During recent years, the government's health expenses have increased to some extent, but they have decreased as a proportion of all health expenses (Table 5.2). Individual residents handled most of their own health expenses. In accordance with the relatively low level of government participation in health care, some health expenses were also unequally distributed between urban and rural areas. This is indicated in the low infant mortality rates in cities relative to rural areas. After the reform and opening-up, the infant mortality rate first declined and then increased rapidly. The increase in the infant mortality rate after the 1990s took place mainly in rural areas. From 1990 to 1995, the infant mortality rate also increased in urban areas, but only by about two per thousand. In rural

Table 5.2   Total health expenses (100 million RMB)

Year	1999	2000	2001	2002	2003	2004	2007
Health expenses in government budget	640.9	709.5	800.6	908.5	1,116.9	1,293.6	2,297.1
Proportion (%)	15.34	15.47	15.93	15.69	16.96	17.04	20.35
Health expenses paid by public contributions	1,064.6	1,171.9	1,211.4	1,539.4	1,788.5	2,225.4	3,893.7
Proportion (%)	25.48	25.55	24.10	26.59	27.16	29.32	34.49
Health expenses paid by individuals	2,473.1	2,705.2	3,013.9	3,342.1	3,678.7	4,071.4	5,098.7
Proportion (%)	59.18	58.98	59.97	57.72	55.87	53.64	45.16
Total health expense	4,178.6	4,586.6	5,025.9	5,790.0	6,584.1	7,590.3	11,289.5

Source: China Statistical Yearbook 2009 (China Statistics Press).

areas, it increased by 12.55 per thousand births. Rural infant mortality was even higher in 1995 than in 1981 (ibid.).

During the early stages of the foundation of new China, the cooperative medical system covering rural areas was established on the basis of the foundation of people's public communities. The collective economic system and the medical-care and prevention systems also extended to rural areas. After that, the original cooperative medical care disintegrated or was dismantled. In recent years, a new type of rural cooperative medical system developed, but progress was irregular. For example, rural-to-urban migrants faced a disconnection between rural cooperative medical care and medical insurance.

Similar inequalities occurred between urban and rural areas with respect to pensions. The urban pension system is improving daily, but no system has yet been established for rural areas.

Regional Inequality under the Decentralization System

The marketization process has fostered cross-regional inequalities in access to public services. Under the system of fiscal decentralization, local financing provided public services. After the implementation of the tax-sharing system in 1994, the amount of funding provided by local governments decreased sharply, but the amount of the expenditures to be financed from the local budgets did not change. Less-developed regions faced stricter fiscal constraints in terms of the provision of public services, exacerbating cross-regional inequalities regarding access to public services.

Under the system of fiscal decentralization, unequal access to elementary education funding across regions became a serious issue. Local financing was the main source of funding for compulsory education. Due to the huge differences in fiscal revenue among different regions, the distribution of financial resources for compulsory education was unequal, and the difference in the development of such education among regions and between urban and rural areas was huge. In 2001, the province with the most funding had a primary education budget ten times that of the province with the least funding. The difference was sevenfold for middle schools. Differences in the quality of school facilities and funding became obvious. The difference among different regions within provinces was greater than that among provinces. Budgetary educational funding per student showed the greatest differences in rural primary schools. In some provinces, it was 1:19, and in middle schools it was 1:25 (State Statistics Bureau, 2003).

County-level governments are required to take responsibility for arranging the funding of local schools, principals, and teaching personnel. However, due to the undesirable financial conditions in some less-developed regions, county responsibility is not always effective. Counties sometimes arrange funding for compulsory education and transfer some of the financial pressure to township governments, which then transfer it to village committees, which transfer it to the peasants. This can cause a compulsory education poverty trap – the poorer the region, the greater the financial pressure, and the worse the quality of compulsory education.

In both urban and rural areas, the degree of governmental financial contributions to medical security varies by the degree of government strength, the level of local economic development, and the lag in the central government's fiscal transfer system. In recent years, economically developed regions (such as Guangdong Province) have begun to set up comprehensive rural cooperative security systems on the basis of established experimental units. At the end of 2002, the proportion of people participating in rural medical care was 30 percent in those regions, but the coverage of rural cooperative medical care in the central and western regions was only 5 percent (ibid.). Since 1994, the establishment of subsistence allowance systems in rural areas began in coastal regions with developed economies, such as Shanghai, Guangdong, and Zhejiang. Provinces with developed economies were able to set up rural subsistence allowance systems early on. In economically backward regions, subsistence allowance systems could not be realized overnight. Until June 2007, only 31 provinces had a subsistence allowance system for rural residents.

Individual Inequality during the Process of Marketization Reform

In the process of marketization, inequalities in public services emerged among individuals in both urban and rural areas. Wu (2003) made a detailed analysis of inequalities in access to social security services within urban populations. Under the traditional system of distributing concrete social security resources through units (*danwei*), individual benefit levels were dependent on the accessibility of resources and the ability of units to access resources under the planned system. This allowed different units to have different levels of access to welfare systems and expenditure levels. These problems have become more and more severe. First, the abolition of people's public communities undermined the rural social security system. The medical services obtained by different people were then directly connected to income. Second, in urban areas, privately owned entities, including both individual and joint-venture enterprises, became stronger. However, a large number of employees in non-SOEs were not covered by the social security system. Third, during the period when pensions and medical welfare were provided by businesses, the financial status of SOEs depended on their performance in the market. This caused inequality in levels of access to welfare among different enterprises. Some badly performing businesses could not guarantee the payment of pensions or the reimbursement of medical expenses.

During the marketization of the housing system, similar inequalities emerged among individuals. Along with economic development, housing prices increased continuously; people who owned houses participated in the value growth of urban fortunes, but people with low incomes were usually renters. Marketization reform of the housing system actually enlarged the income gap among urban residents, which intensified instabilities (Meng, 2007). Before this reform, long-standing urban residents owned many welfare houses and migrants owned none. After the marketization reform, the migrants faced even greater difficulties (Sato, 2006).

5.4 FROM THE PURSUIT OF EFFICIENCY TO THE PURSUIT OF EQUALITY

Adjusting the Pattern of Marketization

Over the past 30 years, achievements in the fields of elementary education, medical care, pensions, and housing can be attributed to marketization reform. This reform took place under the system of decentralization which intensified inequalities in these fields. This does not mean that China should give up marketization reform. The welfare system as operated during the period of the planned economy was inefficient, so China should continue to promote marketization. However, in the face of the real problem of unequal access to public services, the country should also adjust the pattern of marketization to shift the object of reform from the pursuit of efficiency alone to an emphasis on equal access.

When education is considered a public service and provided by local governments, we should ask how a local government with a monopoly of the provision of local public goods could discharge its duties efficiently. There are two ways of promoting the effective distribution of public resources such as education. First, the decentralized system of educational funding can promote efficiency in the allocation of resources across different regions. Because local governments have more information about the territories that they control than other entities do, they are better equipped than the central government to allocate resources to meet actual local demands. Second, under the system of fiscal decentralization, if residents are unsatisfied with local education, they can change their residence, which allows areas to compete to provide the best-quality public services. This increases efficiency. In the US, the residents in each region decide the property tax rate by voting for the local officials who will in turn vote on taxation. If the educational quality of a region is low, then residents with children will leave, causing a decline in economic activity, property values, property tax revenues, and eventually educational financing. In China, although educational financing is not based on property taxes, if residents (especially families with high incomes) select schools by changing their residence, it will still influence the property value, and affect local government revenues. It will also influence the income and education levels of local residents, which in turn affects the fiscal revenue of local governments through the development of the local economy.

The decentralization of educational financing, the ability of residents to vote with their feet, and the use of price mechanisms in the real estate market all favor the efficient allocation of educational resources among different regions. In addition, if residents are not free to relocate, then the local governments may consider residents' demands for education quality difficult to guarantee. Although the *hukou* system creates limitations, free movement among different districts within the same city, or among different cities within the same province takes place on a considerable scale, especially among families with high incomes. The movement of those residents is often key to voting with one's feet. Price mechanisms in the real estate market can cause the quality of education to become capitalized (Feng and Lu, 2010). If real estate prices indicate the quality of education, then the connection between education quality and local government tax revenues may provide an incentive for governments to develop high-quality education.

This system in which elementary education is funded through decentralized finances makes high-quality education more accessible to high-income residents, and thus education is decided according to income. This means that low-income individuals, including children with strong academic abilities, will be denied a high-quality education. This is both inefficient and unjust. Fiscal decentralization only solves the problem of education resource allocation across different regions. Other methods are required to promote the efficient allocation of educational resources across different income groups.

To promote competition among schools, providing scholarships to highly capable children from low-income families would increase both equity and efficiency of education resource allocation. In any market in which public and private schools co-exist, if the government provides residents with education vouchers, competition increases (Epple and Romano, 1998, 2002). In schools, different students interact with each other. A diverse student body is vital to school quality. Competition between public and private schools gives the latter an incentive to provide scholarships to attract highly capable students – especially those from low-income families – to increase the average quality of the student. This both requires and allows schools to charge tuition to high-income families. A mechanism similar to that underlying employment compensation then develops. This increases access to high-quality education for children from low-income families, promoting equity and efficiency. Under general conditions, because private schools are more efficient than public ones, the role of the latter is to provide basic education at a low price (or even for free).

Any effective mechanism of education resource utilization would need to cover three points. First, local governments, rather than the central government, should provide elementary education. Second, private schools should be introduced into the education market. The current problem in China's education market is not the privatization of schools, but the lack of competition among schools. Full competition among private schools and between private and public schools should be encouraged. The privatized schools are usually the best in the region, but the lack of competition allows them to charge high tuition fees. Third, price mechanisms are necessary to adjust supply and demand for elementary education. Even if local governments are able to provide elementary education free of charge, once the movement of residents affects the housing market the quality of education will be reflected in the price of real estate. Thus, residents still have to pay for high-quality education. This is why the government cannot simply abolish education fees and allow residents to compete for education resources. Without education fees, competition will take place only through the real estate market and the resources that would otherwise be used to develop education will flow into that market (Lu and Jiang, 2007).

The marketization reform of the housing market can serve as another example. In August 2007, the General Office of the State Council published documents mandating the upgrade of housing security for low-income urban families and clarified for the first time that low-rent housing is the core of the housing security system. They also implemented limited property rights for occupants of economically affordable houses. The governmental establishment of the housing security system does not mean a regression to the period in which the government directly provided houses to all residents. Housing policies in the future should continue in the direction of marketization. Meanwhile, in order to help those with difficulties in finding housing, the government should implement housing policies that lessen speculation and support the less fortunate.

One well-accepted viewpoint is that in order to help the groups whose interests were ignored during the marketization process, improved housing conditions must mean that everyone has access to acceptable housing. The redistribution of houses should be conducted by pumping financial capital into low-rent housing and offering financial rent compensation, instead of providing funds for construction. The US experience indicates that a large administrative system is required if the government is to build and distribute houses. This costs a great deal. If the government interferes in housing construction, and sets the housing prices below market levels, corruption is almost certain. The implementation of an economically affordable housing system usually lacks flexibility. There is often more access to low-rent housing.

The housing security system should focus on different groups of people rather than rely on market pricing. It should rely on market rather than on governmental administrative forces. That may decrease opportunities for corruption and manipulation of the system among government officials. This kind of policy could be effected in the following ways. First, part of the revenue from land auctions would be distributed to low-income groups that had had difficulty finding housing. Current policies for low-rent and economically affordable housing should also be adjusted. Residents should be encouraged to buy or rent houses in the market. Newly built, economically affordable houses should be rented but never sold, and the houses already distributed should be re-sold, but then re-purchased by the county. Only tenants with low- and medium-income levels should be allowed to rent government houses. Second, there must be equal treatment for renters and buyers in terms of *hukou* applications and access to public services. Third, property taxes should be adjusted. The focus should be on maintenance taxes rather than transaction taxes, and a property tax to replace current taxes should be implemented. This may reduce the number of vacant properties, eliminate housing speculation, accelerate house sales, help low-income groups become homeowners, and improve housing conditions. From 2007 to 2008, the strength of housing security policies was high. In August 2007, the State Council decreed that housing security be included among the functions of the government. This policy promoted the construction of housing by local governments at all levels, which had a significant impact on the housing security system.

Socialization of Public Service Financing and Marketization of Funding

During the 30 years of China's reform and opening-up, the role of government as a provider of public services has grown smaller and smaller. The differences in the financial strength of urban and rural areas and of different regions have created different levels of access to public services. The achievements in the various fields of public services are primarily related to marketization reform; the different types of financing inspired development. The diversification of financing patterns and the diminished role of government as a provider of funding are also critical causes of inequality in access to public services. The future development of public services must involve continued government-organized marketization, but the pattern of that marketization must be adjusted. The socialization of public service financing should be realized to increase the governmental input and to diminish the link between personal income and access to public services so that public welfare can be equalized. The marketization of supply should be enhanced and the monopoly of public service providers should be broken so that efficiency through competition can take place.

NOTES

1. The statistics in this chapter all come from *China Statistical Yearbook 2010* (China Statistics Press) except where specifically indicated.
2. Barefoot doctors are farmers who received minimal basic medical and paramedical training and work in rural villages.
3. *China Health Statistical Yearbook 2009* (China Union Medical University Press).
4. *China Health Statistical Yearbook 2009* (China Union Medical University Press).

6. Developmental imbalances and mechanisms for improving the market system

In previous chapters, we discussed China's economy as part of its status as a large, developing country. In this chapter, we shall examine the challenges faced by its particular model of economic development. China's strategy involves unbalanced development. The current stage of the plan involves the shift from a centralized, planned economy to a market economy. The construction of the market system has made great progress, particularly after 1994. After 1996, market competition intensified further, triggered by structural adjustments in the labor market. Waves of marketization reform were carried out by China's strong government. The low prices and quality work of the labor force and the low RMB exchange rate established after 1995 have increased the international competitiveness of China's products.

While they have caused growth, market-oriented reforms and Chinese-style federalism have also created both internal and external imbalances in the economy. Internal imbalances have widened the gaps in both income and access to public services between urban and rural areas and between social groups. These domestic imbalances have caused insufficient demand for domestic goods and services and high savings and investment rates. This creates a growth pattern dependent on investment and export. Overspeculation first became a problem in the mid-1990s. After 2005, serious external imbalances appeared in the economy. These manifested as soaring foreign trade surpluses, increases in foreign exchange reserves, foreign trade disputes, and increasing pressure on the government to allow the RMB to appreciate. Although many macro and international economists are trying to find short-term countermeasures to address the external imbalances in the economy (such as appreciation of the RMB), the transitional and institutional environment that caused the external imbalances in the first place should also receive due attention.

The histories of other developing and developed countries have shown that timely structural adjustments can prevent internal–external imbalances, the need for high-cost solutions later on, and long-term structural imbalances such as those of some Latin American countries. China will have to either resort to macro means or initiate deeper structural adjustments to set the economy on a balanced and sustainable development. This may provide the country with a smooth path away from the middle-income trap and allow modernization to continue. This chapter describes the internal and external imbalances in the context of the economic growth of the economy over the past 30 years. It analyzes the mechanism by which the mutual relationships between these internal and external imbalances formed, and discusses structural reforms and dynamic mechanisms that may resolve this imbalance.

6.1   INTERNAL IMBALANCES

The internal imbalances of the economy can be viewed at two levels, the micro/meso view shows the widening income and public service gaps, and the macro view shows insufficient demand for domestic consumption and the dependence of economic growth on investment and export.

Costs of Unbalanced Development

Here, we briefly summarize the costs of unbalanced growth in income gaps, access to public services, and market segmentation, based on the previous analysis.

Widening income gap

The most direct cost of transition and development since the beginning of China's reform and opening-up is the widening of the income gap (Li and Sato, 2004). The income gap between urban and rural areas is the biggest component of overall income inequality, and it tends to be self-reinforcing. The cross-regional income gap has a great deal to do with urbanization. Areas with little urbanization tend to have lower per capita income. The contribution of the urban–rural income gap to regional income inequality is as high as 70–80 percent (Chapters 3 and 4).

As we pointed out in Chapter 3, the divergence between the lives of urban and rural residents is closely related to the fiscal decentralization system. Because this system provides the incentive for local governments to develop the local economy and because the assessment system for local government officials is based on the amount of economic growth and investment attracted, the government has focused on urban-biased economic policies. This has significantly decreased the amount of money available for rural production and local financial expenditures (Lu and Chen, 2006a).

The widening cross-regional income gap is related to the decentralized fiscal system. Under this system, local governments must compete with one another in economic development. Eastern areas tend to perform better than other areas because of their history, advantageous location, and the central government's previous policies. This advantage is self-reinforcing: development fosters more development, and it is hard for the backward areas to catch up. Differences that formed during the process of competition manifested during the opening-up process. Generally, China has a large labor force but not much domestic capital. This capital shortage should be addressed. Winning over foreign investors may be key to widespread economic development (Zhang and Xia, 2006).

Competition among regions is also reflected in the grants made to different areas by the central government. Whether because economically developed areas have more bargaining power or because central government pays more attention to overall economic growth than balanced development, economically developed areas receive more investment from the central government. Since tax revenue returns consider the 1993 figures as base numbers, these payments have widened the regional income gap since the late 1990s (Raiser, 1998; Ma and Yu, 2003).

Interpersonal income gaps also widened the income gap between urban and rural areas and among regions.[1] With the existing urban–rural divide, outflow of the rural labor force is restrained, and the marginal products of the rural labor force and the reservation wages of migrant workers have decreased due to the surplus rural labor force. This produces downward pressure on urban sector wages. Under the system of fiscal decentralization, local governments necessarily offer more protection to investors in order to attract more investment, especially because capital is rare. Laborers' rights are often neglected. Under this growth model, the income gap between capital owners and ordinary workers has widened. By 2007, the proportion of national income made up by labor income decreased from its peak in 1995 to less than 40 percent (Figure 6.1).

The widening of the income gap is also related to differences in social and political resources owned by different people. As discussed in Chapter 2, during marketization China's original social and political resources were marketized and capitalized. Social relationships have not only improved the benefits of insiders, but also widened the income gap between insiders and outsiders. When the people with advantageous social relationships are also those with political and economic authority, income mobility may become limited as entrenched individuals monopolize opportunities.

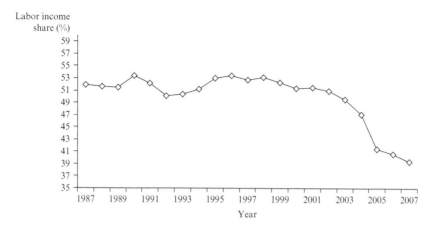

Note: In 2004, the sharp decline in the proportion of labor income was found to be related to the change in statistical criteria (Bai and Qian, 2010; Luo and Zhang, 2010).

Source: *China Statistical Yearbook* (China Statistics Press).

Figure 6.1   Proportion of national income made up by labor income

Access to public services: unfairness and inefficiency
In addition to the great differences in access to medical care, education, and social security between urban and rural areas, there is also a geographical problem. The locations of sources of public services are not themselves problematic. In many federal states, public services are provided by local governments. The short-term objectives pursued by local governments are often at odds with social objectives. Mechanisms that would inspire local governments to pursue long-term objectives have yet to be discovered. The development of education and medical care cannot promote economic growth in the short run, despite their far-reaching long-term significance. Local governments have been eager to shed the burden of education and medical care by carrying out marketization reform. The proportion of local government expenditures in these areas has decreased markedly, and central government expenditure fostering equal access to public services has become deficient. Only recently has the government paid more attention to improving people's livelihoods. Studies have found that fiscal decentralization discourages local governments from increasing expenditure in local public services (Fu and Zhang, 2007). As discussed in Chapter 5, the products and services surrounding medical care and education are sophisticated, and simple marketization reforms on the pattern of financing will exacerbate inequalities in access. This would not favor

regions or individuals with low incomes as they attempt to develop human capital. Continued marketization of these fields creates both inequality and inefficiency.

Both public services and social security are linked to the household registration system, which impedes cross-regional labor mobility. The difficulty of cross-regional flow of factors promotes duplication of industrial structures and homogeneous competition among regions, which causes these regions to downplay their complementary strengths. If laborers cannot move to developed areas freely, economies of scale cannot develop. Thus, the existing public service system is not only in opposition to social equity but also works to the disadvantage of economic efficiency. The 17th CPC National Congress also pointed out that in order to narrow the cross-regional development gap, China must improve equal access to basic public services and promote reasonable factor mobility among regions.

Convergence of regional development strategies: market segmentation, and duplication

When regions compete for economic growth and efficiency, local governments may turn to local protectionism and market segmentation. This has two causes.

First, the misallocation of resources and similar industrial infrastructure developed during the planned economy period. Industries and individual businesses that did not develop local advantages then continue to lack competitiveness under the market economy system (Lin, 2002). However, those industries and businesses still possessed great capacity for production, and they generated financial revenue for local governments. Protecting these local enterprises through market segmentation is, from the point of view of local officials, rational (Lin and Liu, 2004).

Second, increasing returns due to the process of learning by doing exist in many industries (especially growing industries with certain levels of technology). These industries have a first-mover advantage, and various regions are scrambling to develop so-called strategic industries, which leads to rounds of duplication (Lu et al., 2004; Lu and Chen, 2006a). When the issue of duplication arises, market forces determine whether any given relevant enterprise will survive. When a region's strategic enterprises fail to compete, local governments turn to market segmentation and protectionism.

Increasing social costs of economic growth

Unbalanced growth also manifests in the sidelining of other development objectives, which increases high natural resource and environmental costs. The long-standing economic growth pattern adopted in China is highly dependent on exports. Labor is relatively inexpensive. This makes the country attractive to foreign investors, but it also makes its growth dependent on low costs. A great many labor-intensive manufacturing industries consumed resources and degraded the environment. Under the current system, local governments lack incentives to consider environmental and social costs.

Superficially, economic development exists on the basis of low cost. However, if implicit costs such as environmental and social costs are considered, then the price of economic development is much higher. The aggregated emission of air pollutants remains high, and carbon dioxide emissions are the highest in the world. Water quality is still far from satisfactory. On average 54 percent of the water in the seven main rivers is not suitable for drinking. The estimated costs of premature deaths caused by environmental deterioration can amount to 3.8 percent of GDP (World Bank, 1997a).

Local governments are also lacking incentives to regulate labor and promote quality standards. Even if the country has national regulations, these cannot always be implemented at the local level. In recent years, accidents such as mine disasters and failures in product quality have been frequent. For example, according to the data from the State Administration of Work Safety, China produced 1.66 billion tons of coal in 2004, accounting for 33.2 percent of the worldwide total. However, deaths in mine disasters reached 6,027, accounting for 80 percent of the worldwide total. Local governments often skimp on safety regulations so that local businesses can reduce costs.

Pollution and overutilization of resources both reduce the benefits of GDP growth to the public and reduce the country's chances for sustainable development. If the pattern of economic growth is not adjusted in a timely manner, the constraints of the environment and finite resources may cause a bottleneck. China ranks 133 out of 144 on the international Environmental Sustainability Index. Its pattern of economic growth is dependent on the consumption of natural resources. This must be changed quickly. The government must promote a conservation-oriented society.

Macro Imbalances and the Dilemma of Economic Growth

The economy experienced great highs and lows during the 1980s. After the mid-1990s, the macro economy tended to become stable, but structural problems became increasingly evident. The structural imbalances in the macro economy come from the imbalances discussed in Section 6.1. Their ultimate origins can be traced back to the system factors relevant to the pattern of unbalanced growth.

The decentralization reform and other coordinated reforms initiated in

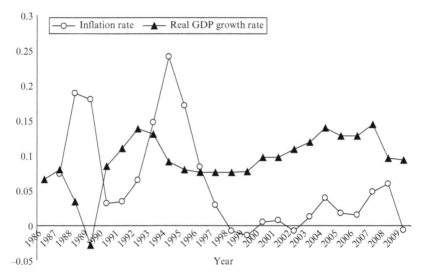

Source: *China Statistical Yearbook* (various years) (China Statistics Press).

Figure 6.2   Growth of real GDP and inflation (1986–2009)

1994 increased the total output of the economy and eliminated the cyclical phenomenon of disorder without management and controlled stagnation,[2] which had troubled China for many years. This could be considered a positive result of decentralization reform. Thus, 1994 was a watershed year in the macro economy. The pattern of government credit and money management and the mechanism of inflation (and deflation) changed markedly.

The macro economy since 1978
If we divide the macro economy into two phases using 1994 as the year of implementation of the tax-sharing system, then the economy can be considered to have been under soft budget constraints from 1978 to 1994. This is common in traditional socialist planning (Kornai, 1986). This period featured expansion of both investment and consumption, but the economy still had many characteristics of a shortage economy, in which the macro economy experienced a cycle of instability without management and controlled stagnation. As shown in Figure 6.2, there were huge changes in the relationship between economic growth and inflation before and after 1994, when the previous economic cycle disappeared.

Consumption and investment in GDP   Over the past 30 years, the pro-

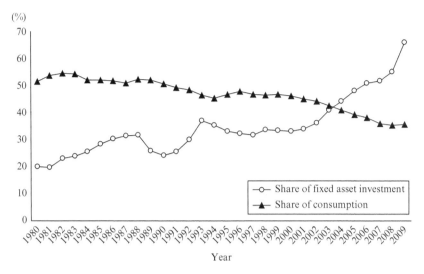

Source: *China Statistical Yearbook* (various years) (China Statistics Press).

Figure 6.3 *Proportion of fixed asset investment and household consumption in GDP (1970–2009)*

portion of GDP comprising domestic (household) consumption has decreased, and that comprising investment has increased. As shown in Figure 6.3, during the ten years prior to economic reform, the investment ratio was about 36 percent. This rose quickly after the 1990s, and in 2003, 2004 and 2005, it reached 43 percent. The long preceding period of high savings rates made this high investment rate sustainable. The savings ratio was as high as 50 percent in 2005. From 2001 to 2005, investment made up over half of the GDP. This was notably higher than the rate of investment in other East Asian countries during the same development phase (Lardy, 2007). Due to the insufficiency of domestic consumption demand, China had to rely on exports to maintain economic growth, and the proportion of exports in GDP has increased yearly. Figure 6.3 shows the changes in fixed asset investment and household consumption during the past 30-plus years. Increases in the proportion of fixed asset investment were in clear opposition to that of consumption.

Excess liquidity since the mid-1990s Many scholars measure excess liquidity from the perspective of the money supply (the ratio of M2 to GDP). However, excess liquidity is not solely a monetary phenomenon. Rather it is the result of structural changes in the economy, both domestically and

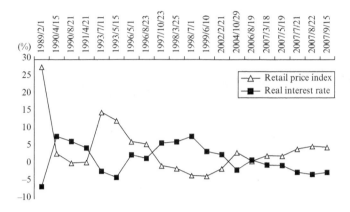

Source: *China Statistical Yearbook* (various years) (China Statistics Press).

Figure 6.4   *Retail price index and real interest rate for saving in China*
(February 1989 to September 2007)

abroad. One practical method of judging whether liquidity is excessive
is to determine whether the real interest rate decreases over time, which
can indicate equilibrium between the supply and demand of liquidity very
precisely. From 1994 to just before the recent economic crisis, the real rate
generally decreased (Figure 6.4).

Micromechanism of the imbalances of the macro economy
One key to understanding the economic decentralization and macro
economy that have existed in China since the reform and opening-up is to
understand how decentralization has changed the degree of governmental
soft budget constraints on SOEs and the creation of liquidity. There are
two other kinds of economic reform: marketization and fiscal decentralization. The first involves the gradual loosening of price controls and the
introduction of market mechanisms in which the decentralized allocation
of resources renders more resources available to non-SOEs in an efficient
manner. The latter involves the transfer of financial activities from the
central government to local governments.

Influence of soft budget constraints on the macro economy before 1994   Soft
budget constraints appeared in the planned economy whenever the central
government had to rescue SOEs, usually when they suffered losses. Even
when the government announced ahead of time that it would not bail out
SOEs in the red, no one believed it (Kornai, 1986). In a highly centralized planned economy, the government is the only investor in SOEs. If an

investment experiences problems, the government increases funding. This prevents the termination of projects that incur losses. It is even harder for the government to shut down operations that provide employment or social security services.

From 1978 to 1994, the reform of marketization and fiscal decentralization were carried out simultaneously. One characteristic of marketization reform is that the market share of the non-state-owned sector increases (both private and township-owned businesses). The deepening of marketization reform increased the amount of resources (including financial resources) allocated to the more efficient non-state-owned sector, which led to economic growth. During this period of incremental reform, the government neither loosened regulations nor privatized the state-owned sector. It only introduced non-state-owned economic entities in the margin, and the government's soft budget constraints on the state-owned sector remained. Fiscal decentralization was indicated by the constant decline of the proportion of the central government's financial revenue and the continuous rise of the revenue of local governments (Chapter 2). During this period, there were no fundamental changes in the governmental soft budget constraints on state-owned entities, and the system of fiscal decentralization limited the financial strength of the central government. When the economy is in a depression, the government lacks sufficient financial resources to give aid to SOEs. The reform of the banking sector also prevents the government from directly interfering with the banks' credit habits. The only method remaining to the government is to pull the economy out of depression by printing more money, which then causes inflation during periods of economic expansion. For this reason, growth and inflation have tended to occur simultaneously in China during this period (Brandt and Zhu, 2000). If the government withdraws power to award in the financial field and directly controls the credit market, then economic depressions will be more frequent. That is the cause of the periodic fluctuation of instability without management and controlled stagnation that occurred in the macro economy during this period.

Changes in the structure of the economy since 1994   The year 1994 was a watershed for economic reform in China. In 1994, the government announced the transition from the previous incremental system of reform to all-round reform. Along with the establishment of the modern enterprise system, reform of the tax-sharing system, and commercial bank reform, the problem of soft budget constraints, which had originally limited SOEs, was fundamentally changed. Reform of the tax-sharing system clearly defined the tax collection rights of the central and local

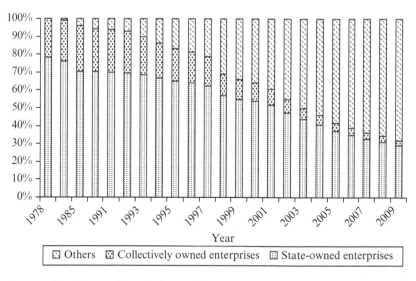

Source: *China Statistical Yearbook 2010* (China Statistics Press).

Figure 6.5   People employed by urban businesses according to ownership (1978–2009)

governments. All previous attempts at separating tax revenue had failed, including those made from 1980 to 1987, and the fiscal contracting system implemented from 1988 to 1993. Under this contracting system, the fiscal retention rate between each region and the central government was set at a one-to-one discussion between local and central governments and based on historical statistics. This kind of arrangement did not clearly define the tax base, and allowed interregional inequities to persist. The fiscal responsibility system also increased the financial revenue of the local governments. The central government's financial revenue continued to decrease. During the early 1990s, half of the central government's expenditures were sustained by debt (Wu, 2003).

The reforms in the tax-sharing system in 1994 clearly defined the tax base and the proportion of tax due to the central and local governments. The influence of these reforms had a far-reaching impact, promoting large-scale privatization of SOEs. Because most taxes went to the central government after the reform of the tax-sharing system on condition that the duties, responsibilities, and expenses of local governments would not decline, great pressure was brought to bear on local financial institutions. The privatization of inefficient SOEs was the usual strategy chosen by local governments (Zhang and Li, 1998; Li et al., 2000). At the end of the

1990s, the non-state-owned economy made up the largest proportion of the national economy, becoming the fundamental power behind economic growth. Changes in the urban ownership structure from 1978 to 2009 are shown in Figure 6.5. Changes in the ownership structure of the main economic indicators of industrial enterprises in 2009 are shown in Table 6.1. Both Figure 6.5 and Table 6.1 show that the non-state-owned economy had become the absolute majority in each indicator.

Reform of the tax-sharing system diminished soft budget constraints. Privatization lessened government constraints on SOEs. However, there were still government constraints on some SOEs. The tax revenue of the central government increased after the reform of the tax-sharing system, which made it unnecessary for the central government to invest in or protect SOEs to produce funds. Both these effects removed some of the motivation of central government to increase money supply. Thus, the pressure of inflation decreased.

Reform of the banking system solved the problem of government soft budget constraints on the state-owned sector. The establishment of the commercial banking system had a late start and the system remained under the administrative control of the central bank for a long time. This is in fact a characteristic of economic depression. The real official interest rate was generally negative. Since the beginning of the reform and opening-up, local banks have made annual plans to distribute credit. Each province also had a fixed investment share for state-owned and non-state-owned enterprises. This prevented capital from being allocated efficiently through the market. As the economy developed, the right to distribute credit was gradually delegated to local banks. This tightened the relationship between local governments and banks, which became capable of interfering with the distribution of credit from local governments, strengthening soft budget constraints. After the delegation, local governments were not willing to re-implement unified credit planning, but instead began to direct the capital under their control more efficiently, especially to non-SOEs. However, the central government still resorts to credit planning management, which it uses to control the loans made by state-owned banks, to limit the loans made out of the credit plans of state-owned banks, and emphasize the personal obligations of local leaders and state-owned bank leaders to implement their credit plans. From 1979 to 1993, 84 percent of the new loans went to SOEs, 33 percent of which were approved by the central bank. These 'loans' were not usually expected to be paid back, creating an unhealthy situation for the banks.[3]

Banking system reform did not move toward marketization until 1994. Then the central bank shifted control of the money supply from a multi-level system to control by the central government. It also established an

Table 6.1 *Main indicators of all state-owned and non-state-owned industrial enterprises grossing more than 100 million yuan in 2009*

Item	Number of enterprises (units)	Total volume of industry (price in relevant year)	Total capital	Revenue of the main business	Total profit	Annual average number of all employees (10,000)
Total	358,988	395,625	369,215	392,259	21,824	6,380.8
SOEs	9,105	45,648	68,685	47,035	24,435	639.10
Proportion (%)	2.53	11.53	18.60	11.99	8.08	10.02
Collective enterprises	10,285	9,587	5,016	9,451	1,973	199.30
Proportion (%)	2.87	2.42	1.36	2.41	2.61	3.12
Others	339,598	340,389	295,514	335,773	21,824	5,542
Proportion (%)	94.60	86.04	80.04	85.60	89.31	86.86

Note: Non-state-owned enterprises grossing more than 5 million yuan per annum are listed.

Source: *China Statistical Yearbook 2010* (China Statistics Press).

indirect controlling system. The object at this stage was also changed from a credit capital scale to a money supply system, and the application of various monetary policy tools became progressive. This weakened local governments' control of the banks, and it became difficult for local governments to allocate credit to banks. More loans then went to businesses that had shown better performance. The financial system was decoupled from the state-owned sector. This also tightened budget constraints.

The comprehensive reforms initiated in 1994 had three general macroeconomic results: first, the inflation cycle, which had been highly problematic from 1978 to 1994, disappeared; second, production overcapacity gradually emerged; and third, excess liquidity began to appear and accumulate.

The reform of the tax-sharing system clarified the manner in which local taxes were to be distributed, making local governments compete fiercely to construct better infrastructure to attract investors and increase local GDP growth. Under the 'small but comprehensive' industrial strategy of the planned economy period, investment was more or less equally distributed across regions, which intensified overinvestment and overcapacity. In China's current development phase, there is a concentration of certain industries in certain places (Lin, 2007). In developed countries, private businesses tend to develop new technology. These businesses also absorb the risk and uncertainty of new ventures. In developing countries, private businesses are usually far from cutting edge. They usually select relatively mature and safe projects to invest in. Many businesses select the same industry or type of project to invest in, which leads to overinvestment and overcapacity.

Overcapacity causes the total supply of many types of products to expand continuously. However, this can tighten the budget constraints of certain types of enterprises. The government no longer bails out SOEs by increasing the money supply. This creates a relatively stable amount of investment demand, but it also increases the gaps between urban and rural areas and among regions. The interpersonal income gap is also enlarged due to the reform of urban marketization. Because of this, consumer demand is relatively small. The slow increase in residents' consumption of Chinese-made goods and services is closely connected to the household registration system and the urban–rural divide. Large numbers of migrants relocating from rural to urban areas, lack official urban registration. Because this makes many basic social services, such as education and pensions, more expensive and less accessible, they must cut back on their consumption of durable commodities and save much of their income for the future. They also face discrimination in the credit market. Migrants' marginal propensity to consume is an estimated 14.6 percent lower than

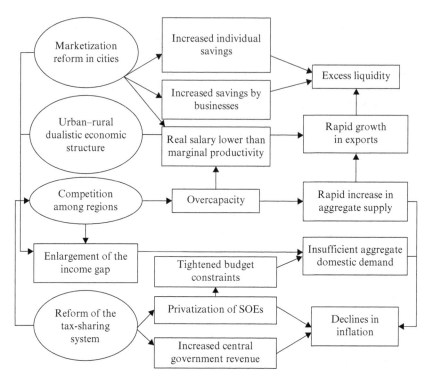

Figure 6.6   Micro foundation of China's macro economy

that of official urban residents (Binkai Chen et al., 2010). The expansion of aggregate supply and the relative insufficiency of aggregate demand has caused increased production and declining prices. This is consistent with the performance of the macro economy after 1994 (Figure 6.6).

The phenomenon of excess liquidity was at first related to the development of the economy, urban marketization reforms, and the urban–rural division of the economy. Because of the way rural-to-urban migration is regulated, the labor supply is greater in rural areas than it would be if China had free labor mobility. Considering rural land and capital resources, this lowers the marginal production of the rural labor force, which in turn determines the reservation wage of migrant workers. In the urban labor market, although the migrant workers face discrimination by the system, they are still able to compete with urban laborers. In this way, the low wages of migrant workers limit all wage growth in the urban sector. Slow increases in wages allow businesses to reap more profits. Savings and investments from the business sector increase rapidly. The reality of low wages and high profits make up for the inefficiency of the domestic banking system by allowing businesses to rely more on internal financing through profits, decreasing their dependence on external financing and relieving the credit constraints brought on by the inefficient financial system. Because it promotes high levels of investment, labor productivity increases much faster than wages (*The Economist*, 2007). A high level of investment increases the production capacity; but sluggish wages limit increases in domestic consumption demand. This leaves the economy heavily reliant on exports and further investment, and structural imbalances gradually become more pronounced.

The comprehensive structural reform of the mid-1990s changed the nature of the economic cycle. The tax-sharing system, among other important reforms, eliminated the phenomenon of soft budget constraints, the recruitment of SOEs through government increases in the money supply, and a great deal of the country's demand–pull inflation. However, the low wages caused by the surplus of rural labor and the minimal leverage of laborers throughout China has also greatly reduced cost–push (especially wage) inflation. Due to the reform of SOEs that took place in 1996, competition within the urban labor market has intensified, creating downward pressure on wages in cities. The widening income gap has limited the growth in demand. On the supply side, more intense regional competition and the rapid development of the non-state-owned economy have led to the rapid growth of production, creating deflation pressure.

Figure 6.6 summarizes the mechanism of the changes in the macro structure after 1994. As shown in the figure, internal imbalances can become external imbalances. When there is insufficient domestic aggregate demand, China must depend on rapidly increasing amounts of exports to maintain the high speed of its economic growth. Increases in domestic wages have lagged behind increases in labor productivity, which have greatly increased the international competitiveness of China's products and created conditions that facilitate increases in exports. After 1994, the long-undervalued RMB helped to keep down the prices of China's products. The rapid expansion of exports eliminated the trade deficit in the mid-1990s, which rapidly became an international trade surplus after 2005, creating an external imbalance. A detailed analysis of these external imbalances is given in the next section.

6.2   EXTERNAL IMBALANCES

This unbalanced growth increased China's international competitiveness and promoted the rapid expansion of international trade but also established external imbalances, which are certainly linked to the internal imbalances in the domestic economy. Fundamental solutions to these problems and strategies for creating external equilibrium, adjusting domestic political and social structures, and realizing balanced domestic growth may be developed only by taking this into account.

Characteristics of External Imbalance

Sharp increases in the foreign trade surplus

Since the mid-1990s, China has had an export-oriented strategy of development involving the devaluation of the RMB. In 2001, China joined the WTO. Since then, the trade dependency ratio has continued to increase, approaching 70 percent in 2006 (Figure 4.1, above). The trade dependency ratio is a common indicator of a country's openness. Under normal conditions, the larger a country is, the higher the proportion of domestic demand in GDP will be, and the lower the degree of openness. Countries with large economies, such as the US and Japan, do not have high trade dependency ratios. China's particular economic conditions cause it to differ from other large countries. In accordance with its high trade dependency ratio, China's foreign trade surplus remained positive after 1994, rising to 8 percent of GDP in 2007. After the outbreak of the recent global economic crisis, the ratio of China's dependence on foreign trade and the relative amount of foreign trade surplus in GDP both decreased (Figure 6.7).

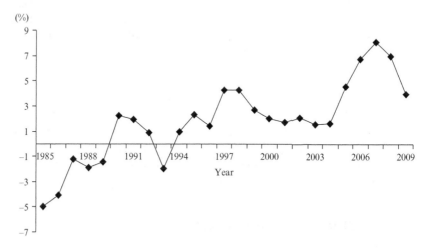

Source: *China Statistical Yearbook 2010* (China Statistics Press).

Figure 6.7   Proportion of foreign trade surplus in China's GDP (1985–2009)

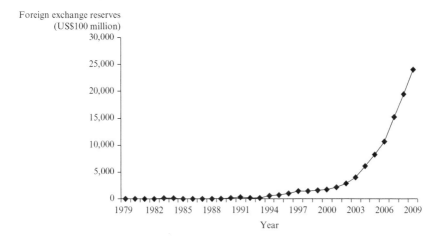

Source:　*China Statistical Yearbook 2010* (China Statistics Press).

Figure 6.8　*China's foreign exchange reserves*

Expansion of foreign exchange reserves

The expansion of the foreign trade surplus caused an increase in foreign exchange reserves (Figure 6.8). Foreign exchange reserves reached US$11.1 billion in 1990. In 1996, it exceeded the critical point of US$100 billion, reaching US$105.1 billion by the end of the year. By the end of 2001, it had reached US$212.1 billion. Foreign exchange reserves increased to US$853.6 billion in February 2006, by which point China had overtaken Japan as the country with the most foreign exchange reserves. As of December 2011, the foreign exchange reserves amounted to US$3.18 trillion. In China, there are limits on the foreign exchange that may be kept by individuals and businesses, and it is difficult to import certain badly needed products, such as raw materials, high-tech products, and military goods, in large quantities. China has used its foreign exchange reserves to purchase a large amount of the US treasury bonds. The liquidity that China provides supports US consumption, and increasing US imports aggravate the trade imbalance between China and the US (Dooley et al., 2004; Bai, 2006).

Increases in trade disputes

In some ways, China's current situation is similar to the periods of high-speed growth that took place in Japan and South Korea. As the amount of Chinese goods in the global trade system increases, the number of trade protections it encounters also increases day by day. The protections

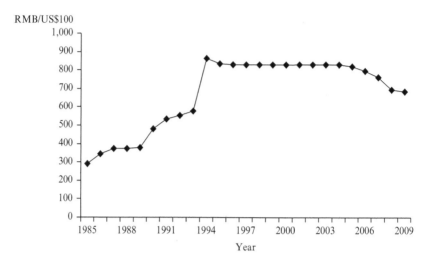

RMB/US$100

Source: *China Statistical Yearbook 2010* (China Statistics Press).

Figure 6.9 *Exchange rate of the RMB against the US dollar (1985–2009)*

are present not only in developed countries such as the US and most European countries, but also in emerging market economies such as those of Mexico and India. However, unlike Japan and Korea, China is still relatively undeveloped. It has already received more anti-dumping investigations than any other country in history. Between 1995 and 2008, China was the target of such investigations 677 times; 73 in 2008 alone.[4]

Pressure for the appreciation of the RMB

As China's foreign trade surplus increases, international pressure to allow the RMB to appreciate increases daily. Although the RMB has tended to appreciate against the US dollar, it is still far from the target required by the US (Figure 6.9). The self-devaluation of the US dollar has also prevented the RMB from appreciating against other major currencies. In the context of the current global financial crisis, many countries are increasing protectionist measures, and the exchange rate of the RMB and the mechanism by which that rate is determined are facing close international scrutiny.

Causes of External Imbalances

The external imbalances of China's economy are indicated by the constant enlargement of its trade surplus. As shown in Figure 6.10, import and

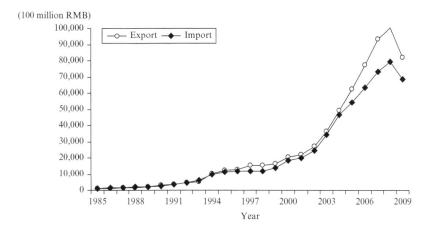

(100 million RMB)

Source: *China Statistical Yearbook 2010* (China Statistics Press).

Figure 6.10   Export and import volume in China (1985–2009)

export volume have both tended to increase over the past 25 years. Before 1994, the volume of imports frequently exceeded that of exports, but the margin slowly decreased, and the first surplus appeared in 1990. However, in 1993, there was again a large deficit. From 1994 to 2004, the volume of exports exceeded that of imports, and the trade surplus remained relatively stable, and its proportion of GDP remained at 2 percent. After 2004, the volume of exports far exceeded that of imports, and the proportion of trade surplus in GDP increased sharply to 8 percent. In 2008, the global financial crisis broke out, and China's imports and exports both shrank. However, exports declined more than imports, and the trade surplus decreased accordingly. Different forces have predominated during different stages of China's foreign trade development. These include long-term characteristics of economic structure and fundamentals and also short-term factors such as economic cycles and the impact of technological developments. Both supply- and demand-side influences have played a role.

Period of trade deficit: before 1994

The period before 1994 can be divided into two stages by changes in the structure of China's export products (Table 6.2): the period during which China exported resource-intensive products, mainly mineral fuels, before 1985, and the period during which China exported labor-intensive products, mainly light textile products.

During the early period of China's development, the country mainly

China's economic development

Table 6.2   Categories of export commodities (US$100 million)

Year	Total volume	Primary products	Food[a]	Mineral fuels[b]	Industrial products	Light textile products[c]	Mechanical products[d]
1980	181.19	91.14	29.85	42.80[I]	90.05	39.99[II]	8.43
1985	273.50	138.28	38.03	71.32[I]	135.22	44.93[II]	7.72
1990	620.91	158.86	66.09[II]	52.37	462.05	125.76[I]	55.88
1995	1,487.80	214.85	99.54[II]	53.32	1,272.95	322.40[I]	314.07
2000	2,492.03	254.60	122.82	78.55	2,237.43	425.46[II]	826.00[I]
2002	3,255.96	285.40	146.21	84.35	2,970.56	529.55[II]	1,269.76[I]
2004	5,933.26	405.49	188.64	144.80	5,527.77	1,006.46[II]	2,682.60[I]
2006	9,689.36	529.19	257.23	177.70	9,160.17	1,748.16[II]	4,563.43[I]
2007	12,177.76	615.09	307.43	199.51	11,562.67	2,198.77[II]	5,770.45[I]
2008	14,306.93	779.57	327.62	317.73	13,527.36	2,623.91[II]	6,733.29[I]
2009	12,016.12	631.12	326.28	203.74	11,384.83	1,848.16[II]	5,902.74[I]

Notes:
1. a: food and live animals meant for human consumption; b: mineral fuels, lubricants, and raw materials; c: light textile products, rubber products, mineral smelting products, and processed products; d: machinery and transportation equipment.
2. I and II: products ranked 1st and 2nd, respectively, in all categories except 'miscellaneous' that year.

Source: China Statistical Yearbook (various years) (China Statistics Press).

exported resource-intensive products. Before 1985, the top exports were mineral fuels, lubricants, and related products. During this period, the strategy of industrialization based on the development of heavy industry was established, and much emphasis was placed on the production of products such as coal and steel. After the mid-1970s, along with the improvements in China's status in the international environment, the export of resource products increased sharply, relieving some of the insufficiency of capital and the difficulties of the scarcity of foreign exchange. Also during this period, there were still two factors promoting increases in the export of resource products from China. First, in order to develop the manufacturing industry, China deliberately suppressed prices, making its resource products more internationally competitive (Lin and Yu, 2007). Second, the energy crisis faced in Western countries due to increasing oil prices increased the importance of preliminary resource products, such as coal (Cyrus, 1985).

However, there are some unstable factors involved in the export of resource products. The first is fluctuations in the international market. The export of resource products is influenced by the internal factors of each import country and by changes in the price of resource products.

As China's economy developed, the demand for energy increased accordingly, and the price advantages caused by the domestic scissors difference have gradually diminished. In the meantime, the cost of exporting resource products was very high and offered few benefits to the public. Because most of the coal resources are far inland, when the infrastructure was less developed, transportation costs were quite high. For a long time, mining and the sale of resource products took place solely through a state-owned monopoly, which could not absorb surplus labor. As China continues to open up, it must become accustomed to the demands of the market, especially the international market, making use of its advantages in global specialization and increase the efficiency of the utilization of resources. This will allow China's resources and foreign trade to translate into opportunities and improved living standards for the public. Since 1986, the export of mineral fuels has gradually been eclipsed by light textile products, which are more competitive internationally. Modern China saw its first trade surplus in 1990.

Period of stable trade surplus: 1994–2004
The trade surplus began in 1994. This year was a critical point for the changing patterns of China's economic variables. The devaluation of the RMB, which took place that year, had a profound effect on foreign trade. This devaluation was to some extent a correction of earlier overestimates of the RMB.

The reform of the right-incentive system has also had considerable impact on the trade surplus. The 1994 reforms of the tax-sharing system led to competition for growth at the regional level (Zhang and Gong, 2005; Zhang and Zhou, 2008). Internally, each region manipulated various resources to expand production. Externally, there was competition to attract foreign capital and expand into the international market. This caused regions to develop preferential policies and set up development zones. During this period, industries that were not relevant to national security, especially labor-intensive industries, were subject to comprehensive opening-up policies, and they attracted a great deal of capital. State-owned capital was utilized inefficiently during this period. Accumulated private capital competed with newly introduced foreign capital to produce and export labor-intensive products. This accelerated the process by which abundant labor resources became specialized on an international scale.

Through international trade, China's market has become integrated into the international market, but its domestic market is not yet integrated. The domestic market could not absorb all of the goods produced by the enormous production system that developed through competition, so producers turned to the international market. In a sense, it was the constant inflow of foreign capital that enabled the non-unified domestic market to be replaced by a more integrated international market (Luo and Zhang, 2008). As production expanded, competition among regions intensified. Because the domestic market had not become integrated, industries tended to be homogeneous, and every region relied increasingly on the export market. In order to obtain a stable market share, they tended to lower prices. The similarities in industrial structure weakened each region's unique advantages, but offering low prices for similar products kept China's products competitive in the international market. However, the development and maintenance of this kind of competitiveness has had high costs. Because of the dilution of profit, businesses had to keep labor costs low and neglect the environment in order to remain competitive. Concurrent with the rapid growth of the economy, the proportion of labor income of total national income decreased, and environmental contamination and depletion of resources became serious.

The rapid expansion in Chinese exports is related to lagging consumption, which in turn is the result of the widening income gap. The distribution of factor income has also had a clear influence on the distribution of income among individuals. When the distribution favors labor, then the share of labor income increases, decreasing income inequality (Daudey and Garcia-Penalosa, 2007). The share of labor income in national income peaked in 1996, after which it began to decline. As of 2012, it has declined to less than 40 percent (see Figure 6.1, above). This has pushed national income more toward capital, increasing savings, especially those of businesses, and finally intensifying external imbalances by allowing new production capacities to form.

Period of increasing trade surplus: 2005 to the eve of the global financial crisis

Since 2005, the increase in the scale of China's foreign trade surplus has been, to some extent, the result of the mutual reinforcement of the expectations of the appreciation of the RMB. The increase in the scale of the foreign trade surplus strengthened other nations' expectations that the RMB would appreciate, and those expectations in turn promoted the enlargement of the surplus. These expectations caused exporters to deliver the goods in advance, which in turn led importers to delay delivery, which also intensified China's trade surplus in the short run.[5] Here we analyze the enlargement of the trade surplus of foreign-invested enterprises and the effects of surpluses in the heavy and chemical industries on the overall trade surplus.

In the decentralized system, a segmented domestic market and the weakness of the labor force have given China several advantages in the international labor market. If there were no abrupt changes in these

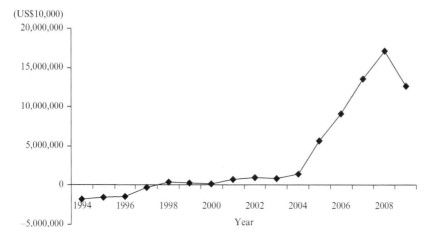

Source: *China Statistical Yearbook* (various years) (China Statistics Press).

Figure 6.11   Trade surplus of foreign-invested enterprises (1994–2009)

structural factors, then their effects on the trade surplus would remain stable. That was one of the reasons why the foreign trade surplus remained at 2 percent from 1994 to 2004. Since 2005, the trade surplus has increased sharply. This increase was closely related to the large-scale trade surpluses of foreign-invested enterprises. After 2001, exports of such enterprises accounted for over half of all China's exports (Wang and Wei, 2008). This tied China's overall trade surplus to that of foreign enterprises (Figure 6.11). Before 1997, foreign-invested enterprises always imported more than they exported, which offset the trade surplus of domestic enterprises to some extent. This was one reason why China's overall trade surplus remained stable. Between 1998 and 2000, the trade balance of foreign-invested enterprises moved from deficit to surplus, but it accounted for less than 10 percent of the country's total trade surplus. However, beginning in 2001, the trade surplus of foreign-invested enterprises began to increase sharply. After 2005, over half of the total surplus was attributable to foreign-invested enterprises (Figure 6.12).

There is some question regarding the origin of this phenomenon. We know that there are two types of foreign capital in China. The first is capital from adjacent countries and other parts of Asia, in which the main participants are businesses that purchase and sell intermediate products abroad. The second is capital from Europe and the US. This generally comes from companies that obtain intermediate products from their home country and sell the final products in the Chinese mainland (Volkswagen,

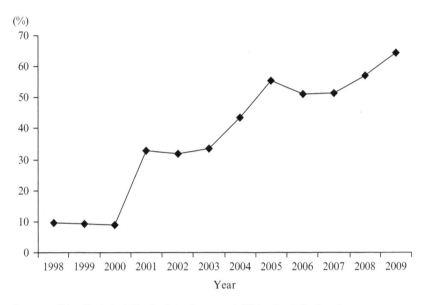

(%)

Source: *China Statistical Yearbook* (various years) (China Statistics Press).

*Figure 6.12   Proportion of trade surplus of foreign-invested enterprises
(1998–2009)*

Fukang). For many years, few foreign-invested companies purchased
intermediate products made on the Chinese mainland. Some economists
have said that China could produce world-class large ships, but all the
ships' intermediate features, even the toilets, have to be imported from
abroad. That is a typical processing trade. However, since 2005, imports
from foreign-invested enterprises have decreased as a portion of total
imports, which indicates that domestic producers are growing stronger,
and that the degree of localization in foreign-invested enterprises' products is increasing. There are two possible causes of this phenomenon. First
is technological improvements that have improved the quality and variety
of intermediate products made in China, meeting some of the demand for
intermediate goods by foreign-invested enterprises (Cui and Sayed, 2007).
Second, the competition among foreign-invested enterprises has increased
within China, compelling them to strengthen their linkages with local
enterprises, especially forward and backward linkages. During the past
few years, the inclination of exclusive investment of foreign enterprises has
become more and more obvious, but their forward and backward linkages with local enterprises may be even closer. If technological progress
motivates foreign-invested enterprises to strengthen their localization,

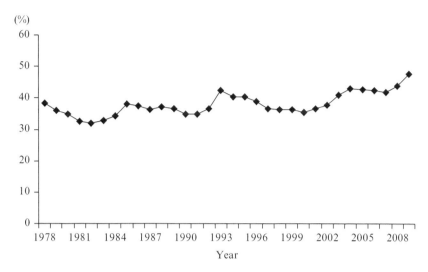

Source: *China Statistical Yearbook* (various years) (China Statistics Press).

Figure 6.13   Proportion of capital formation in GDP (1978–2009)

then this may greatly increase technological improvements in China in the long term.

The open macroeconomics of external imbalances

Lardy (2006) discussed the reasons for trade surplus in China from the angle of open macro economics. He also considered China's foreign trade imbalances to be related to insufficient domestic demand. Under the conditions of opening-up, aggregate demand has four components: consumption, business investment, government expenditures, and net export. In China, investment is the most important factor driving economic growth. Since 2001, half of China's economic growth has come from the increase in investments. As shown in Figure 6.13, in the first decade of the reform, the proportion of investment in GDP was close to 36 percent on average, which was higher than that of most developing countries but was not as high as those of adjacent Asian countries. From the early 1990s, investments began to expand by a large margin. In 1993, and since 2004, the proportion of investments has approached or been more than 43 percent, exceeding the highest value of the high development stage of adjacent Asian countries or regions.

In a clear contrast to the increase in investment, the increase in consumption fell behind economic growth. As shown in Figure 6.14, in the 1980s,

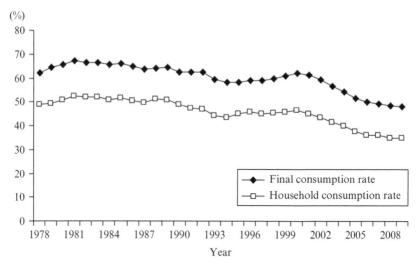

Source: *China Statistical Yearbook* (various years) (China Statistics Press).

Figure 6.14   Proportion of consumption in GDP (1978–2009)

household consumption accounted for a little more than half of GDP. This fell to 46 percent by the end of the 1990s. After 2000, the proportion of household consumption further decreased, to 35 percent by 2009, lower than all other major economic entities in the world. The proportion of household consumption in GDP in the US exceeded 70 percent, with 60 percent for both Britain and India. Even countries with high savings rates still had high household contributions to GDP. For example, that of Japan was 57 percent in 2005 (ibid.). The proportion of government expenditure in GDP remained relatively stable. This proportion decreased relative to the maximum value of 16 percent in 2001, and has since stayed at 14 percent of GDP. The entire consumption comprised both household and government consumption. Household consumption declined from its peak of 67 percent in 1981 to less than 50 percent in 2009. In the first half of the 1980s, the contribution of the growth exceeded 80 percent, but since 2001, its contribution has declined to 40 percent. Under the condition of investment expansion and slow growth of consumption, exports became the main absorbers of surplus products. As of 2005, the net export of products and services has become the main source of the country's economic growth, a phenomenon not observed since 1995. The trade surplus rose from US$32.2 billion in 2004 to US$264 billion in 2007, and its proportion of GDP rose from nearly 2 percent in 2004 to about 8 percent in 2007 (*China Statistical Yearbook*).

6.3 MECHANISM OF CHINA'S TRANSITION FROM INTERNAL AND EXTERNAL IMBALANCE TO BALANCED DEVELOPMENT

During the process of urbanization, industrialization and globalization, the achievements of and problems encountered by China's development are both related to its unique political and social structures. With these structures, China realized rapid growth for 30 years and encountered great challenges, including internal and external imbalances in its development. From the point of view of traditional and international economics, this challenge was also faced by other developing countries. From a political and social perspective, however, the challenges that China has encountered are unique. This uniqueness has increased the complexity of the issues of its development. In order to resolve these internal and external imbalances, China must prepare a strategy for balanced development.

Simultaneous Rapid and Balanced Development

If we compare the first stage of economic development in China to a scenario in which the stronger survivors seek help for others stranded on an island, then in the new historical period, those who reach safety first should not thwart the hopes of others. In the language of economics, if people at a developmental disadvantage do not have opportunities equal to those of developed regions, then the whole society can be adversely affected.

Role of urban–rural integration and harmony in urban–rural joint development
The process of economic development is not a simple matter of combining urbanization and industrialization. These factors have promoted economic development but they have also caused urbanization to lag behind industrialization and this has constantly enlarged the urban–rural gap and increased the scale of labor mobility from rural to urban areas. Migrant workers were not integrated into the urban communities to which they made personal and economic contributions. The social conflict between urban residents and migrant workers became one of the causes of the intense urban–rural divide and harmed urban development in the form of inharmonious social factors.

Currently, urban–rural integration and the development of a harmonious urban society are necessary for both rural development and sustainable urban development. Only by constant promotion of the urbanization process will the rural population decrease, which would increase the quantity of rural resources per capita and remove the difference between urban and rural areas. Through urbanization, the current rural labor force will be utilized for urban development and promotion of the industrialization process. The development of a harmonious urban society is also favorable for cities because it decreases the non-productive expenditures used to handle inharmonious social issues, freeing up productive capital.

Regional division of labor, cooperation, and market integration

Under the current system of fiscal decentralization, regional development strategies have remained largely the same as previously, fostering intense competition. The difference between backward and developed regions may become even larger if competition continues. The natural, geographical, and historical differences among regions suggest that regional division of labor might promote efficiency. This might allow each region to make the most of its strengths, so that all would reap the benefits of economic development, and the economy would realize the advantages of economies of scale.

However, the current system of fiscal decentralization has not facilitated the establishment of a unified market. Under this system, economically developed regions develop faster, and the central government could not fully utilize the central fiscal transfers to control the differences among regions. As a result, local governments had incentives to protect local industries through market segmentation, which increased employment and local taxation. If the central government were to encourage them to participate in the regional division of labor on the condition that fiscal transfers would go toward undeveloped regions, the efficiency of regional division of labor could be raised and equity and efficiency in regional economic development could both be realized (Lu et al., 2004, 2007).

The process of opening-up and marketization of the economy could also affect domestic market segmentation. Empirical research has shown that when the openness of the economy was relatively low, the economic opening-up may have intensified the separation in the domestic market. Foreign trade gave each province a reason to strengthen market segmentation and ignore the domestic market. When the openness of the economy was increased further, market competition became severe, and the cost of market segmentation increased further. We conclude that economic opening-up has favored integration of the domestic market. Research has also shown that privatization of the economy and decreased government intervention can promote market segmentation. The increase in the degree of privatization of the economy has favored domestic market segmentation; the strengthening of government intervention in recent years has been unfavorable to integration of the domestic market. To develop a nationwide free market, China must continue the reform and opening-up process, decrease government intervention, and prevent local governments from avoiding the domestic market (Chen et al., 2007a).

Construction of a Harmonious Society and the Promotion of Economic Development

The target of a harmonious society marked an important turning point in China's development: the government decided to change its strategy. The previous model had created inefficient utilization of resources, overexpansion of production capacities, backward consumption, a large income gap, slow increases in employment, severe environmental pollution, a fragile financial system, and foreign trade conflicts (Lardy, 2006). Under current conditions, the construction of a harmonious society would favor sustainable economic development in several ways.

Role of controlling the income gap and promoting increases in employment and consumption in the growth of the overall economic volume and structural adjustment

The income gaps between urban and rural areas, among regions, and among individuals have all widened considerably. This not only undermines social harmony but also affects the investment environment, and impedes growth of the economy and of consumption (Lu et al., 2005; Wan et al., 2006). The slow increases in employment also indirectly influence the growth of consumption. From 1978 to 1993, employment increased by 2.5 percent annually, but during 1993 to 2004, though the growth in investment was much higher than during the previous period, the increase in employment was only a little more than 1 percent annually (Kuijs and Wang, 2005). From a macro point of view, the increase in consumption has lagged far behind economic growth. In 2004, the GDP per capita in China was 2.5 times that of India, but the consumption per capita was only two-thirds higher than that of India (Lardy, 2006). The slow increase in consumption rendered China's economic growth dependent on investment and exports, potentially creating external imbalances. China must promote consumption by controlling the income gap and increasing employment.

Effects of energy inefficiency and environmental degradation on the improvement of the quality of economic growth

Resource constraints may become a bottleneck in the country's social and economic development. According to the research by Kuijs and Wang (ibid.), from 1978 to 1993, the growth rate of TFP in China was around 4 percent on average, and this was relatively high compared to other countries. However, after 1993, the growth rate of TFP had already declined to

3 percent. This indicated that, along with the constant expansion of investment, production efficiency gradually decreased. However, along with an
inefficient utilization of resources, the rapid expansion of production led
to surplus production capacity. For example, in 2005, steel production
reached 120 million tons, and the profit margin in the steel industry gradually shrank (Lardy, 2006).

During the 1980s and 1990s, the elasticity of China's energy consumption was 0.6 percent on average, which indicates the amount of energy
required for each single unit of production. This figure has doubled in
the past five years, which indicates that a rise in energy consumption
has made energy utilization more efficient. In 2005, China's coal consumption reached 2 billion tons, which was twice as much as that in the
US, but China's economy was only one-sixth the size of that in the US
(ibid.). During this period of inefficient energy utilization, the environment was also seriously damaged. During the 1980s and 1990s, China was
the second largest emitter of greenhouse gases in the world (Hu, 2007).
Considering the negative effects of environmental pollution, the growth
in the Chinese people's well-being must not be assessed solely through the
speed of GDP growth.

In China, both the price of raw materials and the environmental costs
of development were long underestimated. To a certain degree, pollution
was the result of the transfer of high-pollution industries from other parts
of the world to China. China produced massive amounts of goods for the
world market, and environmental degradation remained lower than it
would have been if this production had been dispersed among many countries. The high energy consumption and environmental pollution did have
causes related to technology and China's development stages, but institutional factors were also very important. Under the system of fiscal decentralization, local government officials pursued speedy economic growth
and the indicators of environmental protection and energy consumption
were ignored for quite some time.

The rapid expansion of production capacity can cause a surplus. There
are also the problems of inefficient resource utilization and environmental
pollution. These two factors threaten sustainable economic development. The construction of a resource-conserving, environmentally friendly
society would facilitate quality, sustainable economic growth.

Role of China in the Building of a Harmonious World

In recent years, a new concept came into being in the field of economics: the 'China effect'. Developed countries are currently facing the
problem of a widening income gap between skilled and unskilled labor

and a decline in the share of labor income (Blanchard, 1997). Developing countries have advantages when it comes to making labor-intensive products, especially products produced by unskilled laborers. According to classical trade theories, trade between developed and developing countries fosters competition among unskilled laborers in developed countries, which decreases their income. Globalization has increased the speed of capital flow: investors in countries with high labor costs will transfer their capital to developing countries, diminishing the bargaining power of the workforce in their own country and decreasing their share of labor income (Harrison, 2002). As the largest developing country in the world, China has shown outstanding performance in terms of exports and the attraction of foreign investment, but this has made it a target for criticism from some developed and developing countries. Other developing countries, such as Mexico, have expressed concerns about the crowding-out effect on their exports and the siphoning effect on their foreign capital (Garcia-Herrero and Santabarbara, 2005; Mercereau, 2005). As research has proved, 'the rise of China was an event with mixed results which needs to be analyzed according to the specific conditions' (Eichengreen and Tong, 2005). However, when in economic trouble, these countries tended to conspire against China (ibid.). Adjusting China's internal economic structure, promoting the domestic demand, and changing the pattern of economic growth from reliance on exports to reliance on domestic demand would not only facilitate China's transition to balanced development but also allow it to undertake the responsibilities of a large country and contribute to the formation of a harmonious world.

Conditions for the Shift of Government Responsibilities

Over the past 30 years, China has adopted a development pattern dominated by a strong government, but it has greatly changed the economic structure and constraint conditions. When China entered the new historical period, the government functions were adjusted to match changes in conditions. China's economy already has to meet the following criteria to complete the transition from an administration- to a service-oriented government.

Increase in the complexity of information and the difficulty of governmental administration
During the early stages of economic development, the economic structure was relatively simple, and the technology produced in China was far from the world's best. The government was easily able to obtain

important information on parameters of economic development and was therefore well equipped to play a large role in economic development and social management. However, along with the economic development and post-industrialization, information became increasingly complex and consumer preferences became more diversified. With economic development, people's demands could no longer be met by mere economic growth. People required good-quality medical care, education, and rights to cultural and personal expression. The complexity of information in the field of consumption increased the complexity of information in the field of production. Innovations based on knowledge have played a more important role. The complexity of information rendered the administration of government increasingly difficult. For this reason, the government should gradually withdraw from direct participation in the economy and play the role of rule maker and implementer. It should protect property rights, promote fair competition, and inspire creativity.

Changes in the social and economic structure and requirements for transition

Workers who were once closely affiliated with their organization have now become more like the social workforce. Cross-regional labor mobility has increased, and the connections between families and relationship networks have gradually been loosened and even dismantled. China has gradually transitioned from a society of acquaintances to a society of strangers whose interactions are based on anonymous trades. This kind of change in social structures increases the need for a change in the role of the government, which must provide new social norms and mechanisms for risk sharing. Society's increased requirements for fair trade necessitate a government that acts as a service provider rather than a manager.

Effects of a strong private sector on the conditions required for the government's new role

At the early stage of economic transition and development, one important reason for the large investments in government infrastructure and industries was that the private sector was not yet strong enough to hold up the economy. The tax-sharing reforms of 1994 also motivated local governments to conduct privatization reforms on inefficient state-owned sectors. In retrospect, local governments completed two important missions: the construction and privatization of infrastructure. In the field of production, and even in some fields of public goods, strong private sector companies were found to be more efficient than government-run enterprises. Under these historical conditions, some functions traditionally performed by the government may be performed as well as or better by the market and the public. The government would then take on new duties, including offering public goods such as medical care, education, and social security, that are difficult for the private sector to provide (such as large civilian airplanes). The government also addresses regulation issues involving the environment, the labor force, and product quality standards. It must also become an arbiter of social fairness and a creator of equal opportunities.

NOTES

1. China's interregional inequality may have declined in 2004 and the urban–rural income gap may have declined in 2010, but whether this change is sustainable is still not clear. The confusion comes from constraints on interregional and rural-to-urban labor mobility and on the inequality-reducing effects of subsidies for the poor, neither of which is sustainable.
2. This is a popular description of macroeconomic fluctuations in China in the 1980s and early 1990s.
3. *China Statistical Yearbook* (various years) (China Statistics Press).
4. See http://www.antidumpingpublishing.com.
5. Due to lack of data, we could not take into consideration the activities of international hot money behind the enlargement of the current account surplus.

7. Appropriate institutions and sustainable growth: China's development and its worldwide significance

China's economy has grown at an average yearly rate of nearly 10 percent over the past 30 years. This is practically a miracle for a developing country with a large population, extensive territory, and large-scale economy. The 30 years of rapid economic growth were caused by large-scale, market-oriented reform and opening-up under a governance structure with uniquely Chinese characteristics. Neglecting to acknowledge these characteristics would impede further understanding of China's developmental path and the future of this Chinese-style socialist market economy.

In this book, we have presented a development model with three core elements to illustrate the past and future of China's development: appropriate institutions, and imbalanced economic growth and development. China's economic growth has involved the establishment of appropriate institutions adapted to the early stages of economic development under the decentralized governance structure and relationship-based social structure. Economic decentralization (fiscal decentralization) has given local governments incentives to develop the economy. The Party's leadership promoted political utility and integration of the economy. The relationship-based social structure was able to reduce transaction costs during the early stages of economic development. Market-oriented reform and opening-up were both challenged by development imbalances. During periods when growth was the first priority, local governments upheld urban-biased economic policies, which enlarged urban–rural disparities. Under the background of globalization, coastal areas had a geographical advantage, allowing them to develop greatly, but interregional migration has been constrained, causing a cross-regional gap in development. Given that local governments pay for public services, these differences in development levels can cause interregional inequalities in access to public services. Many administrative powers and social relationships were embedded in the newborn market mechanism, which aggravates interpersonal inequality with respect to income and public services. As these gaps grow larger, domestic demand grows slowly, and economic growth is increasingly dependent on foreign investment and exports. Intensified competition in the domestic labor market reduced labor costs, and the undervalued RMB caused external trade imbalances. Given the objective of sustainable economic development, the dual imbalances that China faces today have necessitated further adjustments of the structure of internal governance and improvements in the mechanisms of the market economy.

In this final chapter, we shall extend our view to the pre-modern era, which will show the past and the future of modern China's reform more clearly.

7.1 CHINA'S PATH OF DEVELOPMENT: PAST, PRESENT, AND FUTURE

Ever since the reign of Emperor Qin Shihuang, China had been a vast and unified country. In the pre-modern history of human society, China was the only country that lowered transaction costs among regions through unified forms of writing and measurement and a developed transportation network, and these benefits remained in place for a long time.[1] One question a large country must answer is how to form an effective governance structure. During the Qin Dynasty, a system of prefectures and counties was established and local government officials were appointed directly by the central government in order to strengthen centralization. However, those policies were implemented for only a very short period. In the Western Han Dynasty, the system of prefectures and counties was maintained, which was good for the empire's unification and centralization, and the enfeoffment system was partially restored, which was, in fact, a form of economic decentralization. Qian (1952 [2001]) maintained that the more prosperous dynasties in Chinese history were decentralized and competitive both politically and economically, particularly the Western Han, Tang, and Song Dynasties. This kind of decentralization had two levels: the separation of imperial power from political power, and economic decentralization.[2] In order to prevent the centralized political system from losing its vigor, political power and education were opened up to the public as early as the Western Han Dynasty, beginning with a system in which government official candidates were recommended on the basis of their filial piety and moral reputation and on a system of civil service exams, which created opportunities for social mobility.[3] For better governance of the country, the Western Han Dynasty chose Confucianism as a political and ethical philosophy, the basic components of which were family ethics and social hierarchy. Economically, the ethics of the state power played a considerable role in coordinating people's actions. Confucianism became the ethical basis of the family-centered, relationship-oriented society, and it met the demands of the bureaucratized administrative hierarchy of the time.

During most of the time since the Western Han Dynasty, China has successfully maintained national unity and economic and social development under a governance structure incorporating economic decentralization, political centralization, Confucian ethics, and the sharing of political power. However, this governance structure could not overcome two important problems. First, the growth of local forces threatened the supremacy of the central government under the decentralized economic system. A more centralized political system was effected during the Ming and Qing Dynasties. Second, effective mechanisms preventing the power of the royal family from declining and the bureaucracy from becoming corrupt were lacking; the political system was centralized and each level of government reported to a higher level. The beginning of each dynastic period was characterized by speedy economic development, but the middle and later parts were marred by serious corruption. In the end, royalty was either replaced by stronger local forces or overthrown by peasant uprisings or foreign invasions. The idea that dynasties first thrive and then decline became a basic law of ancient Chinese history. After the collapse of the empire system, the problem of declining royal power ceased to exist. Maintaining national unity and effective political centralization are still issues in modern China.

Fundamentally, the governance structure incorporating economic decentralization, political centralization, Confucian ethics, and the sharing of political power is still considered an effective system for a large country. After the founding of the People's Republic of China, the Chinese leaders had massive goals, and there was a clear consensus on development strategies. However, the planned economic system of that time could not overcome two fundamental problems. First, China abolished the price mechanism and private economy, pursuing development dependent solely on central planning and state-owned entities. This was subject to the information and incentive problems inherent in this type of economic development. Second, no effective mechanism was put in place to reverse this policy once it failed.

After the reform and opening-up, the realities of poverty and underdevelopment spurred the collective leadership led by Deng Xiaoping to implement the generally agreed development policies. By reestablishing market mechanisms and developing the private economy, China successfully solved its information and incentive problems. Meanwhile, collective leadership and intra-Party democracy were strengthened, which ensured that the policies made would be correct and efficient. The Washington Consensus embodied the transition completed by speedy liberalization, privatization, and macro stability. In the former Soviet Union and Eastern European transition countries, liberalization and privatization were completed in a very short period. However, the objective of macro stability was difficult for these countries to realize due to a vacuum of governance. In China, however, marketization and privatization were implemented under the leadership of the Communist Party. From a macro perspective, despite the business cycles of instability without management and stagnation under control observed in the 1980s, China maintained acceptable levels of macro stability through government intervention in areas in which market mechanisms were not well established. Since the 1990s, which saw improvements in economic privatization and an end to the shortage economy, China has shown greater macro stability than in the 1980s. Thus, China realized the objectives of the Washington Consensus.

China's economy grew rapidly and gradually moved toward a market mechanism. Marketization reform has been pushed forward under a political and social structure suitable to a large, developing country. This has led to both achievements and problems. In the country's 30-year history of reform and opening-up, especially in the 1980s, localism was a constant problem. In order to further propel marketization reform, promote strong unified leadership from the Central Committee, and reduce resistance from local interests, China reformed the system of tax sharing in 1994, which strengthened central financing. It then implemented new systems of performance assessment and instituted fixed tenures and cross-regional rotation for local officials. However, because this system of performance assessment was based on GDP growth, it caused local officials to focus on short-term objectives at the expense of goals helpful to long-term development. Nevertheless, the systems of fixed tenures and cross-regional rotation kept the local governments focused on localism and short-term objectives. In the process of economic development and market growth, weakening local government interventions and promoting legalization and democratization should protect people's interests and encourage sustainable development.

China is attempting to establish a market economy mechanism based on legislation and democracy, and to maintain sustainable development. However, the relationship-based society hinders this process. The market economy, which is an important characteristic of modernity, requires that the principle of equity must be adhered to in all transactions. In order to remove the restraints of the relationship-based society, equitable market transactions, legislation and democratization are key. Institutions are endogenous. If many social relationships are embedded in the market mechanism, then the market may not be able to remove the restraints placed on it by the acquaintance society. Authority is important in relationship-based societies and in political bureaucratic organizations, while the idea that all individuals are equal is inherent in legislation and democracy. Therefore, when we propose reducing governmental intervention on the market and establishing a society based on laws and democratic politics, we find that the current mechanisms of the market economy do not lend themselves to equal transactions.

Choosing between a judicial market economy and a power-and-money-combined market economic system may have serious implications for development, especially now that modern China is standing at the beginning of a new era. Two internal factors require China to choose the judicial market economy system. First, if market growth and economic development widen the scope of transactions, then local social relationships will become weaker, at least with respect to economic activity, and administrative regulations will then be able to integrate the markets and set up economies of scale. When the domestic market becomes sufficiently integrated, the internal power of the economy appears to maintain national unity and market integration. Political centralization is therefore no longer required to perform this function. As China interacts with other countries, it must adapt to an increasing number of international rules and conventions and improve its domestic legal system and level of democracy. Second, the continuous widening of the income gap and the public service gap between urban and rural areas, across regions, and among individuals and the relevant internal–external dual imbalances of development require China to adjust its internal governance structure to improve the market economy system. In this sense, the challenges that China faces today are also the opportunities to sustain development in the future.

After the past 30 years of reform and opening-up, China is on the brink of a new historical era, 60 years after the founding of new China. The whole world is concerned with this issue.

7.2   SIGNIFICANCE OF CHINA'S EXPERIENCE

If China can maintain its level of growth over the next 30 years, then it will become a great power, with the largest total economic output of any country in the world. In this case, China's current development path may serve as a historical modernization model different from that of Europe and the United States. Over the past 30 years, China has developed considerable experience in terms of economic take-off, economic transition, and development specific to a large country.

Appropriate Institutions and Diversity Among Development Models

We have repeatedly used the phrase 'appropriate institutions'. This refers to the particular system that is best adapted to a specific place and time. In terms of place, the system must take into account its country's political and social structure.

The economic modernization process, which began in the West, was accompanied by the development of modern economics as an academic discipline. To be more precise, modern economics seeks a direct theoretical rationale for Western-style modernization. This 'modernity' has four characteristics: a market economy, democratic politics, an active civil society, and a focus on personal dignity. These four factors are assumed to have universal value in the modernization process of any human society. This assumption is widely accepted but it has been corroborated only in Euro-American countries. Modern economics first originated in Britain in the eighteenth century, and it developed in Britain and America through the nineteenth and twentieth centuries. Economics was established on the experiences of modernization in the Western world, particularly the philosophy of individualism, which determined the core of traditional economics. It has been proven that an individualism-based market economy could realize efficiency, growth, and modernization. Likewise, Western democratic politics and civil society also developed in an individualism-based market economy and were found to continuously improve that market economy. That is why mainstream economics prior to the 1980s seldom discusses the interactive relationship between institutional changes and economic development. Regarding the problem of the modernization process, mainstream economists believe that Western-style liberty and democracy are preconditions of economic modernization. In that worldview, industrialization and urbanization are the only two problems left for China to overcome, and the adjustment of political and social structures will be independent of economic development. Western economists have long considered them problems of political science and sociology rather than economics.

As the formal planned economy system is slowly replaced by market economy systems unique to the countries in which they arise, societies will have to face the question of whether modernization is unitary. Economics then changes accordingly. Economists have noted the cross-national diversity of the market economy, especially differences in terms of system, history, and culture, which affects the economic efficiency of all nations.

There is a question regarding whether or not the differences of the market economy system in different countries support or contradict the idea that Western-style modernization is human society's ideal path.

China's experiences indicate that a nation can choose a developmental path suitable to its circumstances on the basis of its history and current needs. Because China is a large, developing country, it is still economically decentralized and politically centralized. Economic decentralization provides local governments with incentives to develop the economy. Political centralization is conducive to national unity and the implementation of coherent policies. Meanwhile, because China is in the early stages of economic development, the country has no sound legal system, and market transactions are often based on relationships instead of rules. Social relationships became the mechanism by which transactions are coordinated. During the early stage of China's development, this reduced the need to make and implement laws. Compared to those of Western countries, China's market economy has more government intervention and embedded social relations. The Chinese market economy mechanism is currently facing the challenge of dual imbalances, but it is constantly adjusting.

The market economy is the most effective resource allocation system to date, and every country's market economy model is unique. Some of the features of the socialist market economy with Chinese characteristics are medium term and some are long term. China's experience has shown once again that each country must adopt a different set of institutions to adapt to the demands of economic development and that these institutions depend on the country's political and social structure. Ignoring the historical and current conditions of one's own country and blindly adopting the systems of other countries would result in inappropriate and inefficient systems.

Relationship between Government, Society, and the Market and the Need for Adjustment of Demands

If each institution is viewed as a series of arrangements facilitating the relationships between government, society, and the market, then institutional adjustments must be made to tailor the developmental process to the demands of the time. In the 30 years after reform and opening-up, China adopted the government-led development model. The market system was established gradually, however, and the government often overrides the market and allocates resources directly. On the macro level, the government makes strategies and policies related to economic development. On the micro level, the government constructs infrastructure, tells financial institutions which loans to make, and even organizes productive business activities. During the early stages of economic development, the government-led development model had significant advantages. The government can compensate for the small size and weakness of the private sector by promoting the development of infrastructure and large-scale manufacturing. However, the private sector has tended to expand gradually once the infrastructure is in place. As standards of living improve, demand for public services increases. Then, the government must withdraw gradually from production and spend more time and money on social services.

China's system of fiscal decentralization should be adjusted in the following ways. During the early period of reform and opening-up, the system of fiscal decentralization provided incentives for local governments to develop the economy. Without effective incentive mechanisms, the developmental model of strong government may fail to promote the development of a healthy market economy. Fiscal decentralization and the system by which government officials are assessed permit China's local governments to form a unified strategy that crosses all levels of government. However, because economic development is accelerating and because people are more concerned with issues such as equal access to public services, sustainable development may not occur unless the present incentive scheme, which focuses on growth, is changed.

The market and the government are key concepts in economics. The term 'the market' refers to non-government-sponsored mechanisms of resource allocation. In economics, both monopolies and imbalances in supply and demand are considered failures of the market to allocate resources properly. Then, the government must serve as a mechanism to resolve these failures. However, when the government allocates resources, inefficiency and corruption often occur. At that point, the market mechanism can supplement government efforts. In political science and sociology, society is also an important mechanism of resource allocation and organization. In Western countries, civil society, democracy, and the market economy are all basic characteristics of modernity. From an economic point of view, the government and market may both fail. Sometimes, market demand occurs due to a lack of scale, or consumer buying power may be inadequate. In that case, supplies from the for-profit private sectors may be insufficient if the economy depends on the market, whereas inefficiency and corruption may occur if the economy depends on the government. Non-profit social organizations may be able to overcome the failures of both the government and the market.

The orthodox view was that China lacked a mature civil society; however, Qian (2001) believed that Chinese society is made up of the family and extended family. He believed that individualism prevails in

Europe but that families prevail in China, stating, 'China-clan roughly equals West-society'. However, in the process of modernization, the scope of transactions continuously enlarges, and the meaning of society stretches beyond the extended family. Lin (1958 [1988]) also recognized the family institution as the foundation of Chinese society. However, there is a contradiction between family and societal values. This diminishes the population's public spirit. In addition, Confucianism ignores the social responsibility of individuals to strangers with whom they have no previous social relationships. Fei (1985) considered China's traditional folk society to be a differential order and that every individual is the center of his or her social circle. This differs from the group order found in the West and is not generally found in modern countries. Because the scope of the markets has widened, interactions between people now frequently cross family and extended family boundaries, weakening those bonds. China needs not only new social organizations to make up for the deficiencies of the market and the government but also new laws and rules to break the family-centered economic relationships and bring a critical public spirit to the operation of modern society.

Institutional Experimentation and Its Role in Economic Transition and Development

Although the country lacks mature theoretical guidance from economics for transition, China has still successfully advanced. The most important part of its economic transition and development has been institutional experimentation. At the beginning of reform and opening-up, Deng Xiaoping said,

> [O]urs is an entirely new endeavor, one that was never mentioned by Marx, never undertaken by our predecessors and never attempted by any other social- ist country. So there are no precedents for us to learn from, we can only learn from practice, feeling our way as we go. . . . [W]e are engaged in an experiment. For us, this is something new, and we have to feel our way. (Deng Xiaoping, Vol. III, 1993, p. 174)

The fundamental feature of China's gradual economic transition is not that it is slower than that of the former Soviet Union or Eastern European countries. Rather, it is China's system of institutional experimenta- tion. There was an internal logical contradiction in the radical reforms adopted by the former Soviet Union and Eastern European countries. Currently, economists have reached an agreement that the failure of the planned economy system was due to the inability of the government to obtain the sufficient information necessary for effective resource allocation. However, the reform pattern adopted by the former Soviet Union and Eastern European countries was promoted by rational planning performed by a small group of people in the hope of completing the transition very quickly through an overnight reform. In other words, the former Soviet Union and Eastern European countries finished the process of dismantling the planned system by means of planning. China's economic transition, however, was logically appropriate. Institutional experiments were used to overcome the shortage of information and knowledge, preventing resistance to reform.

China's institutional experiments have included every field and every period of reform. Rural reform began with a household responsibility system in Anhui Province and other places. The process of opening-up began with the foundation of four special economic zones in 1984. Business reform began with trial locations that aimed to enlarge the autonomy of enterprises in Sichuan Province. After 1994, the market reform process accelerated, and some areas began trials of the modern enterprise system within the country to promote enterprise reform. The development of the stock market can be traced back to experiments in the mid-1980s in which state-owned companies sold stock. The system of labor contracts developed in the 1980s and the process of removing redundant staff in SOEs through reemployment service centers, which was implemented in 1996 in Shanghai, were both significant institutional experiments. Recently, the central government set up comprehensive reform trials: Pudong, a new area in Shanghai; Binhai, a new area in Tianjing; Chongqing; Chengdu; and Wuhan. These experiments were used to promote reform and opening-up.

The reason why institutional experiments were adopted is related to China's status as a large country. Experiments are necessary and feasible for large countries with populations, economies, and territory of a certain size. A large country must allow reform patterns and processes to differ across different regions; large countries must avoid the all-encompassing consequences of failed experiments. As stated by Deng Xiaoping (Vol. III, 1993),

> We should be bolder than before in conducting reform and opening-up to the outside and have the courage to experiment. We must not act like women with bound feet. Once we are sure that something should be done, we should dare to experiment and break a new path. (p. 372)

> Dare to experiment and break a new path. That's the way it was with rural reform, and that's the way it should be with urban reform. (p. 374)

The institutional arrangement of economic decentralization and political centralization created conditions suitable to institutional experiments.

Such experiments usually require special policies for the trial locations, especially when economic growth is the first priority. Innovation in systems may bring new motivations to economic development. Therefore, under the system of decentralization, each local government had an incentive to carry out institutional experiments. Assuming that institutional innovation incentives exist everywhere, political centralization can ensure that important institutional experiments are confined to a relatively small geographical area before widespread implementation. This may create a balance between the risks inherent in reform and the benefits of innovation.

Active Integration into the Global Market and Its Role in Economic Development

If we consider the promotion of reform via experimentation to be an important part of China's experience, then active integration into the global market with open policies is necessary for economic development. Theoretically, economic opening-up and participation in the international division of labor mean that a country could make use of its comparative advantages and realize economies of scale with the help of the international market. For the developing countries that have a relatively large labor force but little capital, income must be increased through international trade and by allowing capital to accumulate gradually in order to upgrade the industrial infrastructure and cultivate comparative advantages. Such countries then become technologically advanced. In this process, opening-up means not only increases in international trade in the commodities market but also the absorption of international capital in the capital market. These both provide developing countries opportunities to learn new techniques, obtain new technology, and develop new institutions.

The history of China shows that development can only be realized through active incorporation with the global economy. Historically, China's less-developed status has been related to its two great divergences from the world. The first occurred during the Ming Dynasty. With the end of Zheng He's voyages to the West and the full ban on maritime trade, China forged an artificial path toward isolation. Zheng He's journeys were supposed to open up the country to the outside world and develop the market, just as the voyages of Columbus and Vasco da Gama during the fifteenth century opened up the first wave of globalization. In Western Europe, such voyages brought a thirst for navigation and the expansion of territory as well as vast changes in the world outlook. However, in China, navigation was strongly resisted by both the government and the public.

After the death of Emperor Yong Le, Ming Xuanzong ordered that Zheng He's 1431 voyage to the West would be the last, after which navigation activities were completely stopped, and China irrevocably stepped into isolation (Luo, 1993).

The second major historical divergence between China and the rest of the world occurred during the Qing Dynasty, and China continued to isolate itself from the outside world for many years after that. In 1792, a special ambassador was sent by the British king to deliver an offer to do business with China. In 1793, Emperor Qian Long stated in his reply that China had a large territory and abundant resources and therefore had no need for international trade. The suggestion of a trade relationship was thereby rejected, and China missed an opportunity to actively integrate itself into the global system. Eventually the Opium Wars forced China to open its doors. During economic central planning, the opposition between China and the Western world left China even more isolated than before. While Western countries were modernizing their economies, extending their markets, establishing rule-based systems, and fostering economic growth, China was moving in the opposite direction. This lasted until 1978, when comprehensive reform and opening-up began. During this period, the economy developed faster than during any other period in history, again proving the importance of economic opening-up. The history of modern human development contains no other similarly isolated country that has succeeded in economic development.

7.3 WORLDWIDE SIGNIFICANCE OF CHINA'S DEVELOPING PATH AS A LARGE COUNTRY

We can understand the nature of economic development in general by analyzing it through the experience of a large, developing country, like China. China's specific characteristics and its differences from Western countries in terms of geography, history, and culture make its development path a useful reference for the future of humankind, especially in other developing countries.

Formation of a New Type of Development

China has experienced a developmental path different from that of any other country. If it requires a name, it should be called a uniquely Chinese socialist market economy. Socialism is the vision of shared prosperity and development; its market economy is the fundamental means of resource allocation, and Chinese characteristics underlie the institutional features that are adapted to both historical conditions and China's current real needs. These characteristics, include four main factors.

The first is the structure of the governance of economic decentralization and political centralization. The right to make developmental policy is delegated to local governments, which allows those governments to make policies adapted to local economic demands. Local governments have the right to share fiscal revenue, and this provides incentives for local governments to make policies favorable to economic development. Political centralization itself favors the unification of the country and the efficient implementation of policies made by central government. Under the system of political centralization, higher levels of government assess local governments, usually using the criterion of economic growth. This, unfortunately, gives local governments an incentive to pursue short-term economic goals. In order to avoid the formation of overly powerful local interests, China has also implemented fixed-tenure and cross-regional rotation systems for local government officials.

The second factor is that strong government promotes economic development. China's reform and opening-up began under a planned system of governmental economic control. As a result, China does not have a developed market system, nor does it have a powerful system of social organization. After reform and opening-up, China introduced a market system, promoted by the government, to allocate economic resources. Government control over the economic development model remained considerable. During the historical period of insufficient capital and a weak private sector, government implementation favored large-scale infrastructure investments and large projects. These projects promote efficiency in policy making and the implementation of policies beneficial to economic development. Because of the consensus on development and incentives for local systems of economic decentralization, the government must encourage economic growth, but problems such as corruption and administrative monopolies are also likely. China's developmental model was also adopted by some other East Asian economies during the early stages of their economic development. Once economic development had reached a certain point, direct governmental intervention in the economy was weakened. The reasons behind Asian decisions to adopt a government-led model of economic development merits further research.

The third factor is Chinese-style political competition. The purpose of democracy is to make sure that politics reflect public opinion. This is effected through both political competition before the government comes into power, and a system of checks and balances afterward. In Western countries, the first condition is realized through party votes, and the latter is realized through the separation of the executive, legislative, and judicial powers. China's unified leadership under the Communist Party fostered political competition among different regions and different government officials. Within the Party, the system of assessing cadres using public opinion was reasonably good at ensuring that the most skilled officials would be the ones who received promotion. Relatively speaking, China's existing political system has failed to deal with checks and balances in an effective way. Sometimes, within a certain organization or bureaucratic system, a balance is achieved between departments with overlapping functions and administrators. However, this kind of balance is not legally recognized in China. Government officials usually have uncontrolled powers, which provides conditions favorable to corruption.

The fourth factor is relationship-based social structures. Family relationships are emphasized in traditional Chinese culture. Because China is still at an early stage of its economic development, and because the range of transactions is rather small, it still has a relationship-based society. The emphasis on relationships can compensate for some of the deficiencies in the market to some degree, and lubricate the market. However, these relationships also affect resource allocation. This is especially visible when interpersonal networks include many individuals with large amounts of public power. In these cases, corruption and inequity are fostered. When the economy and market develop to a certain stage, it is necessary to use legal constructions to prevent social networks from becoming embedded in the new market economy system, which may distort the resource allocation.

China's development could be considered a model for other countries under certain conditions, especially transitional and developing countries. Aside from market mechanisms, privately owned enterprises and opening-up, which are necessary for development, China's success comes from the combination of the following factors:

consensus on development + *necessary implementation power of the government* + *political competition* + *effective incentives* + *institutional experiments.*

A consensus on development is a precondition for continued high-speed development, and the government's implementation of power is the main instigator of development. Political competition and effective incentives can lessen the problems in the governmental development model. At the individual level, effective incentives can help society maintain a high level of openness and mobility. Experiments in institutional transition may prevent China from implementing costly incorrect policies.

Over the past 30 years, China's economy has developed at an extremely fast rate, especially among transitional and developing countries. China was lucky in that it enjoyed favorable economic conditions after its reform and opening-up, as this may be very difficult for a developing country. In other words, China was fortunate that it had the right conditions after its reform and opening-up. By comparison, many other transitional and developing countries lack a consensus on development (such as some countries in South America), or governmental implementation power and effective incentive mechanisms (such as some countries in South Asia), or political competition which can avoid governmental adoption of incorrect policies (such as some dictator nations), or institutional experiments, and if an inappropriate scheme is pushed forward on a large scale, irrevocable loss to the country is inevitable (for example, transitional countries in Eastern Europe).

The Formation of a New World Structure

China is currently an important force in the international economic system. It has become one of the world's largest manufacturing centers, providing the world with low-cost commodities and products. China is also the world's largest emerging market, and the preferred destination of investment for consumer commodities from many countries. The rapid economic growth and large volume of China's economy have made it a new engine of the world's economic growth, alongside the US, Europe, and Japan. Increasingly powerful, China is endeavoring to participate in the construction of a harmonious world and to become a partner with other countries. China is currently standing at a new historical starting point of openness and reform. Looking back on the country's modernization process, it becomes clear that its development is in some ways similar to that of other countries. However, the current practices of various countries indicate that the world will not necessarily limit itself to a single unitary development model.

The first modern societies developed in Europe and North America. There, the income inequality caused by completely free market economies appeared early during development. However, during the late nineteenth century and twentieth centuries, European countries and the US made some adjustments to their economic system, extending civil rights, implementing social security systems, protecting labor, and limiting monopolies. This caused their income gaps to shrink and they began to move toward sustainable development. In economics, the Kuznets curve, which is based on the history of developed countries, tells us that income inequality increases during the early stages of economic development and it narrows as the economy develops further (Kuznets, 1955). However, the Kuznets curve does not indicate that the income gap will necessarily be enlarged as the economy develops or that it will automatically shrink after further economic development. There are a few clear counterexamples, such as Taiwan, in which economic growth did not increase income inequality. In Taiwan, education was popularized early during economic development. This policy favored economic growth and reduced income inequality (Bourguignon et al., 2001). Second, economic growth does not automatically narrow the income gap. Rather, the government must adopt certain policies. Income gaps can harm economic growth, as has been seen in Latin American countries. The economies of certain countries are consistent with the Kuznets curve not because of any natural economic phenomenon but rather because of a series of institutional reforms and policy adjustments undertaken by those countries' governments. The current consensus among economists is that the Kuznets curve is a historical fact only under particular conditions, rather than a law in economics. If modern China narrows the income gap by adjusting its institutions and policies to promote societal development and sustainable economic growth, then its economy will also follow the Kuznets curve. In this sense, China's developmental path is similar to those of Western developed countries.

However, after the Second World War, especially after the oil crisis of the 1970s, the developmental paths of Europe and the United States showed some differences. Continental European countries developed extensive welfare systems, but the US and the UK focused on privatization and free market competition. Countries that followed the Anglo-Saxon model, especially the US, saw more economic growth and larger income gaps and more social conflict than other countries. In the continental European countries following the Rhine model where more social benefits were available, the income gap was smaller, but there was less economic growth. The reasons for these different effects, the influences of each model on the rest of the world, and which of the two will be more enduring are the subject of perennial debate among economists.

Russia, which was once an underdeveloped agricultural society, used to follow the Western development path, which accelerated its industrialization process. After many years, the former Soviet Union adopted a planned economy system, but it failed. Japan also attempted a European model, and, at one point, it was the second largest economy in the world. Aside from some labor systems, which were thought to have strong Japanese characteristics, Japan has demonstrated a spirit of openness and a willingness to learn, fostering industrial policies that encourage and reward the acquisition of experience. However, adoption of the European model damages Japan's identity despite its powerful economy.

India has enjoyed rapid economic growth over the last ten years and has been called the fastest-growing democratic country. India has gained a great deal of experience, especially in the development of modern service industries. However, India's system is derived from Britain, and it is not certain whether India's own traditions can be integrated into the modernization process. For example, a long period of social segmentation prevents India's large rural population from sharing fully in the country's achievements.

In the foreseeable future, if China can realize sustainable economic growth through continuous adjustments of both political and social structures, then its modernization process will be very different from that of other countries. China's experience may provide other developing countries with a reference, showing that modernization of human society is polynary, rather than unitary.

Hopefully, humankind will have a long future. China's modernization process and the dissolution of its planned economy, as happened in other transitional countries, will not be the end of human history, as Fukuyama (1992) has claimed. And it will not necessarily instigate great conflict among civilizations, as predicted by Huntington (1996). There still exist complementary civilizations, abundant in subtle differences; history and culture also develop and change over time in each country. What we ultimately learn is that each country's development has yet to be understood and that there is much that different civilizations can learn from one another.

NOTES

1. Europe, Japan, and India were once composed of numerous small countries, and Europe still is, with some unified large countries and empires occupying their territories for short periods (Jin and Liu, 1984).
2. Fei (2006) maintained that squires were the actual leaders of the units of local self-government in ancient China. The squires governed their communities' affairs and reported public opinion to the central government.
3. Admittedly, neither the system of recommending people on the basis of filial piety and moral reputation nor the system of civil service exams prevented corruption and stagnation.

References

ENGLISH

Acemoglu, Daron, Philippe Aghion and Fabrizio Zilibotti (2006), 'Growth, development, and appropriate versus inappropriate institutions', working paper, MIT and Harvard University, Cambridge, MA.

Alesina, A. and E.L. Ferrara (2000), 'The determinants of trust', NBER Working Paper No. 7621, Cambridge, MA.

Au, Chun-Chung and J. Vernon Henderson (2006a), 'Are Chinese cities too small?', *Review of Economic Studies*, **73**(3), 549–76.

Au, Chun-Chung and J. Vernon Henderson (2006b), 'How migration restrictions limit agglomeration and productivity in China', *Journal of Development Economics*, **80**(2), 350–88.

Bai, Chong-En (2006), 'The domestic financial system and capital flows: China', working paper, Tsinghua University, September.

Bai, Chong-En and Z. Qian (2010), 'The income distribution factor in China: 1978–2007', *China Economic Review*, **21**(4), 650–70.

Baicker, K. (2005), 'The spillover effects of state spending', *Journal of Public Economics*, **89**, 529–44.

Bao, Shuming, Örn B. Bodvarsson, Jack W. Hou and Yaohui Zhao (2007), 'Interprovincial migration in China: the effects of investment and migrant networks', IZA Discussion Paper No. 2924, Institute for the Study of Labour, Bonn.

Bates, Roberts (1981), *Markets and States in Tropical Africa*, Berkeley, CA: University of California Press.

Benhabib, J. and A. Rustichini (1996), 'Social conflict and growth', *Journal of Economic Growth*, **1**(1), 129–46.

Besley, T. and A. Case (1995), 'Incumbent behavior: vote-seeking, tax-setting, and yardstick competition', *American Economic Review*, **85**, 25–45.

Blanchard, Oliver (1997), 'The medium run', *Brookings Papers on Economic Activity*, **2**, 89–158.

Blanchard, Oliver and Andrei Shleifer (2001), 'Federalism with and without political centralization: China versus Russia', *IMF Staff Papers*, **48**, 171–9.

Bourguignon, F., M. Fournier and M. Gurgand (2001), 'Fast development with a stable income distribution: Taiwan, 1979–1994', *Review of Income and Wealth*, **47**(2), 1–25.

Brandt, L. and X. Zhu (2000), 'Redistribution in a decentralized economy: growth and inflation in China under reform', *Journal of Political Economy*, **108**, 422–39.

Brooks, Ray and Ran Tao (2003), 'China's labor market performance and challenges', IMF Working Paper, Washington, DC, November.

Buchanan, J.M. (1965), 'An economic theory of clubs', *Economica*, **31**, 1–14.

Byrd, W. (1989), 'Plan and market in the Chinese economy: a simple general equilibrium model', *Journal of Comparative Economics*, **13**, 177–204.

Cai, Hongbin and Daniel Treisman (2005), 'Does competition for capital discipline governments? Decentralization, globalization and public policy', *American Economic Review*, **95**(3), 817–30.

Chen, Aimin (2002), 'Urbanization and disparities in China: challenges of growth and development', *China Economic Review*, **13**, 407–11.

Chen, Chunlai (2007), 'Foreign direct investment in China: trends and characteristics after WTO accession', in Ross Garnaut and Ligang Song (eds), *China: Linking Markets for Growth*, Canberra: Asia Pacific Press, pp. 197–224.

Chen, Min, Qihan Gui, Ming Lu and Zhao Chen (2007a), 'Economic opening and domestic market integration', in Ross Garnaut and Ligang Song (eds), *China: Linking Markets for Growth*, Canberra: Asia Pacific Press, pp. 369–93.

Chen, Zhao and Ming Lu (2008a), 'Is China sacrificing growth when balancing interregional and urban–rural development?', in Yukon Huang and Alessandro Magnoli Bocchi (eds), *Reshaping Economic Geography in East Asia*, World Bank, pp. 241–57.

Chen, Zhao, Shiqing Jiang, Ming Lu and Hiroshi Sato (2010), 'How do social interactions affect peer effects in migration decision? Empirical evidence from rural China', working paper, Fudan University.

Chen, Zhao, Yu Jin and Ming Lu (2006), 'Economic opening and industrial agglomeration in China', in Masahisa Fujita and Akifumi Kuchiki (eds), *Asian Regional Economic Integration from the Point of View of Spatial Economics*, Joint Research Program Series No. 138, Tokyo Institute of Developing Economies, pp. 97–132.

Cui, L. and M. Sayed (2007), 'The shifting structure of China's trade and production', IMF Working Paper No. 214, Washington, DC.

Cyrus, B. (1985), *The Economics of the Oil Crisis*, New York: St. Martin's Press.

Daudey, E. and C. Garcia-Penalosa (2007), 'The personal and the factor distributions of income in a cross-section of countries', *Journal of Development Studies*, **43**(5), 812–29.

Démurger, Sylvie (2001), 'Infrastructure development and economic growth: an explanation for regional disparities in China?', *Journal of Comparative Economics*, **29**, 95–117.

Démurger, Sylvie, Jeffrey D. Sachs, Wing Thye Woo, Shuming Bao, Gene Chang and Andrew Mellinger (2002), 'Geography, economic policy, and regional development in China', *Asian Economic Papers*, 146–205.

Dewatripont, M. and E. Maskin (1995), 'Credit and efficiency in centralized and decentralized economies', *Review of Economic Studies*, **62**(4), 541–55.

Djankov, Simeon, Rafael La Porta, Florencio Lopez-de-Silanes and Andrei Shleifer (2002), 'Appropriate institutions', working paper, World Bank, Washington, DC, Yale University, New Haven, CT, and Harvard University, Cambridge, MA.

Dooley, M.P., D. Folkerts-Landau and P. Garber (2004), 'The US current account deficit: collateral for a total return swap', working paper, Deutsche Bank, August.

Eichengreen, B. and H. Tong (2005), 'Is China's FDI coming at the expense of other countries', *Journal of the Japanese and International Economies*, **21**(2), 153–72.

Epple, Dennis and Richard E. Romano (1998), 'Competition between private and public schools, vouchers, and peer-group effects', *American Economic Review*, **88**, 33–62.

Epple, Dennis and Richard E. Romano (2002), 'Educational vouchers and cream skimming', NBER Working Paper No. 9354, Cambridge, MA.

Fujita, Masahisa, J. Vernon Henderson, Yoshitsugu Kanemoto and Tomoya Mori (2004), 'Spatial distribution of economic activities in Japan and China', in V. Henderson and J.-F. Thisse (eds), *Handbook of Urban and Regional Economics*, Amsterdam: North-Holland, Vol. 4, pp. 2911–77.

Fukuyama, Francis (1992), *The End of History and the Last Man*, New York: Free Press.

Garcia-Herrero, A. and D. Santabarbara (2005), 'Does China have an impact on foreign direct investment to Latin America', LAEBA Working Paper No. 31, Inter-American Development Bank.

Gill, Indermit, Homi Kharas et al. (2007), *An East Asian Renaissance: Ideas for Economic Growth*, Washington, DC: International Bank for Reconstruction and Development/World Bank.

Groves, Theodore, Yongmiao Hong, John McMillan and Barry Naughton

(1994), 'Autonomy and incentives in Chinese state enterprises', *Quarterly Journal of Economics*, **109**(1), 183–209.

Groves, Theodore, Yongmiao Hong, John McMillan and Barry Naughton (1995), 'China's evolving managerial labor market', *Journal of Political Economy*, **103**(4), 873–92.

Harrison, A.E. (2002), 'Has globalization eroded labor's share? Some cross-country evidence', working paper, University of California-Berkeley and NBER, Cambridge, MA, October.

Hayek, F.A. (1945), 'The use of knowledge in society', *American Economic Review*, **35**(4), September, 519–30.

Hu, Angang (2007), 'Five major scale effects of China's rise in the world', Discussion Paper No. 19, China Policy Institute, Nottingham University,

Huang, Yasheng (2002), 'Managing Chinese bureaucrats: an institutional economics perspective', *Political Studies*, **50**, 61–79.

Huntington, Samuel P. (1996), *The Clash of Civilizations and the Remaking of World Order*, New York: Touchstone Books.

Jian, Tianlun, Jeffrey D. Sachs and Andrew M. Warner (1996), 'Trends in regional inequality in China', *China Economic Review*, **7**(1), 1–21.

Jin, H., Y. Qian and B. Weingast (2005), 'Regional decentralization and fiscal incentives: federalism, Chinese style', *Journal of Public Economics*, **89**, 1719–42.

Kanbur, Ravi and Xiaobo Zhang (2005), 'Fifty years of regional inequality in China: a journey through central planning, reform, and openness', *Review of Development Economics*, **9**(1), 87–106.

Knight, John, Shi Li and Renwei Zhao (2006), 'Divergent means and convergent inequality of incomes among the provinces and cities of China', in R. Kanbur, A. Venables and G. Wan (eds), *Spatial Disparities in Human Development: Perspectives from Asia*, Tokyo: United Nations University Press, pp. 133–57.

Knight, John and Lina Song (1993), 'The spatial contribution to income inequality in rural China', *Cambridge Journal of Economics*, **17**, 195–213.

Knight, J. and L. Yueh (2002), 'The role of social capital in the labor market in China', Economics Series Working Papers No. 121, Oxford University.

Kranton, R. (1996), 'Reciprocal exchange: a self-sustaining system', *American Economic Review*, **86**(4), 830–51.

Krueger, Anne, Maurice Schiff and Alberto Valdes (eds) (1991), *The Political Economy of Agricultural Pricing Policy*, Baltimore, MD: Johns Hopkins University Press.

Kuijs, Louis and Tao Wang (2005), 'China's pattern of growth: moving to sustainability and reducing inequality', World Bank Policy Research Working Paper No. 3767, Washington, DC, November.

Kuznets, S. (1955), 'Economic growth and income inequality', *American Economic Review*, **45**(1), 1–28.

Lardy, N.R. (2006), 'China: Toward a Consumption-Driven Growth Path', Policy Brief, No. 6, Institute for International Economics, Washington, DC.

Lardy, N.R. (2007), 'China: rebalancing economic growth', in C.F. Bergsten, B. Gill, N.R. Lardy and D.J. Mitchell (Project Directors), *The China Balance Sheet in 2007 and Beyond*, Washington, DC: Center for Strategic and International Studies and Peterson Institute for International Economics, pp. 1–24.

Lau, Lawrence J., Yingyi Qian and Gérard Roland (1997), 'Pareto-improving economic reforms through dual-track liberalization', *Economics Letters*, **55**(2), 285–92.

Lau, Lawrence J., Yingyi Qian and Gérard Roland (2000), 'Reform without losers: an interpretation of China's dual-track approach to transition', *Journal of Political Economy*, **108**(1), February, 120–43.

Leman, Edward (2005), 'Metropolitan regions: new challenges for an urbanizing China', paper presented at the World Bank and Institute of Applied Economic Research 'Urban Research Symposium', Brasilia, April 4.

Lewis, W. Arthur (1954), 'Economic development with unlimited supplies of labour', *The Manchester School*, **22**(2), 139–91.

Li, Hongbin and Li-An Zhou (2005), 'Political turnover and economic performance: the incentive role of personnel control in China', *Journal of Public Economics*, **89**, 1743–62.

Li, John Shuhe (2003), 'Relation-based versus rule-based governance: an explanation of the East Asian Miracle and Asian crisis', *Review of International Economics*, **11**(4), 651–73.

Li, Shaomin, Shuhe Li and Weiying Zhang (2000), 'The road to capitalism: competition and institutional change in China', *Journal of Comparative Economics*, **28**(2), 269–92.

Li, Shuang, Ming Lu and Hiroshi Sato (2009), 'Power as a driving force of inequality in China: how do Party membership and social networks affect pay in different ownership sectors?', *CESifo Economic Studies*, **55**(3–4): 624–47.

Lin, Justin Yifu (1992), 'Rural reform and agricultural growth in China', *American Economic Review*, **82**(1), 34–51.

Lin, Justin Yifu and Z. Liu (2000), 'Fiscal decentralization and economic growth in China', *Economic Development and Cultural Change*, **49**(1), 1–21.

Lin, Justin Yifu and Miaojie Yu (2007), 'The economics of price scissors: an empirical investigation for China', Working Paper, CCER, Peking University.

Lipton, M. (1977), *Why Poor People Stay Poor: Urban Bias in World Development*, Cambridge, MA: Harvard University Press.

Liu, Yuanli, Keqin Rao and Shanlian Hu (2002), *People's Republic of China: Towards Establishing a Rural Protection System*, Beijing: Asian Development Bank.

Lu, Ming and Zhao Chen (2006a), 'Urbanization, urban-biased policies and urban–rural inequality in China: 1987–2001', *Chinese Economy*, **39**(3), 42–63.

Luo, Changyuan and Jun Zhang (2010), 'Declining labor share: is China's case different?', *China & World Economy*, **18**(6), 1–18.

Martinez-Vazquez, Jorge and R.M. McNab (2003), 'Fiscal decentralization and economic growth', *World Development*, **31**, 1597–616.

McKinnon, R. (1997), 'Market-preserving fiscal federalism in the American monetary union', in B. Mairo and T. Ter-Minassian (eds), *Macroeconomic Dimensions of Public Finance*, New York: Routledge, pp. 73–93.

McMillan, John, John Whalley and Lijing Zhu (1989), 'The impact of China's economic reforms on agricultural productivity growth', *Journal of Political Economy*, **97**, August, 781–807.

Meng, Xin (2007), 'Wealth accumulation and distribution in urban China', *Economic Development and Cultural Change*, **55**(4), 761–91.

Meng, Xin and Nansheng Bai (2007), 'How much have the wages of unskilled workers in China increased: data from seven factories in Guangdong', in Ross Garnaut and Ligang Song (eds), *China: Linking Markets for Growth*, Canberra: Asia Pacific Press, pp. 151–75.

Mercereau, B. (2005), 'FDI flows to Asia: did the dragon crowd out the Tigers?', IMF Working Paper, Washington, DC.

Miguel, E., P. Gertler and D.I. Levine (2006), 'Does industrialization build or destroy social networks', *Economic Development and Culture Change*, **54**(2), 287–317.

Morduch, J. and T. Sicular (2001), 'Risk and insurance in transition: perspectives from Zouping County, China', in M. Aoki and Y. Hayami (eds), *Communities and Markets in Economic Development*, Oxford: Oxford University Press, pp. 215–45.

Naughton, Barry (1994), 'Chinese institutional innovation and privatization from below', *American Economic Review*, **84**(2), 266–70.

Naughton, Barry (2000), 'How much can regional integration do to unify China's markets?', Working Paper 58, Center for Research on Economic Development and Policy Reform, Stanford University.

North, Douglass C., John Joseph Wallis and Barry R. Weingast (2006), 'A conceptual framework for interpreting recorded human history', NBER Working Paper No. 12795, Cambridge, MA.

Oates, W.E. (1972), *Fiscal Federalism*, New York: Harcourt Brace Jovanovich.

Peng, Yusheng (2004), 'Kinship networks and entrepreneurs in China's transitional economy', *American Journal of Sociology*, **109**(5), 1045–74.

Polanyi, Carl (1957), *The Great Transformation: The Political and Economic Origins of Our Time*, Boston, MA: Beacon Press.

Poncet, Sandra (2003), 'Measuring Chinese domestic and international integration', *China Economic Review*, **14**(1), 1–21.

Qian, Yingyi and G. Roland (1998), 'Federalism and the soft budget constraint', *American Economic Review*, **77**, 265–84.

Qian, Yingyi and Barry R. Weingast (1997), 'Federalism as a commitment to preserving market incentives', *Journal of Economic Perspectives*, **11**(4), 83–92.

Qian, Yingyi and Chenggang Xu (1993), 'Why China's economic reforms differ: the M-form hierarchy and entry/expansion of the non-state sector', *The Economics of Transition*, **1**(2), 135–70

Qian, Yingyi, G. Roland and C. Xu (1988), 'Coordinating changes in M-form and U-form organizations', mimeo, European Center for Advanced Research in Economics and Statistics, Université Libre de Bruxelles.

Qian, Yingyi, G. Roland and C. Xu (1999), 'Why is China different from Eastern Europe? Perspectives from organization theory', *European Economic Review*, **43**(4–6): 1085–94.

Raiser, M. (1998), 'Subsidising inequality: economic reforms, fiscal transfers and convergence across Chinese provinces', *Journal of Development Studies*, **34**(3), 1–26.

Ravallion, Martin and Shaohua Chen (2007), 'China's (uneven) progress against poverty', *Journal of Development Economics*, **82**(1), 1–42.

Rozelle, Scott (1994), 'Rural industrialization and increasing inequality: emerging patterns in China's reforming economy', *Journal of Comparative Economics*, **19**, 362–91.

Sato, Hiroshi (2006), 'Housing inequality and housing poverty in urban China in the late 1990s', *China Economic Review*, **17**, 37–50.

Schultz, T.W. (1978), *Distortions of Agricultural Incentives*, Bloomington, IN: Indiana University Press.

Shi, Anqing (2006), 'Migration in towns in China, a tale of three provinces: evidence from preliminary tabulations of the 2000 census', World Bank Policy Research Working Paper No. 3890, Washington, DC, April.

Stiglitz, Joseph E. (1994), *Whither Socialism?*, Cambridge, MA: MIT Press.

Stiglitz, Joseph E. (1999), 'Quis custodiet ipsos custodes? Corporate governance failures in the transition', *Challenge*, **42**(6), 26–67.

The Economist (2007), 'How fit is the Panda', September 27.

Tian, Qunjian (2001), 'China's new urban–rural divide and pitfalls for the Chinese economy', *Canadian Journal of Development Studies*, **22**(1), 165–90.

Tiebout, Charles M. (1956), 'A pure theory of local expenditure', *Journal of Political Economy*, **64**, 416–24.

Townsend, James R. and Brantly Womack (1986), *A Country Study: Politics in China*, 3rd edn, Boston, MA: Little, Brown & Co.

Tsai, K. (2002), *Back-Alley Banking: Private Entrepreneurs in China*, Ithaca, NY: Cornell University Press.

Tsui, K. and Y. Wang (2004), 'Between separate stoves and a single menu: fiscal decentralization in China', *China Quarterly*, **177**, 71–90.

Wan, Guanghua (2007), 'Understanding regional poverty and inequality trends in China: methodological issues and empirical findings', *Review of Income and Wealth*, **53**(1), 25–34.

Wan, Guanghua, Ming Lu and Zhao Chen (2006), 'The inequality–growth nexus in the short and long runs: empirical evidence from China', *Journal of Comparative Economics*, **34**(4), 654–67.

Wan, Guanghua, Ming Lu and Zhao Chen (2007), 'Globalization and regional income inequality: empirical evidence from within China', *Review of Income and Wealth*, **53**(1), 35–59.

Wang, Yongqin (2007a), 'Interlinking markets, relational contract and economic transition', *The Studies in Regional Development*, **39**(1), 161–87.

Wang, Yongqin and Ming Li (2008), 'Unraveling the Chinese miracle: a perspective of interlinked relational contract', *Journal of Chinese Political Science*, **13**(3): 269–85.

Wang, Zhi and Shang-jin Wei (2008), 'What accounts for the rising sophistication of China's exports', NBER Working Paper No. 13771, Cambridge, MA.

Weingast, B. (1995), 'The economic role of political institutions: market-preserving federalism and economic development', *Journal of Law and Economic Organization*, **11**, 1–31.

Wen, Mei (2004), 'Relocation and agglomeration of Chinese industry', *Journal of Development Economics*, **73**, 329–47.

World Bank (1997a), *Clear Water, Blue Skies: China's Environment in a New Century*, Washington, DC: World Bank.

World Bank (1997b), *Sharing Rising Incomes – Disparities in China*, Washington, DC: World Bank.

World Bank (2008), *World Development Report 2009*, Washington, DC: World Bank.

Xu, Bin (2007), 'Measuring China's export sophistication', working paper, China Europe International Business School, Pudong, China.

Xu, Chenggang (2011), 'The fundamental institutions of China's reforms and development', *Journal of Economic Literature*, **49**, 1076–151.

Xu, Xinpeng (2002), 'Have the Chinese provinces become integrated under reform?', *China Economic Review*, **13**, 116–33.

Yang, Dennis Tao (1999), 'Urban-biased policies and rising income inequality in China', *American Economic Review*, **89**(2), 306–10.

Yang, Dennis Tao and Fang Cai (2000), 'The political economy of China's rural–urban divide', Working Paper No. 62, Center for Research on Economic Development and Policy Reform, Stanford University.

Yang, Dennis Tao and Hao Zhou (1999), 'Rural–urban disparity and sectoral labor allocation in China', *Journal of Development Studies*, **35**(3), 105–33.

Yao, Shujie (2000), 'Economic development and poverty reduction in China over 20 years of reform', *Economic Development and Cultural Change*, **43**, 447–74.

Yao, Shujie and Zongyi Zhang (2001), 'On regional inequality and diverging clubs: a case study of contemporary China', *Journal of Comparative Economics*, **29**, 466–84.

Yao, Yi (2006), 'Equalizing or not? Assessing the intergovernmental grants and their incentive effects in China's fiscal reform', paper presented at the Chinese Economists Society Annual Meeting, Shanghai: July 9–12.

Young, Alwyn (2000), 'The razor's edge: distortions and incremental reform in the People's Republic of China', *Quarterly Journal of Economics*, **115**(4), 1091–135.

Zhang, Dandan and Xin Meng (2007), 'Assimilation or disassimilation? The labour market performance of rural migrants in Chinese cities', paper presented at the 6th conference on Chinese economy, CERDI-IDREC, Clermont-Ferrand, France, October 18–19.

Zhang, Junsen, Yaohui Zhao, Albert Park and Xiaoqing Song (2005), 'Economic returns to schooling in urban China, 1988 to 2001', *Journal of Comparative Economics*, **33**, 730–52.

Zhang, T. and H. Zou (1998), 'Fiscal decentralization, public spending, and economic growth in China', *Journal of Public Economics*, **67**, 221–40.

Zhang, Z., A. Liu and S. Yao (2001), 'Convergence of China's regional income, 1952–1997', *China Economic Review*, **12**, 243–58.

Zhao, Yaohui (1999a), 'Leaving the countryside: rural-to-urban migration decisions in China', *American Economic Review, AEA Papers and Proceedings*, **89**, 281–6.

Zhao, Yaohui (1999b), 'Labor migration and earnings differences: the case of China', *Economic Development and Cultural Change*, **47**, 767–82.

Zhao, Yaohui (2003), 'The role of migrant networks in labor migration: the case of China', *Contemporary Economic Policy*, **21**(4), 500–511.

Zimmer, Z. and J. Kwong (2003), 'Family size and support of older adults in urban and rural China: current effects and future implications', *Demography*, **40**(1), 23–44.

CHINESE

Anderson, Gerard F. and Junjie Mei (2006), 'Medical reform and hospital management in China', *Social Observer*, No. 4, 15–16.

Bai, Chongen, Yinjuan Du, Zhigang Tao and Yueting Tong (2004), 'The determinants and trend of local protectionism and industrial concentration', *Economic Research Journal*, No. 4, 29–40.

Bai, Chongen, Jiangyong Lu and Zhigang Tao (2006), 'Empirical study of the effects of SOEs' ownership transformation', *Economic Research Journal*, No. 8, 4–13, 69.

Cai, Fang, Yang Du and Meiyan Wang (2003), *The Political Economy of Labor Mobility*, Shanghai: Sanlian Press, People's Press.

Chen, Binkai, Ming Lu and Ninghua Zhong (2010), 'Household consumption constrained by the Hukou system', *Economic Research Journal*, No. S1, 62–71.

Chen, Jianbo (1995), 'The ownership structure and its impact on resource allocation efficiency', *Economic Research Journal*, No. 9, 24–32.

Chen, Min, Qihan Qui, Ming Lu and Zhao Chen (2007b), 'How can Chinese economic growth sustainably enjoy scale economy? An empirical study on economic openness and domestic market segmentation', *China Economic Quarterly*, **7**(1), 125–50.

Chen, Zhao and Ming Lu (2008b), 'From segmentation to integration, the political economy of urban–rural economic growth and social harmony', *Economic Research Journal*, No. 1, 21–32.

Dai, Yuanchen (2005), 'The winding development road of private economy: enterprises in red hats', *Southern Economic Journal*, No. 7, 26–34.

Deng Xiaoping (1993), *Selected Works by Deng Xiaoping*, Vols II and III, Shanghai: People's Press.

Development Research Centre of the State Council (2005), *Research Report of SOEs' Ownership Transformation and Restructuring*, Centre for Enterprise Research, Development Research Centre of the State Council.

Ding, Ning and Yougui Wang (2005), 'Chinese households' income mobility and its composition', paper presented at the 2005 Annual Conference of the Chinese Economics Association, December 10–11.

Economic and Trade Committee of Zhejiang Province (2006), 'A development report of economic cluster in Zhejiang', mimeo.

Fan, Gang (1994), 'Dual track transition: the achievements and problems of China's gradualist marketization reform', in Gang Fan, Yang Li and Zhenhua Zhou (eds), *Towards a Market Economy (1978–1993)*, Shanghai: People's Press, pp. 1–42.

Fan, Jianyong (2004), 'Market integration, regional specialization and industrial agglomeration: their effects on interregional disparity', *Chinese Social Science*, No. 6, 39–51, 204–5.

Fan, Jianyong (2006), 'Industrial agglomeration and interregional labor productivity differentials', *Economic Research Journal*, No. 11, 72–81.

Fan, Jianyong (2008), *Industrial Agglomeration and China's Interregional Disparity*, Shanghai: Gezhi Press, Sanlian Press, People's Press.

Fan, Ziying and Jun Zhang (2010a), 'Fiscal decentralization, fiscal transfer and domestic market integration', *Economic Research Journal*, No. 3, 53–64.

Fan, Ziying and Jun Zhang (2010b), 'How does China lose efficiency for balance: from the angle of fiscal transfer', *World Economy*, No. 10, 117–38.

Fei, Xiaotong (1985), *Rural China*, Shanghai: Sanlian Press.

Fei, Xiaotong (2006), *Chinese Gentry*, Beijing: Chinese Social Science Press.

Feng, Hao and Ming Lu (2010), 'School choice through housing purchase', *World Economy*, No. 12, 89–104.

Feng, Jing and Yangyang Yu (2007), 'Chinese rural income inequality and health', *Economic Research Journal*, No. 1, 79–88.

Fu, Yong and Yan Zhang (2007), 'Decentralization with Chinese style and the bias of fiscal expenditure: the cost of competition for growth', *Management World*, No. 3, 4–12.

Gui, Qihan, Min Chen, Ming Lu and Zhao Chen (2006), 'Is the Chinese domestic market being segmented or integrated? An analysis based on prices', *World Economy*, No. 2, 20–30.

Hu, Yifan, Min Song and Junxi Zhang (2006), 'The performance of Chinese SOEs' privatization', *Economic Research Journal*, No. 7, 49–60.

Jin, Guantao and Qingfeng Liu (1984), *Prosperity and Crisis: On the Super Stable Structure of China's Feudal Society*, Hunan: People's Press.

Jin, Yu, Zhao Chen and Ming Lu (2006), 'China's regional industrial agglomeration: economic geography, new economic geography, and economic policy', *Economic Research Journal*, No. 4, 79–89.

Kornai, J. (1986), *Economics of Shortage*, Beijing: Economics Science Press.

Li, Shi (2003), 'Review and prospects of studies on Chinese individual income distribution', *China Economic Quarterly*, **2**(2), 379–403.

Li, Shi and Sai Ding (2003), 'The long-term trend of China's urban returns to education', *Chinese Social Science*, No. 6, 58–72.

Li, Shi and Hiroshi Sato (eds) (2004), *The Price of Economic Transition: Empirical Analyses of Urban Unemployment, Poverty and Income Inequality*, Beijing: Chinese Fiscal & Economic Publishing House.

Li, Wei (1993), *Agricultural Surplus and Industrial Capital Accumulation*, Kunming: Yunnan People's Press.

Lin, Yifu (2002), 'Development strategy, self-sustainability and economic convergence', *China Economic Quarterly*, **1**(2), 269–300.

Lin, Yifu (2007), 'The tide phenomenon and the reconstruction of macroeconomic theory in developing countries', *Economic Research Journal*, No. 1, 126–31.

Lin, Yifu and Peilin Liu (2004), 'Viability and reform of SOEs', *Economic Research Journal*, No. 9, 60–70.

Lin, Yifu, Fang Cai and Zhou Li (1994), *China's Miracle: Development Strategy and Economic Reform*, Shanghai: Sanlian Press and People's Press.

Lin, Yifu, Fang Cai and Zhou Li (1997), *Sufficient Information and SOE Reform*, Shanghai: Sanlian Press, People's Press.

Lin, Yutang (1958 [1988]), *Chinese People*, Hangzhou: Zhejiang People's Press.

Liu, Yongping and Ming Lu (2008), 'On the sustainability of Chinese economic growth with aging population from the angle of household support for the aged', *World Economy*, No. 1, 65–77.

Lu, Jiangyong and Zhigang Tao (2006), 'Regional industrial agglomeration in China and international comparisons', *Economic Research Journal*, No. 3, 103–14.

Lu, Ming and Zhao Chen (2004), 'Urbanization, urban-biased policy and urban–rural inequality', *Economic Research Journal*, No. 6, 50–58.

Lu, Ming and Zhao Chen (2006b), *Market Integration and Industrial Agglomeration in China's Regional Economic Development*, Shanghai: Sanlian Press, People's Press.

Lu, Ming and Hui Pan (2009), *Government–Enterprise Connections – Growth of Private Entrepreneurs and Development of Enterprises*, Beijing: Peking University Press.

Lu, Ming and Shiqin Jiang (2007), 'Rethinking the rethinking of education industrialization: the theory and policy of education resource utilization efficiency', *World Economy*, No. 5, 14–22.

Lu, Ming and Shuang Zhang (2008), 'Influences of labor mobility on public trust in Chinese rural areas', *World Economic Papers*, No. 4, 77–87.

Lu, Ming, Zhao Chen, Min Chen and Qihan Gui (2006), 'The interregional differentials of local protectionism and market segmentation', in Shah et al. (eds), pp. 356–97.

Lu, Ming, Zhao Chen and Guanghua Wan (2005), 'Equality for growth: the interwoven relationship between China's inequality, investment, education and growth', *Economic Research Journal*, No. 12, 4–14, 101.

Lu, Ming, Zhao Chen and Ji Yan (2004), 'Increasing returns, development strategy and regional economic segmentation', *Economic Research Journal*, No. 1, 54–63.

Lu, Ming, Zhao Chen and Zhenzhen Yang (2007), 'Equity and growth hand in hand: a model of strategic labor division based on increasing returns', *China Economic Quarterly*, **6**(2), 443–68.

Lu, Ming, Zhao Chen and Shuang Zhang (2009), 'Cost of public ownership: cases of corruption and transformation of enterprise in China', *Journal of Nanjing University*, No. 2, 49–60.

Luo, Changyuan and Jun Zhang (2008), 'FDI in China's transition', *World Economic Papers*, No. 1, 27–42.

Luo, Rongqu (1993), 'Great navigation in the 15th century and the different development orientations of China and Western Europe', in Rongqu Luo (eds), *A Cross-Country Comparative Study of Modernization*, Xi'an: Shaanxi People's Press, pp. 3–31.

Ma, Shuanyou and Hongxia Yu (2003), 'Fiscal transfer and interregional economic convergence', *Economic Research Journal*, No. 3, 26–33, 90.

Mao Zedong (1956), 'On the ten major relationships', in *Selected Works of Mao Zedong* (Vol. 5), Beijing: People's Press, 1977.

Ministry of Public Health (2004), *Survey on China's Health Services: 3rd Report on National Health Services Survey, Information Statistics Center in China's Ministry of Health*, Beijing: China Union Medical University Press.

Poncet, Sandra (2002), 'Is the Chinese market disintegrating? A comparative analysis of China's domestic and international market integration', *World Economic Papers*, No. 1, 3–17.

Qian, Mu (1952 [2001]), *The Gains and Losses of Chinese Ancient Politics* (Zhongguo Lidai Zhengzhi Deshi), Beijing: Sanlian Press.

Qian, Mu (2001), *New Comments on Chinese History* (Guoshi Xinlun), Beijing: Sanlian Press.

Shah, Anwar, Chunli Shen and Heng-fu Zou (eds) (2006), *The Economic Analysis of China's Regional Disparities*, Beijing: People's Press.

Shankar, Raja and Anwar Shah (2006), 'Bridging the economic divide with countries: a scorecard on the performance of regional policies in reducing regional income disparities', in Shah et al. (eds), pp. 21–50.

Sheng, Laiyun (2008), *Mobility or Migration: The Economic Analysis of Chinese Rural Labor Mobility*, Shanghai: Fareast Press.

Sheng, Laiyun, Ran Wang and Fang Yan (2009), 'The effects of global financial crisis on the employment of migrant workers', *Chinese Rural Economy*, No. 9, 4–14.

State Statistics Bureau, Rural Social and Economic Survey Team (2003), *Monitoring Report of Chinese Rural Poverty*, Chinese Statistics Press.

Sun, Ang and Yang Yao (2006), 'The effects of serious sickness of laborers on household education investment: a study in the Chinese country-side', *World Economic Papers*, No. 1, 26–36.

Wan, Guanghua (1998), 'An empirical analysis on inter-regional income inequality of Chinese rural residents', *Economic Research Journal*, No. 5, 37–42, 50.

Wan, Guanghua (2006), *Economic Developemnt and Income Inequality: Methodology and Evidences*, Shanghai: Sanlian Press, People's Press.

Wang, Hui, Zhao Chen and Ming Lu (2009), 'Hukou, social segmentation and trust: evidence from Shanghai', *World Economy*, No. 10, 81–96.

Wang, Yongqin (2005), *Reputation, Commitment and Organizational Form: A Comparative Institutional Analysis*, Shanghai: People's Press.

Wang, Yongqin (2006a), 'Inter-linked market, relational contract and economic transition', *Economic Research Journal*, No. 6, 80–92.

Wang, Yongqin (2006b), 'Inter-linked relational contract, endogenous institution and economic development', *Academic Monthly*, **38**(11), 78–82.

Wang, Yongqin (2007b), 'Understanding the East Asia model: the dynamics from relation-based society to rule-based society', in Jingpin Wu (ed.), *Embracing the New Age of Asian Development: Volume 3 of Asian Studies*, Shanghai: Fudan University Press.

Wang, Yongqin, Yan Zhang, Yuan Zhang, Zhao Chen and Ming Lu (2006), 'Chinese economy at the crossroads: an analysis based on litera-tures', *World Economy*, No. 10, 3–20.

Wang, Yongqin, Yan Zhang, Yuan Zhang, Zhao Chen and Ming Lu (2007), 'China's development path as a large country', *Economic Research Journal*, No. 1, 4–16.

Wang, Yuesheng (2006a), 'The analysis of modern Chinese family struc-ture', *Chinese Social Science*, No. 1, 96–108, 207.

Wang, Yuesheng (2006b), 'The change of modern Chinese family structure', *Society*, No. 3, 118–36, 208.

Wang, Yujian, Xiongwen Lu, Zhigang Tao, Qingyun Jiang, Qifa Shao and Yimin Sun (2007), *Back to the Center of the Stage: The Integration and Transition of the Regional Economy in the Yangtze River Delta*, Shanghai: Century Press, People's Press.

Wei, Houkai (ed.) (2001), *From Duplicate Construction to Orderly Competition: A Study of China's Industrial Duplicative Construction and Cross-Regional Capital Restructuring*, Beijing: People's Press.

World Bank (2003), *Improving Investment Environment and Better Cities' Competitiveness: The Ranking of Investment Environment of China's 23 Cities*, Washington, DC: Research Bureau of the World Bank.

Wu, Jinglian (2003), *Modern Chinese Economic Reform*, Shanghai: Fareast Press.

Xie, Zhiqiang (1999), *Breakthrough: The Great Transformation of the Chinese Housing System*, Beijing: Social Science Literature Press.

Xu, Qing (2008), 'Separation and unity? The change, summary and prospect of China's rural land system since the reform', *World Economic Papers*, No. 1, 93–100.

Xu, Zheng, Zhao Chen and Ming Lu (2010), 'The core–periphery model of Chinese urban system: an empirical study of geography and economic growth', *World Economy*, No. 7, 144–60.

Yan, Shanpin (2007), 'Human capital, institution and wage differentials: an empirical study of dual labor market in large cities', *Management World*, No. 6, 4–13.

Yan, Wei and Nan Jiang (2007), 'Strictly save land when speeding up urbanization', *Social Science Outlook*, August 9.

Yan, Yuanyuan, Linxiu Zhang, Scott Rozelle and Holly Wang (2006), 'An economic analysis of the new cooperative medical system in rural China', *Chinese Rural Economy*, No. 5, 64–71.

Yuan, Zhigang (1994), *Non-Walrasian Dis-equilibrium and Its Application in Chinese Economy*, Shanghai: Sanlian Press.

Zhang, Jun (1997), *Dual Track Economics: China's Economic Reform (1978–1992)*, Shanghai: Sanlian Press, People's Press.

Zhang, Jun and Yuan Gao (2007), 'Government officials' tenure, rotation and economic growth: evidence from provincial-level data', *Economic Research Journal*, No. 11, 91–103.

Zhang, Jun and Li'an Zhou (eds) (2008), *Competition for Growth*, Shanghai: People's Press.

Zhang, Weiying (1995a), 'Principal–agent relationship in a publicly-owned economy: theoretical analysis and policy implications', *Economic Research Journal*, No. 4, 10–20.

Zhang, Weiying (1995b), *Entrepreneur of Enterprises*, Shanghai: Sanlian Press.

Zhang, Weiying and Shuhe Li (1998), 'Inter-regional competition and the privatization of Chinese SOEs', *Economic Research Journal*, No. 12, 13–22.

Zhang, Xiaobo (2003), 'Inequality in China's education and medical care', *China Economic Quarterly*, **2**(2), 405–16.

Zhang, Yan (2005), *Fiscal Policy and Economic Growth under the Decentralization System*, Shanghai: People's Press.

Zhang, Yan (2007), 'Fiscal decentralization, FDI competition, and local government behavior', *World Economic Papers*, No. 2, 22–36.

Zhang, Yan and Liutang Gong (2005), 'Tax sharing reform, fiscal decentralization, and Chinese economic growth', *China Economic Quarterly*, **5**(1), 75–108.

Zhang, Yan and Jijun Xia (2006), 'A review of tax competition: with an analysis on the competition of tax reduction at local level', CCES Working Paper, Fudan University, Shanghai.

Zhang, Yan, Jijun Xia and Wenjin Zhang (2010), 'Downward yardstick competition and spillover effect differences of provincial public spending in China', *Zhejiang Social Science*, No. 12, 20–26.

Zhao, Yaohui (1997), 'China's rural labor mobility and the role of education', *Economic Research Journal*, No. 2, 37–42, 73.

Zheng, Yusheng and Chonggao Li (2003), 'The efficiency loss of China's regional segmentation', *Chinese Social Science*, No. 1, 64–72.

Zhu, Lin (2000), 'Government and the choice of rural basic medical care system', *Chinese Social Science*, No. 4, 89–99.

Zhu, Lin (2007), 'One of the impressions of Xinjiang: active trade on the border', *Teahouse for Economists*, No. 5, 45–50.

Index